Bloody Sunday

About the Author

A print journalist since 1969 and a lobby correspondent in the Commons since 1978. Ian Hernon covered the Troubles in Northern Ireland and more mayhem in the Middle East. He ran the oldest Parliamentary news agency for fifteen years. For five years until 2018 he was deputy editor of *Tribune*. He is the author of fourteen books including the best-selling *Britain's Forgotten Wars* and *Anti-Semitism and the Left*.

Bloody Sunday

A Fifty-year Fight for Justice

Ian Hernon

AMBERLEY

Dedicated to the Bloody Sunday families
and
For Reuben, Freya and Theo, in the hope they never witness such events

This edition published 2024

Amberley Publishing
The Hill, Stroud
Gloucestershire, GL5 4EP

www.amberley-books.com

Copyright © Ian Hernon, 2021, 2024

The right of Ian Hernon to be identified as the Author
of this work has been asserted in accordance with the
Copyright, Designs and Patents Act 1988.

All rights reserved. No part of this book may be reprinted
or reproduced or utilised in any form or by any electronic,
mechanical or other means, now known or hereafter invented,
including photocopying and recording, or in any information
storage or retrieval system, without the permission in writing
from the Publishers.

British Library Cataloguing in Publication Data.
A catalogue record for this book is available from the British Library.

ISBN 978 1 3981 1955 0 (paperback)
ISBN 978 1 3981 0799 1 (ebook)

1 2 3 4 5 6 7 8 9 10

Typeset in 10.5pt on 13.5pt Sabon.
Typesetting by SJmagic DESIGN SERVICES, India.
Printed in India.

Contents

Acknowledgements

This is a narrative, rather than a polemic. I have tried to be as fair and balanced as I can, although it is difficult to find balance in terrorist acts and indiscriminate violence, whether the perpetrator is wearing a uniform or not.

Most of the lethal action on Bloody Sunday took place in a small urban area over around ten minutes. It was complex, with simultaneous events adding to the confusion for witnesses and participants alike. I have tried to describe them as clearly as possible, but inevitably the timeline of the narrative was not always clear. Similarly, in the heat of the deadly drama, witnesses often gave conflicting and mistaken accounts. That is understandable and reflects the combination of terror, adrenalin, some degree of self-interest and genuine confusion rather, in the case of most civilians at least, than outright fabrication. In any case, such conflicting testimony when innocently given produces snapshots of the turmoil of the time.

Naturally, I have been well aware of the feelings of the families in writing this book. I understand that forensic details of the injuries suffered by the dead and wounded may be upsetting but feel that they are necessary to show the full horror of that day. If I appear to give more space to certain of the casualties than others, I mean no disrespect to the latter – it was necessary to avoid repetition and to aid the tragic flow of the narrative. Any mistakes or misjudgements in that narrative are mine alone, and not those of my sources or the two million-word Saville report on which I have drawn extensively.

I have assumed that anyone picking up this book will have knowledge of the history of the island of Ireland and the counties of the North; I have therefore rattled through pre-1960s history in a few pages. In any case, it has often been said that Northern Ireland has too much history.

Acknowledgements

Praise must go to the journalists, reporters, photographers and camera crew who put their own lives on the line to report Bloody Sunday and, indeed, the whole of the Troubles.

Some of my sources would not welcome my thanks if it meant identifying them, so I will refrain from naming any. They know who they are, and my thanks go to all.

My thanks also go to the team at Amberley.

And, as always, my family.

Introduction

The North Antrim coast has a wild, rugged beauty which made it the go-to location for the producers of *Game of Thrones*. Sheer cliffs overlook a sparkling sea and inland from the Giant's Causeway, rolling green hills are cut by rivers and scattered lakes. It is idyllic, with village pubs where locals chatter about football – Association and Gaelic – rugby union and cricket. An hour's drive away through winding lanes is the city of Derry, and further on the metropolis of Belfast, hotspots of the forty-year nightmare known as the Troubles. And for most of the twentieth century, Northern Ireland was marked by discrimination and hostility in what future First Minister David Trimble called a 'cold house for Catholics'. The reasons for this division were simply deep-seated hatreds and prejudices dated back centuries.

Since the Anglo-Norman invasions in the twelfth century, the British monarchy tried and failed to control Ireland in the face of constant rebellion. The English-controlled Kingdom of Ireland was declared by Henry VIII in 1542, but Irish resistance made English control fragmentary at best. After some decisive victories over the Irish lords in the early seventeenth century, the Catholic Irish aristocracy fled to Continental Europe. James I of England took draconian action by moving the ordinary Catholic Irish off their lands, mainly in the more prosperous North, and replacing them with Protestant settlers from England and Scotland in what became known as the Plantation of Ulster. These settlers soon outnumbered the indigenous Irish in the North but were a minority in the rest of Ireland where they were deeply resented. They relied on Britain for protection and so became fiercely loyal to the British Crown. Unlike English settlers in previous centuries, these Loyalists never integrated into Irish society and never adapted to Irish ways, seeing themselves as a group apart. They, for natural and obvious reasons, developed a siege mentality. That became reality in 1688 when the Protestant community within the walls of Derry came under siege from the Catholic King James II. The siege was broken by the Protestant William of Orange who later went on to defeat James at the Battle of the Boyne in 1690. The Loyalists were jubilant, adopted the colour orange as a symbol of their loyalty to William and the British Crown, and instituted marches to celebrate the victory and to intimidate Catholics.

In the face of open institutional discrimination, the eighteenth century saw the growth of secret militant societies across sectarian and political lines, including the Protestant Peep O'Day Boys and the Orange Order, and the Catholic Defenders and the Society of the United Irishmen. The latter led a disastrous rebellion in 1798 inspired by the French Revolution which aimed to break the constitutional ties between Ireland and Britain and unite Irish people of all religions. Following this, in a bid to prevent the spread of French-style republicanism, the British government in 1801 formally merged both sides of the Irish Sea into the United Kingdom of Great Britain and Ireland, with a single government and parliament based in London.

The Loyalists remained as a group apart and in control until Irish Home Rule dominated the political agenda in the first two decades of the twentieth century. The nationalist fight for self-determination led to the 1916 Easter Rising in Dublin, and the Irish War of Independence between 1919 and 1921 which ended with a truce. The Loyalists in the North reacted furiously to any form of independence, fearing that they would be swallowed up in a hostile, Catholic Ireland. They had earlier formed the Ulster Volunteers militia and threatened to oppose Home Rule by force if necessary. Eventually, the British, the Loyalists and the Irish nationalists reached an uneasy compromise that meant most of Ireland would gain partial independence and have a parliament in Dublin, but the six counties of Ulster that contained large Loyalist majorities would have their own separate parliament and remain part of the United Kingdom. The deal pleased no one, least of all the Catholic minority in the six counties, and sparked an Irish civil war which pitted former comrades against each other, but it passed into law with the Government of Ireland Act of 1920. It created a new parliament for Northern Ireland in Stormont Castle, Belfast, and, recognising that the Catholic minority would always be outvoted in elections to the new parliament, introduced proportional representation, to ensure that the Catholics would at least have some voice in government.

The first prime minister of Northern Ireland was Sir James Craig of the Ulster Unionist Party, a committed Loyalist who from the outset described Stormont as a Protestant parliament for Protestant people. Over the next forty years, Craig and his successors ensured that the Unionists always had a stranglehold on power in Northern Ireland. Proportional Representation was abolished in favour of first past the post to ensure an eternal Unionist majority vote. Electoral boundaries were gerrymandered to further bolster their supremacy. The electoral dice was weighted to the extent that even areas with heavy Catholic majorities such as Derry would return Unionist representatives. The electoral system meant only ratepayers and their wives could vote in local council elections. Adults who lived with parents and so did not pay rates were disenfranchised. As Catholics were more likely to be unemployed and so dependent on their parents, this too helped Unionists to retain electoral power. The Unionist position was further bolstered by the police force, the Royal Ulster Constabulary (RUC), which was more than 90 per cent Protestant even though Catholics made up more than 30 per cent of the population.

By the late 1950s, the Unionists controlled every aspect of Northern Ireland and blatantly ran it to benefit their own narrow community. Another Northern Ireland prime minister, Lord Brookeborough, criticised Protestant business owners who employed Catholics and said that he 'wouldn't have one about the place'. Unionists controlled all the arms of government, got all the best jobs, all the best housing and all the best opportunities. The Catholic minority were treated as second-class citizens and became increasingly isolated and powerless. They had no political influence in their own state, and they got very little support from the recently formed Republic of Ireland, which although it still laid claim to the North, showed little interest in doing anything about it.

The younger Catholic generation looked to the civil rights movements making progress across the Atlantic. They were better educated than previous generations thanks to the passing of school reforms and were not prepared to suffer the injustices and the lack of prospects endured by their parents. Above all, they wanted to enjoy the same rights and opportunities as their Protestant neighbours. Increasingly, sensible Unionists saw that the world was changing and that they would have to change with it – to a certain degree, that is.

In 1963, the diehard, old-school, bigoted Loyalist Lord Brookeborough resigned and was replaced as Northern Ireland prime minister by Captain Terence O'Neill. An Eton-educated former officer with the Irish Guards, his cut-glass English accent aroused fears amongst the more extreme Loyalists that he was not really one of them. They were right – he knew that the old ways of total Unionist domination could not continue. Between 1963 and 1969, he tentatively reached out to the Catholic community in a bid to engage them in the political process. He was sympathetic to the civil rights movement and wanted reform, all of which swiftly put him in a near-impossible situation. The Unionists were alarmed by his conciliatory approaches to the Catholics, while the Catholics felt he was not going nearly far enough. O'Neill then met the Irish Taoiseach, Sean Lemass, in a bid to work together through trade, investment, and tourism, the first ever meeting between an Irish Taoiseach and a Northern Ireland premier. Unionists were appalled and suspicious. They were even more outraged the following year when Lemass visited O'Neill in Belfast, and they started plotting to remove him.

The loudest ultra-Loyalist voice – in every sense – was provided by the 'Reverend' Ian Paisley, a firebrand preacher with a hatred of Catholicism. He demanded 'no surrender' to any change that would weaken the Loyalist hold on power or the strength of the union with Britain. In 1964, he was furious to discover that the Irish tricolour was being flown in the West Belfast election office of a republican candidate for the forthcoming election to the British Parliament and vowed to lead a march of Loyalists to remove it. Rather than run the risk of a violent confrontation, the police removed the flag, and the Catholic population were in turn outraged, seeing it as police appeasement of Loyalist bullyboys. That led to two days of rioting in the Divis Street area of Belfast. Petrol bombs were thrown at police who responded with water cannon and baton charges. No one was killed and there was no gunfire, but it was a shock to both sides of the community. The Catholics were alarmed at the ruthlessness of the police and their willingness to give in to Paisley. The Unionist community were alarmed at the rioting. The growing civil rights movement also alarmed them; in the early days, the movement contained many Protestants who accepted that change was necessary. They fell away, however, as attitudes hardened and as violence increased, all of which made Loyalists less willing to make concessions and so the extremist views of Paisley and others gathered momentum.

Meanwhile, O'Neill came under further pressure when water installations were bombed. The IRA was blamed, and critics turned up the pressure on the premier, saying that he had lost control. O'Neill resigned on 28 April 1969 saying that the bombs had blown him out of office. It later emerged that the bombs had not been the work of the IRA, which was still quite ineffectual, but had been set by the Loyalist paramilitary group the Ulster Volunteer Force (UVF) with the express intention of undermining O'Neill. O'Neill was succeeded by Major James Chichester-Clark and shortly afterwards by Brian Faulkner, but neither could stop the escalating violence and both were reluctant to concede any reforms.

Few outside the Province had heard of the crumbling collections of tower blocks, run-down housing and poorly maintained streets known as the Bogside. It would soon become infamous across the world.

1

Flashpoint Derry

The name of the island of Ireland's fourth-largest city comes from the ancient Irish word *Doire*, meaning an 'oak grove'. Officially called Londonderry to reflect the building of its stout city walls by London guilds, Derry is also known as 'Stroke City' due to the dual name Derry/Londonderry sometimes used by the BBC. Those spectacular mile-long city walls, the last to be built in Europe, are in summer festooned in flowers reflected in the languid waters of the River Foyle. Their beauty does not reflect the cause of their construction in 1613–19 by the Honourable The Irish Society as defences for early settlers from England and Scotland. The city is also nicknamed the Maiden City as the walls were never breached despite being besieged three times in 1688–89 in a war pitching Jacobites against the forces of the Protestant King William. In the first, Protestant apprentice boys locked out the army of King James. A subsequent 105-day siege in which James tried to starve out the occupants also failed. Around 10,000 died, most of them civilians. Such events went to the core of Protestant Unionism. The walls are therefore more than a spectacular tourist walkway around the city, but a symbol of centuries of oppression from the viewpoint of the Catholic majority. Outside them is the Bogside, originally swampy ground allowed by the Protestant rulers for Catholic families. It should therefore surprise few that it was the setting not just for the sparks that inflamed the Troubles, but also for the single bloodiest atrocity inflicted on civilians during that seemingly endless conflict.

By 1969 Catholic nationalists regarded the City of Derry as the epitome of fifty years of Unionist misrule. Ultimately, the Protestant elite did themselves no favours by the disreputable, sometimes illegal, methods employed to keep Catholics in 'their place' while enriching themselves. Blatant gerrymandering which robbed poorer Catholics of the vote while giving property owners multiple votes meant that the City Corporation always returned a Unionist majority even though Catholics on paper enjoyed a two-to-one majority. In the early 1960s, due to the division of electoral wards, Unionists had a majority of twelve seats to eight. Nationalists comprised 61.6 per cent of parliamentary electors, but only 54.7 per cent of local government electors.[1] Whenever it seemed likely that nationalists might take another ward, boundaries were redrawn to maintain Unionist control. That gave them power over the allocation of public housing, which was used, almost openly, to keep the Catholic population confined in a limited number of wards. The overall effect was to create a chronic housing shortage for Catholics and a refusal to renovate and repair existing properties, which left the housing stock in an appalling state. Catholics languished in a fetid, insanitary, built-up but neglected swamp.

There was also widespread discrimination in jobs. The Census showed that Protestant male unemployment was 6.6 per cent compared to 17.3 per cent for Catholic males, while the equivalent rates for women were 3.6 and 7 per cent respectively. Catholics were over-represented in unskilled jobs and Protestants in skilled employment – Catholics made up 31 per cent of the economically active population but accounted for only 6 per cent of mechanical engineers, 7 per cent of 'company secretaries and registrars' and 'personnel managers', 8 per cent of university teachers, 9 per cent of local authority senior officers, 19 per cent of medical practitioners, and 23 per cent of lawyers.[2]

Derry was starved of public investment by the Stormont overlords and motorways were not extended to it. A university was opened in the relatively small, Protestant-majority town of Coleraine rather than Derry. As a result of all the above, and more, the city became a significant focus of the civil rights campaign led by such organisations as the Northern Ireland Civil Rights Association (NICRA).

Formed in Belfast in 1967, the movement's membership included trade unionists, communists, liberals, socialists, and even some members of the Young Unionists,[3] republicans eventually constituting five of the thirteen members of its executive council. From the start, NICRA imitated the tactics used by the resurgent American civil rights movement and, to a lesser extent, the British-based National Council for Civil Liberties. It held marches, pickets, sit-ins and protests, singing 'We Shall Overcome' and 'We Shall Not Be Moved'.[4] Derry civil rights leader Finbar O'Doherty referred to Northern Irish Catholics as Ulster's 'white negroes'. Widespread attention in the US helped NICRA secure a much wider international and internal support than more traditional nationalist protests had done.[5] However, there were inevitable tensions between those advocating militant and confrontational methods, in particular the socialist and republican elements of the movement such as Eamonn McCann, Michael Farrell and Cyril Toman, and those who remained wedded to the pacifist American civil rights model.

The Northern Ireland government accused NICRA of being a front for republicanism and Unionists in general regarded it as a front for the IRA. That proved true to a certain extent. While many genuine pacifists and social reformers signed up, overtly Republic groupings such as the Wolf Tone Society provided high-profile members. After the failure of their border campaign in the early 1960s the IRA infiltrated NICRA along with the Northern Ireland Labour Party and trade unions, something its commanders publicly admitted in 1968. The IRA could not control the movement's direction but could influence it by the choice of protest marches. A commission set up by the British government in 1969 and headed by Scottish judge Lord Cameron reported that 'certain at least of those who were prominent in the Association had objects far beyond the "reformist" character of the majority of Civil Rights Association demands, and undoubtedly regarded the Association as a stalking-horse for achievement of other and more radical and in some cases revolutionary objects, in particular abolition of the border, unification of Ireland outside the United Kingdom and the setting up of an all-Ireland Workers' Socialist Republic'.[6] Despite such views, most active NICRA members were non-sectarian and did not aggressively pursue the objective of a united Ireland.[7]

In July 1968 NICRA organised a march from Coalisland to Dungannon Market Square to highlight public housing being allocated preferentially to Protestants in County Tyrone and the significance of the market square was that it was historically a Protestant/Unionist gathering place. A counter-protest was planned by Ian Paisley's Ulster Protestant Volunteers. RUC officers prevented the march from entering Dungannon while 1,500 counter-demonstrators jeered. Civil rights campaigner Gerry Fitt roared: 'My blood is boiling at the police ban and let me tell the County Inspector and District Inspector who are in charge of the police here tonight that they are only a pair of black bastards of Gestapo and we are not afraid of the blackthorn sticks and batons and but for the presence of women and children I would lead the march into The Square.'[8] The crowds dispersed without major incident.

Radicals considered the march a 'disappointing anti-climax' as some felt that the police barricade should have been broken. Another event was planned for 5 October 1968 along a route commonly followed by Protestant and Loyalist processions – from the Waterside railway station, east of the River Foyle, crossing the river along Craigavon Bridge and proceeding to the Diamond within the city's walls. Unsurprisingly, local Unionists objected. When IRA chief of staff Cathal Goulding televised a statement that his organisation were actively supporting the civil rights campaign – an act of blatant and cynical provocation – Unionist opposition hardened.[9] At the turn of the month, the Derry Apprentice Boys announced they would march the same route on the same day and time. Northern Ireland home affairs minister William Craig banned both marches on police advice. Some members of the NICRA's executive believed that they should withdraw their support for the march and unsuccessfully lobbied the Derry Housing Action Committee to call it off. South Derry IRA decided to push any of the politicians present on the day of the march into the police lines if marchers were blocked. The banned march attracted 400 protesters while a further 200 watched from the pavements. At the head of the march were several republican and Labour MPs, including Gerry Fitt and John Hume.

As they set off, they were stopped by baton-flailing Royal Ulster Constabulary (RUC) and Fitt and several others were bludgeoned to the ground. The marchers sat in the road as TV cameras recorded a blood-drenched Fitt being carried off to hospital. Some marchers retaliated with stone-throwing but film of the RUC chasing unarmed demonstrators and hitting those who fell had the greatest impact. Some demonstrators, mainly local youths who had not taken part in the march, filtered into the Diamond where the police baton-charged, forcing them back to the Bogside. Overnight, disturbances saw petrol bombs thrown and shops looted.[10]

Watching TV broadcasts at home with two schoolmates was fourteen-year-old Sean O'Callaghan, a Catholic imbued with romantic ideals concerning anti-Vietnam War protests and civil rights movements in America and across the island of Ireland. He recalled: 'We saw RUC officers kick, punch and baton completely defenceless and peaceful marchers. We were really shocked by the naked hatred and violence of some of the police ... nothing could excuse the brutality with which the police enforced the banning order. That even had a huge effect on me. All my sympathy was with the marchers and I formed the opinion there and then that the RUC were a totally bigoted police force on a par with the Nazis; this conviction was to remain with me powerfully for many years. My two friends and I, who sat and watched the events of that day, were all to join the Provisional IRA.'[11] O'Callaghan became in turn an assassin, informer, prisoner and peace advocate.

The TV footage broadcast initially by Eire-based RTÉ also brought to a global audience the scale of brutal sectarianism in what had previously been considered an unimportant backwater. Northern Ireland premier Terence O'Neill appealed for calm and signaled upcoming reforms. NICRA in turn declared a halt to marches until 11 January 1969.[12]

A week before that deadline, around 300 Loyalists, including several off-duty B-Specials, attacked civil rights demonstrators at Burntollet Bridge. Dozens of marchers, including civil rights firebrand Bernadette Devlin, were injured by stones, clubs and nails as RUC officers looked on but did nothing to protect those under attack. At the end of March, Loyalists detonated a bomb at an electricity station near Belfast, the first explosion of the Troubles. It marked the start of a two-month Loyalist campaign of bombing water and electricity stations; the perpetrators figured that the attacks would be blamed on republicans (*see Introduction*). On April 19 Samuel Devenny, a Catholic from Bogside, was severely beaten in his home by RUC officers. He died from his injuries three months later. Orange Order parades proved flashpoints for rioting. On 14 July, a sixty-seven-year-old Catholic civilian, Francis McCloskey, died after being batoned during an RUC push in Dungiven, County Derry. McCloskey's death is considered by many to be the first of the Troubles. On 2 August Patrick Corry, a sixty-one-year-old Catholic, was beaten around the head by RUC officers during rioting in Belfast. He died four months later.[13]

Passions heightened by such incidents swiftly escalated the violence, culminating in August 1969 when the annual Apprentice Boys of Derry march was attacked as it went through the city's walls and past the Bogside perimeter. The RUC tried to clear a path through for the marchers but were answered by a barrage of stones. The police launched a baton charge and the Catholic youths responded with petrol bombs. The police then fired tear gas – the first time it had been used in Ireland or Britain. Barricades went up all around the area, open-air petrol bomb factories were established, dumpers hijacked from a building site were used to carry stones to the front. Teenagers went on the roof of the block of high flats dominating Rossville Street, the main entrance to the Bogside, and began lobbing petrol bombs at the police below.

Eamonn McCann recalled: 'This was a brilliant tactical move and, afterwards, there was no shortage of people claiming to have thought of it first. As long as the lads stayed up there and as long as we managed to keep them supplied with petrol bombs, there was no way – short of shooting them off the roof – that the police could get past the high flats. Every time they tried, it rained petrol bombs... Throughout the battle, all the doors in the area were open. Tea and sandwiches were constantly available on the pavement. The police started using tear gas after a few hours, which nonplussed us momentarily. A call to the offices of the Red Mole in London – they seemed the most appropriate people – produced an antidote involving vinegar and a series of instructions for lessening the effects. Soon there were buckets of water and vinegar stationed all over the battle zone. As an alternative, Molly Barr was dispensing free Vaseline from her shop under the high flats... Four walkie-talkie radio sets were taken from a television crew. One was installed in Paddy Doherty's house and the other three used to report back on the state of play in the battle. Our possession of those instruments was later to be adduced as evidence of the massive, subversive conspiracy behind the fighting. When the batteries ran out after a few hours, the sets were given back to their owners... Three first-aid stations, manned by local doctors, nurses and the Knights of Malta, were treating those overcome by the gas or injured by missiles thrown by the police. The radio transmitter, now operating from Eamon Melaugh's house in Creggan, was pumping out republican music and exhortations to "keep the murderers out. Don't weaken now. Make every stone and petrol bomb count."[14]

Police riot shields proved too small for the onslaught from above and uniforms were not flame resistant. Police were under orders not to use armoured cars or police-issue firearms and there was no relief rota; some officers served for three days without proper rest, catnapping in doorways whenever they could. But they flooded the area with CS gas which caused a wide range of respiratory injuries among local people. A total of 1,091 canisters, each containing 12.5g of CS, and fourteen canisters containing 50g of CS were released in the densely populated residential area. On 13 August, Irish Taoiseach Jack Lynch, in a televised speech, said that he 'could not stand by and watch innocent people injured and perhaps worse'.[15] Catholics saw that as a promise of rescue, while Loyalists saw it as a threatened invasion. By 14 August, the 'Battle of the Bogside' peaked following false rumours that St Eugene's Cathedral had been attacked by the police. Restrictions on the police using firearms were loosened and two rioters were shot and injured in Great James Street. The notorious B-Specials, a reserve quasi-military, mostly Protestant, police force with no training in crowd control were sent to Derry, inflaming Catholic fears of a massacre.[16]

Billy McVeigh, seventeen, faced down army vehicles with stones in his hand, an image romantically immortalised in republican murals. He was in the thick of street-fighting, later boasting: 'I used to do shifts and go home and get a sleep and come back again. It was like a full-time job. The adrenalin was unreal. It was like going into a boxing ring. Everybody started building barricades and it was like a conveyor belt system making petrol bombs. There were people gathering bottles, people bringing crates, people coming with flour and sugar and petrol, all doing their bit and then passing them down to us on the front line.' Carmel McCafferty, a twenty-one-year-old hairdresser, said: 'The electricity was there, and it just needed to be ignited. It was like somebody had popped a balloon.' She would work all day, and then riot all night: 'I had two sets of clothes, one for work and one for rioting. I didn't go home, I hid my [rioting] clothes at the bottom of the flats.' French students blooded in the recent Paris riots showed Bogsiders how to make petrol bombs – 'they told us not to throw them, to lob them', said McCafferty. 'I'll be honest, I really enjoyed it. I was brought up in a political house. I knew about gerrymandering, I knew about bad housing, I knew about bad wages and jobs. You needed to have had blinkers on in Derry then not to realise what was happening. This name we give it, the Troubles, it was war. There's no other way to put it. This was war.'[17]

McCann later wrote: 'The police were making charge after charge up Rossville Street. Phone calls were made to contacts in other areas begging them to get people on to the streets and draw off some of the police from Derry. We appealed through Telefis Eireann for "every able-bodied man in Ireland who believes in freedom" to come to Derry and help us. We need you, we'll feed you. In the main battle area, Rossville Street, the fighting was being led by Bernadette Devlin who had seemingly developed an immunity to tear gas and kept telling people, implausibly, that "it's OK once you get a taste of it". On the morning of the 14th, we heard reports of fighting in Belfast, Coalisland, Dungannon, Armagh and other places; we took this as encouragement. Other people were coming to our aid. The Tricolour and the Starry Plough were hoisted over the high flats. Two people were shot and wounded by the police in Great James' Street. The tear gas came in even greater quantities until it filled the air like smog. People were running through it, crouching, eyes closed, to hurl a petrol bomb at the police lines and then stagger back. In William Street, a group breaking into Harrison's garage to steal petrol was stopped by a priest who told them it was wrong. "But, Father, we need the petrol". "Well," said the priest dubiously, "as long as you don't take any more than you really need". And, thus absolved in advance, they went at it with a will...'[18]

Rioter Peter Maloney, then eighteen, said: 'There isn't a drug that compared to the buzz from rioting. You just knew you were part of something bigger, that this was going to change history. The only time that I felt fear was when word came down that the B-Specials were going to attack the Long Tower chapel. I went up, and they had their rifles with them and they attacked down the street.' He and the other rioters ran, abandoning a crate of petrol bombs. 'It was the only time I saw a shotgun,' said Moloney decades later. 'This guy with a shotgun said to me, "go up and get the petrol bombs, I'll cover you". I was mad enough, I went up and picked up the crate, but what I didn't know was the army had just arrived. It was all over.'[19]

A NICRA call for people to aid the Bogsiders led to rioting in Belfast and elsewhere which left seven Catholics and two Protestants dead and more than 130 injured. A Loyalist mob burned all of the Catholic homes on Bombay Street. Over 1,800 people, mostly Catholics, were expelled from their homes in Belfast. After their failure to break through barricades in Derry, the police used armoured cars with machine guns to try to disperse the crowds. The guns were fired in bursts along the Catholic Falls Road area and a bullet ripped through the wall of a block of flats and killed a nine-year-old boy who was asleep at the time. Police then staged baton charges through the protesters and were followed by Protestant youths who attacked and burned the homes of Catholics. Houses were ablaze and thousands of people fought in the streets of West Belfast. It was clear that the RUC could not cope. Civil unrest had turned into a three-way armed conflict between nationalists, state forces and Unionists. The Troubles had begun.

Premier Chichester-Clark looked on with a growing desperation. The RUC were unable to quell the rioting; indeed, they were being accused of colluding with Loyalists and turning a blind eye to attacks on Catholics. In London, Prime Minister Harold Wilson and Home Secretary James Callaghan reluctantly accepted that they would have to get more directly involved as it was clear the Stormont government was out of its depth. Callaghan arranged to have British troops on standby, but he did not want to order the troops in himself, believing that such high-risk action should be at the request of the Northern Ireland government. That request was not long in coming. Chichester-Clark contacted British officials on 13 August to ask for military help, warning of unimaginable consequences for the Catholic community if troops were not deployed. Callaghan was aboard an RAF aeroplane when the message came through and he agreed immediately. The moment had already been planned for and British troops were on the streets of Derry within hours – a company of the 1st Battalion, Prince of Wales Own Regiment of Yorkshire were dispatched from their standby station on HMS *Sea Eagle* in the first direct intervention of the London government in Ireland since partition. Operation Banner was supposed to be a temporary measure; it was just the start of a thirty-eight-year marathon, Britain's longest ever military campaign. They managed to restore calm and were welcomed by the Catholic families who rewarded them with tea and toast. More troops arrived in Belfast the following day and met with the same response. Such amity was not to last.

In Derry, the Yorkshires were ordered to separate the police and the Bogsiders but not to enter Bogside itself. McCann was among the first to speak to them: 'The first thing I said was, "what are your intentions? What are you doing here?" and as we were asking them they were unrolling coils of barbed wire. They said they were not coming into the area – we established that straight off – and that was important to the way we saw it because they put up a barbed-wire barricade with the RUC on the other side of it, away from us. That was the RUC being kept out of our area, and that was a triumph.' Rioter Peter Moloney said: 'The Bogside was effectively sealed off. The Liberation *Fleadh* afterwards was one of the best musical events ever. I remember lying on the roof of a block of flats very late at night, early in the morning, listening. It was absolutely wonderful.'[20]

Over 1,000 people had been injured in the rioting in Derry, but no one was killed. A total of 691 policemen were deployed, of whom around 350 were injured. The number of Bogsiders injured is not reliably known as many did not report wounds for fear of retaliation.[21] In Belfast and other trouble spots ten people were killed, 154 wounded by gunfire and 745 were injured in other ways. More than 1,800 families had been driven from their homes, 1,500 of them Catholics. Television pictures of the violence were beamed across the world, demonstrating the deep scars between the Catholic and Protestant communities and the volatility in their relationship. In his subsequent official inquiry, Lord Scarman concluded: 'We are satisfied that the spread of the disturbances [in Derry in August 1969] owed much to a deliberate decision of some minority groups to relieve police pressure on the rioters in Londonderry. Amongst these groups must be included NICRA, whose executive decided to organise demonstrators in the Province so as to prevent reinforcement of the police in Londonderry.'

In the Irish Republic, Taoiseach Jack Lynch was horrified by the violence. Until then, Dublin politicians had been ambivalent about getting involved in the affairs of the North, but no longer. Lynch's ministers debated whether to send arms or even troops to defend Catholic communities. Lynch himself refused to seriously consider what would have been seen as an invasion of the North but he did take some action that reassured the Catholics and outraged the Unionists. He broadcast: 'It is clear that the Irish government can no longer stand by and see innocent people injured and perhaps worse.' He said the RUC no longer had the confidence of the nationalist community and warned that British troops would not be acceptable either. He urged Britain to send in a United Nations peacekeeping force, and he set up field hospitals near the border to treat the Catholic wounded. He then allocated £100,000 for the relief of distress and also arranged for the Irish Army to provide men from Derry with arms training. Successive British governments from then on acknowledged that there would have to be an 'Irish dimension' to any political solution for Northern Ireland.

Attacks on Catholics led to the resurgence of the IRA. During the 1960s, after the failure of sporadic bombing campaigns, the IRA was looking feeble and dispirited. Between 1956 and 1962, the IRA had mounted what became known as the Border Campaign, which involved some shootings and bombings of installations, but they had little effect. By the end of the decade, the IRA was largely a spent force, toothless and lacking in numbers and arms. A British intelligence report revealed a few years later estimated that they would 'have trouble putting together 50 handguns and a mismatched arsenal of antiquated, ex-Army issue rifles'.[22] They were directed largely from Dublin by ageing leaders who had turned their attention to Marxist politics as much as Irish Nationalism following the failure of the Border Campaign. The Battle of Bogside and similar confrontations in the late 1960s changed all that. Catholics did not trust the police to protect them, and they soon lost faith in the British Army. They felt a need for a security.

Most Catholics in Northern Ireland did not support the IRA or approve of its tactics but would turn to it for protection in times of high tension. Yet, during the Battle of the Bogside and the riots in Belfast, the IRA had been conspicuous only by its absence. IRA commanders faced scathing criticism and scorn from the Catholic community for failing to protect them against attacks from Loyalists and the RUC. Graffiti with the words 'IRA – I Ran Away' appeared on walls. The words could equally have been written by angry Catholics who felt let down or scornful Protestants who felt triumphant, but either way it was a humiliating experience for the organisation. It began to re-examine its role and soon its numbers were swelled by hundreds of new recruits who had been radicalised by their experiences in the rioting. These were younger and more militant than most existing IRA members. Another slogan from the time captured this development from the rioting. The Bombay Street area had been particularly hard hit by Loyalist violence. A piece of graffiti read: 'Out of the ashes of Bombay Street rose the Provisional IRA.'

Every example of police or army brutality acted as a recruiting sergeant for the IRA and its membership swelled. The new generation soon lost patience with the leaders of the old guard and looked for change. In 1969, they set up the Provisional IRA to represent the new generation who wanted direct action to oppose the police and the British troops. The name was only meant to be temporary, but it stuck and was soon shortened to the Provos. Loyalist paramilitaries also grew in numbers and strength. It was only a matter of time before violence erupted on a scale never seen before in Northern Ireland. The role of the RUC was undermined by its failure to control the rioting and its failure to win the trust of the Catholics, and so the discredited B-Specials were disbanded. The Ulster Divide was given a physical manifestation as the Army began to erect what it called peace lines – barricades to keep the warring factions apart. At first, they were simple lines of barbed wire but later developed into huge constructions of concrete and metal, making residential areas look like war zones.

Within weeks of the Army's deployment, Home Secretary Callaghan told Richard Crossman that 'life was very bleak ... no prospect of a solution'. Crossman recorded in his diary: 'He had anticipated that the honeymoon wouldn't last long and it hadn't. The British troops were tired and no longer popular and the terrible thing was that the only solutions would take ten years, if they would ever work at all.'[23] In other words, the intractability of both sides was now clear to Westminster policymakers, but they felt powerless. The deployment of troops, which premier Wilson had long delayed, was seen as the minimum response possible even though it brought direct rule that much closer. Historians Paul Bew and Gordon Gillespie wrote: 'It is arguable that the decision to send in the troops, while leaving the Stormont regime intact, was the greatest mistake of British policy during the Troubles. The effect was to allow the Provisional IRA to present the British Army as the tool of the "Orange" Stormont Ascendancy regime.' Then, and for many years after, many argued that if Wilson had suspended Stormont then, it would have saved many lives subsequently lost. Callaghan responded: 'Public opinion would not have been ready. We would not have been in a position to handle the situation. We did not have enough understanding of it at that time.'[24]

As we have seen, the British troops were at first welcomed by the Bogside residents as a neutral force compared to the police and especially the B-Specials. Only a handful of radicals in Bogside, notably Bernadette Devlin, opposed the deployment of British troops. It was a brief honeymoon period and the troops soon took their place alongside the RUC as hate figures seen to be propping up Unionist dominance and British oppression. The troops were there to maintain order as defined by the Stormont government and the British government. That definition did not coincide with the nationalist view – they saw their homes raided, and their lives disrupted. The way the troops behaved while carrying out their duties also provoked anger and widespread criticism. Catholics complained that not only were they subjected to more raids, roadblocks and curfews than their Protestant neighbours, but the troops were unnecessarily heavy-handed, even brutal. A notorious later example came in July 1970 when Army commanders decided to impose a thirty-four-hour curfew on the Lower Falls Road area of Belfast. The move was later deemed to be illegal as they had acted beyond their powers. During the curfew, they confined 20,000 people, including children, to their homes while 5,000 house searches were carried out. During this process, three men were shot dead and a fourth was crushed by an armoured car. None turned out to have any connection with terrorist organisations. A further sixty people were wounded by army gunfire. Catholics complained that during the searches, their homes were ransacked, many of their possessions were deliberately destroyed and, in some cases, looted by the troops. The Catholic community was outraged, and the Army never regained their trust. During four turbulent decades, British troops were largely supported by Loyalists but went from heroes to hate figures in the eyes of the nationalist/Catholic community. They were constantly the men in the middle between warring paramilitaries and rival demonstrators. Nearly 700 of them lost their lives to bullets and bombs, and in turn they killed more than 300 people; some of their victims were paramilitaries but many were innocent civilians.

Broadly, the competing participants switched from stones and slingshots to bombs and bullets. The immediate aftermath saw a succession of grisly 'firsts'. A Catholic man, John Gallagher, became the first civilian to be shot dead during the Troubles; David Linton was the first Protestant shooting victim; while fifteen-year-old Gerard McAuley was the first IRA volunteer to be shot and killed. Also among the dead were nine-year-old Patrick Rooney, the youngest fatal victim thus far. For several weeks in October the Ulster Volunteer Force for the first time detonated several bombs across the Republic of Ireland, including police stations. During riots and unrest in the Loyalist area of Shankill in Belfast, British soldiers shot dead two Protestant civilians, and police officer Victor Arbuckle was shot by Loyalists, the first of more than 300 RUC officers to die in the Troubles. A Loyalist paramilitary volunteer, Thomas McDowell, was killed when a bomb he was carrying detonated prematurely in County Donegal. He was the first person killed by an explosion during the Troubles.[25]

In December 1969 and January 1970, both the IRA and its political wing, Sinn Féin, formally split into 'Official' and 'Provisional' organisations due to internal feuds and different interpretations of the 'bullet and ballot box' scenarios. A Provisional Army Council statement slammed the IRA old guard for compromise and parliamentary politicking which had undermined 'the basic military role of the IRA'. It went on: 'The failure to provide the maximum defence possible of our people in Belfast is ample evidence of this...' After the split, the Provisional IRA planned for an 'all-out offensive action against the British occupation'.[26] Provo Chief of Staff Sean Mac Stiofain decided they would 'escalate, escalate and escalate' until the British agreed to go.[27] The Provos, and their Loyalist foes, duly stepped up the violence, while their more moderate ex-comrades fought a losing battle to seek a political solution.

1970 saw rioting all over Derry and Belfast, with atrocities committed on all sides. The year also saw a British general election that returned a Conservative and Unionist government in London under Edward Heath. The Conservatives, who traditionally had close ties with Unionists, allowed Faulkner to step up security, with predictable results. Tit-for-tat violence became evermore deadly throughout the year. At the end of March an Orange Order parade sparked riots in the Springfield Road area of Belfast in which dozens of soldiers and civilians were injured. The summer brought no respite: three PIRA members were killed while assembling a bomb in Creggan, County Derry, along with two sisters aged nine and four. Five Loyalists and a Catholic IRA member were killed in street violence and gun battles across Belfast. The British Army imposed another curfew in the Falls district of Belfast after gun battles with Official IRA personnel. Four civilians, three of them Catholics, were shot dead by British troops; another sixty were injured. A nineteen-year-old Catholic was shot dead by a British soldier during more street violence in Belfast. Security forces used rubber bullets for the first time in Northern Ireland. Two RUC officers died in Crossmaglen, County Armagh, after opening an abandoned car booby-trapped by the IRA. An IRA member was killed in Belfast when a bomb he was carrying accidentally detonated. A civilian was executed in his home in the Shankill by Loyalists. In November two Catholics were executed in Belfast for alleged criminal activity, and two days before Christmas a sixty-five-year-old Protestant civilian was shot dead at home by unknown assailants.[28] There was worse to come.

Every week in the first half of 1971 saw murder, maiming and mayhem. In January, IRA gunmen executed a twenty-eight-year-old Catholic man in Belfast. In February, twenty-year-old Robert Curtis was the first British soldier to die, having been shot dead along with two Catholic men during gunfights in Belfast; a Protestant man was shot dead in Ballyhill; a Provisional IRA landmine killed five workers near a radio transmitter in County Tyrone, their Land Rover having been mistaken for an army vehicle; another British soldier was shot and killed by an IRA sniper while on patrol in western Belfast; two RUC officers were killed in a gun battle with the IRA in western Belfast; and an eighteen-year-old soldier was suffocated by the contents of a fire extinguisher after his vehicle was firebombed in Bogside. In March a twenty-one-year-old Catholic man was shot dead by British soldiers during rioting in the Lower Falls; IRA member Charles Hughes was executed in Belfast as part of an internecine feud; Provisional IRA members kidnapped three off-duty British soldiers from a Belfast bar and murdered them at Squire's Hill (*see following chapter*). That atrocity sparked rage amongst serving soldiers and a crisis for the Stormont government. Unionists demanded increased security measures, while Ian Paisley demanded the administration's resignation, saying: 'We can no longer tolerate your weakness. You must go before the whole land is deluged with the blood of innocent men and women.' Four thousand shipyard workers took to the streets of Belfast to demand internment of republican suspects and sympathisers.[29] Northern Ireland prime minister Chichester-Clark flew to London to request more troops, and when the numbers were not what he wanted, he resigned.[30] On 23 March 1971, Brian Faulkner was elected leader of the Ulster Unionist Party and appointed premier.[31]

And so it went on through spring and early summer. Two small boats attached to British naval vessel HMS *Hecate* were stolen by IRA members and blown up off the coast of Baltimore, Republic of Ireland. Isabella McKeague, sixty-seven, died in a house fire after Loyalists firebombed an adjacent shop. IRA volunteers and British soldiers fought more gun battles in Belfast; an IRA member was killed and two British soldiers wounded. Another British soldier was killed by an Official IRA sniper while patrolling in Belfast. An IRA bomb was thrown into a British Army base in Belfast, killing one soldier and injuring twenty-seven others. The dead man, Sergeant Michael Willetts, was awarded the George Cross for using his body to shield civilians from the blast. Two Catholic men were shot dead by soldiers during rioting in Bogside. A British soldier was killed by an IRA sniper in Lower Falls, Belfast. An Army patrol was ambushed by three IRA volunteers in south-western Belfast; one soldier was killed by machine-gun fire. Soldiers opened fire on a civilian driving past their base in Belfast, killing him – they had mistaken the backfiring of his car for gunfire. The following day an IRA sniper shot dead a soldier on patrol in Ardoyne, Belfast.[32]

In response to the escalating violence, the British government introduced internment without trial on 9 August 1971 at the request of Faulkner. Approval was given by British Home Secretary Reginald Maudling who was unenthusiastic about the move but feared a Loyalist backlash if he did not act with such draconian measures. The British Cabinet recommended 'balancing action', such as the arrest of Loyalist militants, the confiscation of weapons held by generally Unionist rifle clubs in Northern Ireland, and an indefinite ban on parades, most of which were held by Unionist/Loyalist groups. However, Faulkner argued that a ban on parades was unworkable, that the rifle clubs posed no security risk and, bizarrely, that there was no evidence of Loyalist terrorism. It was eventually agreed that there would be a six-month ban on parades but no interning of Loyalists.

On the initial list of those to be arrested, drawn up by RUC Special Branch and MI5, there were 450 names. Key figures on the list, and many who never appeared on it, had got wind of the swoop before it began. The list included leaders of the non-violent NICRA such as Ivan Barr and Michael Farrell. Writer Tim Pat Coogan wrote: 'What they did not include was a single Loyalist. Although the Ulster Volunteer Force had begun the killing and bombing, this organisation was left untouched, as were other violent Loyalist satellite organisations such as Tara, the Shankill Defence Association and the Ulster Protestant Volunteers. Faulkner was urged by the British to include a few Protestants in the trawl but, apart from two republicans, he refused.'[33]

The British Army, in co-operation with the RUC, mounted Operation Demetrius to round up and intern 342 people. British intelligence was seriously flawed and the round-up included many with no links to the IRA. Within forty-eight hours, 116 were judged innocent and released. The IRA had gone underground or fled across the border and fewer than 100 of those arrested were IRA members.[34] Many of the arrestees reported that they and their families were assaulted, verbally abused and threatened by the soldiers, and that soldiers smashed their way into houses without warning and fired baton rounds through doors and windows. Many also reported being ill-treated during their initial three-day detention at holding centres. They complained of being beaten, verbally abused, threatened, harassed by dogs, denied sleep, and starved. Some reported being forced to run a gauntlet of baton-wielding soldiers, having their heads forcefully shaved, being kept naked, being burnt with cigarettes, having a sack placed over their heads for long periods, having a rope kept around their necks, having the barrel of a gun pressed against their heads, being dragged by the hair, being trailed behind armoured vehicles while barefoot, and being tied to armoured trucks as a human shield.[35] Some were hooded, beaten and then thrown from a helicopter. They were told they were hundreds of feet skywards but were actually only a few feet from the ground.

For seven days, when not being interrogated, they were kept hooded and handcuffed in a cold cell and subjected to a continuous loud hissing noise. Here they were forced to stand in a stress position for many hours and were repeatedly beaten on all parts of their body. They were deprived of sleep, food and drink. Some of them also reported being kicked in the genitals, having their heads banged against walls, being shot at with blank rounds, and being threatened with injections. The result was severe physical and mental exhaustion, severe anxiety, depression, hallucinations, disorientation and repeated loss of consciousness.[36] Internees were then held at the new Long Kesh camp near Lisburn, later known as the Maze Prison; Magilligan British Army camp in County Derry; and on the prison ship HMS *Maidstone* in Belfast Harbour. Most Unionists supported the move at the time although the Reverend Ian Paisley opposed it because he was concerned some Loyalists would eventually be interned.

Fourteen of those arrested, the so-called Hooded Men, were subjected to 'interrogation in depth' which involved five techniques: wall-standing, hooding, subjection to white noise, sleep deprivation and deprivation of food and drink. The Irish government took a case to the European Court on Human Rights, who found the five interrogation methods amounted to torture. That judgment was appealed by the British government and the court slightly moderated the judgment to say the men were subjected to 'inhuman and degrading treatment'. The Irish government set up five camps to accommodate families of internees and refugees from the Troubles. Almost 2,000 people were interned up until its ending in December 1975.[37]

The fourteen Hooded Men were the only internees subjected to the full five techniques. Over the following months, some internees were subjected to at least one of the five techniques, as well as other interrogation methods. These allegedly included waterboarding, electric shocks, burning with matches and candles, forcing internees to stand over hot electric fires while beating them, beating and squeezing of the genitals, inserting objects into the anus, injections, whipping the soles of the feet, and psychological abuse such as Russian roulette.[38]

When the interrogation techniques became known to the public, there was outrage, especially from Irish nationalists. English Lord Chief Justice Lord Parker chaired a committee of inquiry which found the five techniques to be illegal under domestic law, and premier Heath pledged they would not be used in future. Despite directives expressly forbidding them, the five techniques were still being used by the British Army until 2003. In 2013, declassified documents revealed the existence of the interrogation centre at Ballykelly which had not been mentioned in any of the inquiries.[39] In June 2014, an RTE documentary entitled *The Torture Files* uncovered a letter from the UK Home Secretary Merlyn Rees in 1977 to the then British prime minister James Callaghan which confirmed that a policy of 'torture' had in fact been authorized by the British government's ministers – specifically the Secretary for Defence, Peter Carrington – in 1971.[40]

No UVF or UDA men were interned until nearly two years later, even though they had killed over 100 people between them. Internment, and the uneven way it was deployed, inflamed sectarian tensions and increased overwhelming feelings of injustice while failing in its goal of arresting key members of the IRA. As fathers, sons and brothers were locked up, it became a major recruiting tool for the IRA and nationalist hard-liners. The list's lack of reliability and the arrests that followed, complemented by reports of internees being tortured, led to more nationalists identifying with the IRA and losing hope in non-violent methods. After Operation Demetrius, recruits came forward in huge numbers to join both the Provisional and Official wings of the IRA. There was a subsequent sharp increase in violence. In the eight months before the operation, there were thirty-four conflict-related deaths in Northern Ireland; in the four months following it, 140 were killed. A serving officer of the British Royal Marines declared: 'It (internment) has, in fact, increased terrorist activity, perhaps boosted IRA recruitment, polarised further the Catholic and Protestant communities and reduced the ranks of the much-needed Catholic moderates.'[41]

The swoops caused huge Catholic and nationalist alienation from the Unionist state. Almost fifty years later journalist Gerry Moriarty wrote: 'Internment ramped up the Troubles. It is estimated that from August 9th, 1971 until the end of that year that close to 150 people were killed, with many hundreds injured. The following year almost 500 people were killed, the worst year of the Troubles.'[42]

All that was in the future, however. The immediate outcome of internment was predictably bloody, with twenty-four people killed in three days of rioting. Of the casualties, fourteen were Catholic civilians, six Protestant civilians, two British soldiers and two PIRA volunteers. The youngest victim, Desmond Healey, was fourteen. On 10 August, Bombardier Paul Challenor became the first soldier to be killed by the Provisional IRA in Derry when he was shot by a sniper on the Creggan estate. A further six soldiers had been killed in Derry by mid-December 1971. At least 1,332 rounds were fired at the British Army, who also faced 211 explosions and 180 nail bombs and who fired 364 rounds in return. In Belfast, soldiers of the Parachute Regiment shot dead eleven Catholic civilians in what became known as the Ballymurphy Massacre (*see following chapter*).

Thirty British soldiers were killed in the remaining months of 1971, in contrast to the ten killed during the pre-internment period. Both the Official IRA and the Provisionals established no-go for the British Army and the RUC in Derry through the use of barricades. By the end of 1971, twenty-nine barricades were in place to prevent access to what was known as Free Derry, sixteen of them impassable even to the British Army's 1-ton armoured vehicles. IRA members openly mounted roadblocks in front of the media, and daily clashes took place between nationalist youths and the British Army at a spot known as 'aggro corner'. Due to rioting and damage to fire-bombed shops, an estimated total of £4 million worth of damage had been caused to local businesses.[43]

Another flashpoint was Ardoyne in North Belfast, where soldiers had shot dead three people on 9 August. Many Protestant families fled Ardoyne and around 200 burnt their homes as they left, lest they fall into Catholic hands. Protestant and Catholic families fled to either side of a dividing line, which would provide the foundation for the permanent peace line later built in the area. Catholic homes were burnt in Ardoyne and elsewhere too, and in all around 7,000 people, most of them Catholics, were left homeless. Around 2,500 Catholic refugees fled south of the border, where new refugee camps were set up.[44]

On 15 August, the nationalist Social Democratic and Labour Party (SDLP) announced a campaign of civil disobedience in response to internment and within two months it was estimated that around 16,000 households were withholding rent and rates for council houses. Over the same period, over 8,000 workers went on strike in Derry alone. Around 130 non-Unionists announced that they would no longer sit on district councils. The SDLP also withdrew its representatives from a number of public bodies. In October, five Northern Ireland MPs began a forty-eight-hour hunger strike close to Downing Street. But such civil disobedience was overshadowed by the men and women who embraced violence.

The dance of death was again ratcheted up: Eamon McDevitt, a deaf Catholic civilian, was shot dead by the Army in Strabane, while two British soldiers were shot and killed by IRA snipers in western Belfast. September saw yet another brutal escalation: IRA men fired on British soldiers in Belfast and a ricochet hit and killed seventeen-month-old Angela Gallagher; the IRA later apologised. An Ulster Defence Regiment (UDR) soldier was also killed by the IRA in County Fermanagh. An eighteen-year-old soldier was killed by an IRA landmine in County Down. Fourteen-year-old Catholic Annette McGavigan became the 100th civilian fatality of the Troubles, shot in the head by a British soldier. A British soldier was killed in Drumankelly while attempting to disarm an IRA bomb. A Loyalist volunteer, aged twenty-one, was injured when a bomb exploded prematurely in Belfast; he died a month later. A British soldier was killed by an IRA sniper in Derry's Creggan estate, while another was shot dead by the IRA in County Tyrone, and another was fatally shot on the Falls Road. A Catholic civilian was shot by a British Army sniper in Derry. A Protestant civilian was murdered in Belfast, probably killed by Loyalists. Another soldier was shot and killed by an IRA sniper in Ardoyne. A twenty-year-old RUC officer was shot dead by IRA gunmen while patrolling in central Strabane, County Tyrone. Two teenagers were killed when a bomb exploded prematurely at an Official IRA location. A bomb attack on a Protestant pub filled with football fans in Shankill Road, Belfast, killed two men and injured twenty-seven others.

The following months were just as bad, another litany of snipings, bombings, gunfights and so-called 'friendly fire' incidents. A Catholic civilian on his way to work was killed during a gun battle between British soldiers and the IRA in Falls Road. The Official IRA bombed a British Army post in Belfast, killing a twenty-two-year-old Scots Guard. The UVF bombed the Fiddler's House bar in Belfast, killing one man and injuring others. Two RUC officers were shot dead by IRA gunmen while parked near Twaddell Avenue in Belfast. A British soldier is also shot by the IRA in Belfast and died two days later. On 23 October five people were killed by the British Army: three men in Newry and two women in Belfast. All were presumed to be IRA members. The following day a nineteen-year-old IRA member was shot dead by RUC officers while attempting to bomb a nightclub in Belfast. The IRA abducted a Protestant man; his body was found bound, gagged and shot through the head in East Belfast. On 27 October alone two British soldiers died after the IRA bombed their post in

Derry; another British soldier was killed in Kinawley after his vehicle hit an IRA landmine; and an RUC officer was shot dead by an IRA sniper in Country Antrim.

By this time all sides knew that, for whatever reasons and for whatever motives, they were engaged in open warfare. And in a largely urban battle zone, with only some participants wearing uniforms, the outcomes were both messy and tragic. The Army shot dead a man standing in the doorway of his home in Ardoyne. The IRA bombed a pub and shops near an RUC station in Belfast, killing two men and a woman. A fifty-one-year-old Belfast woman was shot in the face and blinded by a rubber bullet fired into her window by a British soldier. In a Provisional IRA attack on British soldiers near Strabane, a stray gunshot killed a female Catholic civilian. The UVF exploded a bomb in McGurk's Bar in Belfast, a meeting place for Catholics and known republicans, killing fifteen people including two children and injuring seventeen others, the highest Belfast death toll to date. Security forces initially claimed that the bomb had exploded prematurely while being handled by IRA terrorists inside the pub, implying that the victims themselves were partly to blame. Relatives alleged that the security forces deliberately spread disinformation to discredit the IRA. UVF member Robert Campbell was eventually sentenced to life imprisonment for his part in the bombing and served fifteen years.[45]

The bombing sparked yet another series of tit-for-tat bombings and shootings. Two off-duty UDR soldiers were shot dead by the Provisional IRA while driving to work near Strabane. In the run-up to Christmas, the IRA detonated a bomb at a furniture company in Shankill Road, a Loyalist area of Belfast, killing four civilians, two of them babies sharing a pram. Ulster Unionist senator John Barnhill was shot and killed by the Official IRA near his Strabane home, the first politician to be murdered during the Troubles. The Army shot dead sixteen-year-old Martin McShane outside a youth centre in County Tyrone. Within hours the IRA had shot and killed a twenty-two-year-old British soldier in the Lower Falls. Three IRA volunteers were killed when the bomb they were carrying exploded in County Derry. In Belfast, the UVF bombed a pub, killing a sixteen-year-old civilian. A Catholic publican was also killed while attempting to remove an IRA bomb from his bar.[46]

My reason for listing such individual and communal tragedies – and there were many more – is to show how mutual hostility based on prejudice, injustice and self-interest snowballed into blood feuds involving every side. Catholics, Protestants, republicans and socialists, Unionists and the Establishment, rich and poor families, terrorists, paramilitaries and street hooligans, criminal elements, the RUC, the B-Specials, politicians on both sides of the Irish Sea, and the Army all fell prey to a bloodlust justified, in their own minds at least, by their competing causes. There was never going to be a happy outcome.

In the republican strongholds of the Bogside and the Creggan in Derry, peace of sorts had been largely maintained following the 1969 riots. In the early summer of 1971, the RUC was patrolling almost everywhere in the area on foot and the Army was little in evidence. At the beginning of July, however, gunmen appeared again. Despite considerable violence the authorities decided to reduce the level of military activity in the hope that moderate opinion would prevail, and the IRA gunmen would be isolated from the community.[47] Bogside and Creggan residents threw up or repaired over fifty barricades, including one in Rossville Street which was to figure prominently in subsequent events. The RUC and the Army patrols stayed clear of the area. Apart from one Company location at the Bligh's Lane factory in the centre of the area, all military posts were located round the edges of the district. The law was not effectively enforced within the barricade perimeter. In the view of the authorities, the military policy of 'passive containment' was not working.

At the end of October, 8 Infantry Brigade was ordered to regain the initiative in a step-by-step fashion and reimpose the rule of law on the Creggan and Bogside with 'vigorous' snatch and arrest operations against 'hooligans', the clearing of barricades and the forceful searching of suspects' homes. The soldiers duly went in at battalion strength and employed aggressive tactics which even Lord Widgery described as hardening the attitude of the community against the Army, 'so that the troops were operating in an entirely hostile environment and as time went on were opposed by all elements of the community when they entered the Bogside and Creggan'. The Army's observation posts were fired upon and large numbers of unemployed youths gathered daily at points of entry to attack soldiers with stones and petrol and nail bombs. Gunmen made full use of the cover offered by such mayhem. The Creggan became a fortress. Whenever troops appeared at night car headlights were switched on and car horns blazed.[48] From August 1971 in Derry, according to figures given to Widgery, 2,656 shots were fired at the security forces, 456 nail and gelignite bombs were thrown and there were 225 explosions, mostly against business premises. In reply the security forces fired back 840 live rounds. Two RUC officers were killed when snipers fired on their vehicle.

Lord Saville would later sum up: 'The police had become regarded by many in the nationalist community not as impartial keepers of the peace and upholders of the law, but rather as agents of the unionist Northern Ireland government, employed in their view to keep the nationalist community subjugated, often by the use of unjustifiable and brutal force. On 14th August 1969, after there had been particularly violent clashes between civilians and the police in Londonderry, the authorities brought into the city units of the British Army as an aid to the civil power, in other words to restore law and order.'[49] The situation in Derry in January 1972 was serious. Parts of the city to the west of the Foyle lay in ruins, and largely nationalist streets were a 'no-go' area where ordinary policing could not be conducted and where even the Army ventured only in large numbers.[50]

In the New Year, the security authorities worried that the violence was now spreading northwards from William Street, the line on the northern fringe of the Bogside. Bombing and arson attacks on shops, offices and commercial premises increasingly occurred in Great James Street and Waterloo Place. The Londonderry Development Commission estimated that between August 1971 and February 1972 damage amounted to more than £6 million.[51] Local traders feared that the whole of this shopping area would be extinguished within the next few months. At the beginning of 1972 Army foot patrols were not able to operate south of William Street by day because of sniper fire, although the Army continued to patrol in the Bogside at night.

Major General Robert Ford, then Commander of Land Forces in Northern Ireland, visited Londonderry and wrote a confidential memorandum to Lieutenant General Sir Harry Tuzo, his senior and the General Officer Commanding Northern Ireland, in which he reported that the 'Derry Young Hooligans' were responsible for the continued destruction of the city and that the Army was 'virtually incapable' of dealing with them. General Ford ordered that an additional Army battalion be sent to the city to be used to arrest rioters if, which was expected to happen, any proposed civil rights march was followed by rioting. Initially he believed that such a force might be able to arrest a large number of rioters and by that means significantly decrease the activities of the 'Hooligans'.[52] To that end General Ford ordered that 1st Battalion, The Parachute Regiment (1 PARA), which was stationed near Belfast, travel to Derry and be used as the arrest force.

Although for most of January Derry was the centre of the violence, the rest of the Province was hardly quiet. In that month, an IRA sniper shot dead a British soldier patrolling the Lower Falls, British troops killed an IRA member during a gun battle in Belfast, and IRA squads shot and killed two off-duty RUC officers in the capital. An IRA sniper shot dead a UDR soldier in County Antrim. A Catholic civilian from Belfast was murdered after he allegedly gave police information about an IRA operation, and a British soldier was fatally wounded after treading on an IRA landmine.

On 18 January 1972, Northern Ireland premier Brian Faulkner banned all parades and marches in Northern Ireland until the end of the year in a bid to prevent more bloodshed. That proved to be a forlorn hope. By then, passions had been roused on all sides. With the benefit of hindsight, we must go back to two incidents in the previous months that explain why the desire for 'payback' was paramount.

2

Honeytrap Killings and the Ballymurphy Massacre

'It's alright son, I'm coming to you.'

In the opening weeks of 1971, two teenage brothers were learning the crafts of soldiery in Scotland and a teenage dad in Belfast was getting used to married life while a neighbour just out of his teens shunned alcohol but enjoyed a flutter at the bookies. In another environment, in another life, they would probably all have got along well. Although every death during the Troubles can be regarded as a tragedy whatever the deceased's age, their fatal involvement in two separate incidents can be used to illustrate how mutual hatreds led to Bloody Sunday.

* * *

Brothers John and Joseph McCaig from Ayr, aged seventeen and eighteen, were privates serving with the 1st Battalion, The Royal Highland Fusiliers, stationed at Girdwood barracks in Belfast.[1] They were lads of their age and of the age – their ethos was to train hard, work hard and play hard, within reason. Like most young squaddies, they had signed up for adventure and as an escape from a working-class poverty of aspiration.

Off-duty and with off-base passes on the afternoon of 10 March, they hooked up with their mate, twenty-three-year-old Private Dougald McCaughey, whose younger brother serving in the same unit was on duty and unable to join them. Dressed in civvies, they were cheerfully ready for a session of booze and, they hoped, girls after a tense tour of duty. Soldiers at that time were allowed to visit local bars and mingle with the locals; they felt safe as until then just three British soldiers had been killed in separate incidents and each during a riot. There were no riots that day.

They headed into the city. McCaughey needed to withdraw cash from the General Post Office in Royal Avenue and the brothers went with him. Friends and fellow Fusiliers believe that the soldiers were first spotted by a republican sympathiser – with a British military background – as they entered the GPO and after that, their fate was sealed.[2] Later evidence suggested that eight days before the Metropolitan Police had received intelligence that the IRA was planning to kill off-duty soldiers. Whether what followed was opportunist or well-planned – or maybe both – remains unclear.

The young Fusiliers strolled to the Abercorn Bar, where they were spotted at around 3 p.m. drinking with two men with 'southern Irish accents'. One of their new-found pals sported a distinctive Van Dyke beard. Two attractive, well-dressed women in their mid-twenties flirted with the soldiers. One was a blonde wearing a black, tight-fitting sweater with a silver buckled belt and a black miniskirt with black tights; the other was a brunette whose shortish hair left one ear uncovered. Their next pint stop was Mooney's, a Cornmarket bar which was then considered one of the safer places for soldiers. They were then invited to Kelly's Cellars – they were seen there at 6.30 p.m., the time they were due back in barracks. Fifteen minutes later McCaughey telephoned his aunt at her home in Glasgow. Recognising that he was phoning from a busy, noisy pub, she warned him to 'watch himself'. At around 7 p.m. a known republican entered the bar and minutes later the soldiers left with the group, still holding their pint glasses. By then they had been drinking heavily for at least six hours and were enticed into a saloon car when the two women, who seem to have been with them for most of the afternoon, invited them to a party. One witness suggested they were heading for the Glen Inn near Squire's Hill. In the car were 'three fellows ... speaking with Scottish accents' and 'the girls'. It is not clear whether the three other men cited by the witness were crammed in the same car or in a following blue Vauxhall or lying in ambush by the side of the road.

At White Brae, a remote and narrow lane roughly 4 miles outside the city limits which ended at the pub, the Fusiliers got out to relieve themselves in a ditch. As they did so, they were shot with a .38 revolver and a 9mm semi-automatic pistol. Two were shot in the back of the head and the other in the chest.[3] Witnesses spoke of seeing an Austin Cambridge and a red Mini leaving the scene. The Mini's occupants appeared to be covered by a white sheet. The bodies left behind were heaped on top of each other alongside two empty beer mugs and twenty-five domino pieces. After failing to return to their barracks by 6.30 p.m. the three were listed as absent without leave. Three hours later they were found by local children.[4]

The day after the killings, Home Secretary Reginald Maudling told the Commons that security arrangements for off-duty soldiers were being reviewed and suggested that the aim of the killers was to provoke the security forces into reprisals. He said that: 'The battle now joined against the terrorists will be fought with the utmost vigour and determination. It is a battle against a small minority of armed and ruthless men whose strength lies not so much in their numbers as in their wickedness.'[5]

The inquest in August 1971 was not able to establish the exact sequence of events. It was established, however, that all three were shot at very close range, probably in a line. All had been drinking, and Joseph was found to be severely intoxicated. The jury was told that the three were probably shot whilst relieving themselves beside the road, although rumours persisted that their unbuttoned flies were in expectation of a sexual encounter. Their commanding officer described them as 'just boys'. The coroner commented: 'You may think that this was not only murder, but one of the vilest crimes ever heard of in living memory.'

The funerals were held in Scotland with John and Joseph McCaig buried together in Ayr. Their older brother, a serving Royal Marine, was flown home from Singapore for the service. Around 10,000 people attended a rally around the cenotaph opposite Belfast City Hall in a gathering that stopped the traffic in the city centre. Many wept openly. The crowd laid dozens of wreaths, observed a two-minute silence, and sang a hymn and the national anthem. The mother of the two McCaig brothers visited the scene of their deaths in May 1972. She expressed a wish to leave a monument to her sons but was advised that it might well be damaged by vandals. She later said that she was touched by the wreaths and flowers that had been left at the spot. Given John McCaig's youth, the British Army raised the minimum age for active service in Northern Ireland to 18.[6]

No one was ever convicted of the killings. The RUC was unable to provide solid evidence on several suspects and the Metropolitan Police and Special Branch were sent to break the case. The RUC gave the squad a list of names. By the time the Met's inquiries ended, they had come up with the exact same names, and they, too, lacked the necessary evidence.[7] In November 2007 it was reported that three Provisional IRA men were responsible: Michael Meehan, who had been questioned that year, but not charged; the goatee-bearded Patrick McAdorey, who had been shot and killed in August 1971 during a gun battle in the Ardoyne (he was also suspected of the fatal shooting, hours before his own death, of Private Malcolm Hatton of the Green Howards); and a third unnamed man. The case was reopened by the Police Service of Northern Ireland's Historical Enquiries Team which, like the RUC and the Met, failed to unearth enough new evidence to bring charges.[8]

In February 2020 the BBC unearthed evidence that former Paratrooper Paddy O'Kane, who had switched allegiance to the IRA, was the main killer. The documentary *The Killings of the Three Scottish Soldiers* included witness statements that he had shared a drink with them before taking them away to their deaths. Members of O'Kane's family confirmed that he boasted he was involved in the killings, while former IRA intelligence chief Kieran Conway said O'Kane spoke openly about his role. He said: 'I believe any man that could execute three young soldiers in that manner must have been a psychopath.'[9] Multiple sources confirmed that O'Kane was a lead suspect for the Kingsmill massacre in January 1976, when ten Protestant workmen were shot dead by the IRA. He was also implicated in the 1979 Warrenpoint massacre which left sixteen Paras and three Queen's Own Highlanders dead. He fled to County Clare in the Republic and worked as a labourer. He was given an 'immunity letter' after the Good Friday Agreement and died in 2009.[10]

Also in February 2020, the *Mail on Sunday* confirmed O'Kane as one of up to ten conspirators including the two women involved in the 'honeytrap'. One of the women, whose father and brother were IRA members, was reportedly living in England. The other allegedly acted as a lure in a similar murder of three more off-duty soldiers in Belfast two years later.[11] A 1973 wanted poster described her as smartly dressed, well-built, attractive with dark wavy hair and a small turned-up nose. The newspaper claimed she had been a member of the IRA's women's division, *Cumann na mBan*, and was then, aged seventy-one, living in Dublin.[12]

Such new evidence from multiple sources put more pressure on the government to open a new inquest, especially as 200 former members of the British security forces were still being investigated for alleged historic crimes. Lawyer Matthew Jury, representing the families of the dead soldiers, said: 'There are a number of unanswered questions and suspects who were not previously spoken to by the police. Those who are still alive must be brought to justice and all avenues pursued. The families will not rest until these people answer for their crimes.'[13]

In 1971 the impact of the killings was immediate and widespread. On-the-spot reporter Martin Lindsey recalled: 'It was the first multiple killing of the so-called Troubles. But the IRA murder of three young Scottish Fusiliers sent shock waves through a country which had not yet witnessed the wholesale slaughter of civilians and security force members at the hands of terrorists. Narrow Water, Kingsmill, Loughinisland

and Enniskillen had yet to happen. But that chilly night ... the unrest witnessed up to then was suddenly and brutally overshadowed.'[14]

An on-the-run Provisional told another reporter: 'We had buried young lads of our own ... it was high time the army did the same.'[15] The Army understandably took a different view. The murders, not in battle, not in a riot, were seen as cowardly and deserving of vengeance. From then on it was not just two tribes who went to war.

A memorial was eventually raised at White Brae, in 2011. It has been vandalised several times since.

***

The Parachute Regiment was born during the Second World War and over two generations had a proud if bloody history as a light infantry unit sent swiftly into the worst trouble spots. The 1st Battalion was set up in 1940, when No. 2 Commando trained as parachutists. In 1941, the battalion was assigned to the 1st Parachute Brigade as part of the 1st Airborne Division. Hitler's *blitzkreigs* employed massed parachutists, most notably in the invasion of Crete, and it was believed this was the future of warfare.

The battalion took part in operations in Tunisia in late 1942 and early May 1943, suffering heavy casualties. They fought bravely in the subsequent invasion of Sicily but again suffered such heavy losses that they were withdrawn to England in late 1943 to train and prepare for what became known as D-Day. At the start of the Allied invasion, they were held in reserve to wreck Nazi counter-attacks which never really materialised. Finally, they were dropped into Arnhem with the rest of the 1st Airborne Division, as part of the disastrous Operation Market Garden and the few uninjured survivors did not see combat again for the rest of the war. The battalion was reconstituted in 1946, affiliated to the Brigade of Guards, and served in Palestine but the days of going into battle by parachute were numbered, although arduous training for that eventuality continued. The battalion was deployed to Northern Ireland in 1969 as part of the Operation Banner incursion. It is fair to say that, given their illustrious para predecessors, the new generation did not always cover themselves in glory.

On the streets, they quickly established a reputation for casual, unnecessary brutality in their dealings with civilians and for a mindset which saw all Catholics, nationalists and republicans as either potential terrorists or actual ones. Their training also imbued a 'don't ask why, just get it done' mentality. Given the Army's rising casualty rate, that is understandable but not necessarily justifiable. At the time they had suffered minimal casualties but took a more draconian line that those regiments who had, including the Fusiliers. A 1 Para veteran said: 'We were in it for the ruck, pure and simple.'[16] Their operational methods were neither nuanced nor subtle and their sense of professionalism was not always matched by the quality of their officers. The 'Ruperts' were, with exceptions, prone to panic.[17]

Such issues came to the fore in three bloody days from Monday 9 August when 1 Para was deployed in Ballymurphy, a suburb of Belfast, as part of the round-up of suspects earmarked for internment. As elsewhere, army intelligence was faulty to the degree of guesswork. Shortly after dawn at 5 a.m., 600 Paras descended on the sleeping community, kicking down doors, smashing windows and dragging sleep-drugged civilians from their beds. Uncoordinated groups of youths protested noisily, and some stones were thrown. Paras claimed that they were shot at by republicans, a claim ardently disputed by the affected families.[18] Riflemen had taken positions on the roof of a block of flats, unaware that they were overlooking fellow soldiers. One theory, dismissed at the time but which gained traction later, was that their fields of fire overlapped and one side briefly came under 'friendly' fire. True or not, the word that they were facing an armed enemy spread rapidly amongst the Paras, with tragic consequences.

At roughly 8.30 p.m. in Springfield Park, local man Bobby Clarke was trying to take children in open ground to safety when he was shot. Other locals tried to go to his aid but were pinned back by para gunfire. Corpus Christi Parish priest Father Hugh Mullan telephoned the Henry Taggart army post to tell them he was going onto the field to help the injured man. He then did so, waving a white baby-grow as a flag of truce. He anointed Clarke and, having seen that he was suffering a flesh wound and was not fatally wounded, he tried to leave the field, only to be fatally shot in the back. Nineteen-year-old Frank Quinn left his place of safety to help the fallen priest, but before he could reach him was fatally shot in the back of the head. Their bodies lay where they fell until local people could safely reach them.[19]

Understandably, tensions soared in the community as the round-up continued through the morning. Families fleeing their homes in the Springfield Park area known locally as the Manse came under attack from Loyalist youths from the Springmartin district. Catholic youths targeted the Henry Taggart army base with stones. Parents frantically searched for their children gathered at the bottom of Springfield Park. Among them were local amateur boxer Joseph Murphy who was returning from the wake of a local boy who drowned in a swimming accident, while Joan Connolly and her neighbour Anna Breen were searching for their daughters. Daniel Teggart stopped after checking on his brother's safety as his home was close to the army base. Noel Phillips, nineteen, had just finished work and walked to Springfield Park to check on the situation. With no apparent warning the Army opened fire directly at the gathering. Panic-stricken people ran in all directions, but many took refuge in a field directly opposite the army base. The Army focused their fire on them.

Noel Phillips was shot in the buttocks, an injury that was later described in his autopsy as a flesh wound. As he lay crying for help, Joan Connolly, a forty-four-year-old mother of eight, went to his aid. She was heard calling to the teenager: 'It's alright son, I'm coming to you.' She was shot in the face. When the gunfire stopped Noel Phillips, Joan Connolly, Joseph Murphy and many others lay wounded. Window cleaner Daniel Teggart, a forty-four-year-old father of fourteen, lay dead having been shot fourteen times mainly in his back, allegedly as he lay injured on the ground. A short time later a British Army vehicle left the Henry Taggart army base and entered the field. A solider exited the vehicle and executed the wounded Phillips by shooting him once behind each ear with a handgun.

Soldiers then threw injured and dead into the back of the vehicle and took them into the army base. Joseph Murphy, who had been shot once in the leg, Noel Phillips and others still breathing, were severely beaten. It was later reported that soldiers punched and kicked the victims, jumped off bunks onto the injured and forced objects into existing wounds. Murphy died three weeks later from his injuries; from his hospital death bed he claimed that he had been shot again while in custody. That was strenuously denied, but when his body was exhumed in October 2015, a second bullet missed in his initial autopsy was indeed discovered in his body.

Joan Connolly was left in the field where, according to eyewitnesses, she cried out for help for several hours before dying untended, her body lying where she fell for the rest of the day and evening. Her body was finally removed from the field around 2.30 the following morning. Autopsy reports found that, having been repeatedly shot, she bled to death. It was claimed she was shot by three soldiers and that she could well have survived had she been given medical attention. Family members remain convinced that after the initial wounding she, Teggart and maybe others were used as 'target practice' by Paras as they lay prone and no threat to anyone.

The Tuesday broke with what was described as a 'calm numbness'. Soldiers compiled reports. Families double-checked on each other. Medical professionals stemmed wounds. Prayers were said. People mourned. Life went on. For most.

Father-of-two Eddie Doherty from the St James' area of West Belfast visited his elderly parents in the Turf Lodge area in the evening to check on their safety during the ongoing unrest. While walking home along the Whiterock Road he saw a barricade at the corner of Brittons Parade which had been erected to keep out the Army. He chatted to an acquaintance about the ongoing trouble as an army digger and Saracen armoured car moved in to dismantle the barricade. From the digger, a para opened fire. Doherty was shot in the back as he ran away. Local people carried him to a house close by in a bid to provide medical attention, but he died, aged thirty-one, a short time later from a single gunshot wound.[20]

At roughly 4 a.m. on 11 August, twenty-year-old John Laverty from Whitecliff Parade was shot and killed by Paras whose bullets had hit him in the back and one leg. Father-of-seven Joseph Corr was also shot several times and died of his injuries sixteen days later aged forty-three. The Parachute Regiment insisted that both men were firing at the Army and were killed as the Army responded. Neither was armed and ballistic and forensic evidence tested at the time disproved the Army's testimony.

The Army had imposed a curfew and Pat McCarthy, a London community worker who had transferred to Ballymurphy to work for a tenants' association, knew it prevented essential bread and milk vans from entering the area. He was shot in the hand as he left the local community centre waving a Red Cross flag to distribute essentials. A few hours later, nursing his wounded hand, McCarthy decided to continue with the deliveries. He was stopped and punched by Paras. Eyewitness watched in horror as the soldiers carried out a mock execution by placing a gun in his mouth and pulling the trigger. The gun was unloaded, but McCarthy suffered a massive heart attack. The same soldiers stopped local people who tried to help as he died.[21]

Father-of-eight John McKerr, a carpenter from Andersonstown Road, was carrying out repair work in Corpus Christi chapel but took a short break for the funeral service of the local boy who had drowned in a swimming accident. As he waited outside for the mass to end, the forty-nine-year-old was shot once in the head by a Para. An ambulance was called but initially soldiers refused to let it take McKerr to hospital. They relented after severe barracking from the church congregation. He died of his injuries nine days later having never regained consciousness.[22]

For the families of the dead and dying, there was little respite in their grief. Frank Quinn and his wife had married when they were both seventeen in St Peter's Cathedral shortly before the birth of their first child. He was described as 'a practical joker and full of fun'. One of six siblings, he was an avid fan of Glasgow Celtic and Everton and played the mouth organ to a not-always-receptive audience. Frank's younger brother recalled the moment his father came home from work and told the family that Frank had been shot. 'I said "was he wounded? Was he wounded?" and he said "no, he's dead". Those three words changed me and my family's lives forever.'[23] His young widow gave birth to a second daughter shortly after his death. As Frank's parents lived in a mixed-religion community, his wake was held in the Divis area of West Belfast as shots were fired outside. Mourners moved back from the windows for their own safety, but his mother never left his side. Both parents suffered sectarian abuse and had to leave their home on the Ravenhill Road to move across the city to the New Lodge.

Joan Connolly, the second youngest of eight children, had the first four of her eight children while living in the Shore Road area of Belfast, a mixed area where the family had many friends from both sides of the community. With only two bedrooms, their home became small and cramped for a fast-growing family. When a bigger home became available in Ballymurphy, she and her husband jumped at the chance. They became an integral part of the close-knit community and in May 1971 she became a grandmother. She didn't drink and rarely socialised but did enjoy a game of bingo and a cigarette. Her daughter, Briege Voyle, said her mother was shocked by the start of the Troubles, saying that she 'just couldn't get her head around' what was happening, and previously she had made tea and sandwiches for British soldiers at her house.

The extent of her injuries was so horrific – half her face was blown away – that her husband could only identify her body on the third attempt by her red hair. He immediately sent their six youngest children south of the border to stay with family members. Two daughters were held first in a refugee holding centre and the first they knew that their mother was dead and buried was on the evening news. Joan's widower and the elder children who stayed in Belfast were harassed by soldiers who sang the current pop hit 'Chirpy Chirpy Cheep Cheep', which included the words 'where's your momma gone'. Widower Denis, already suffering from poor health, had a nervous breakdown; his health never fully recovered, and he died of cancer in May 1982. Joan's eldest daughter, having married a soldier, was posted in Germany with her husband. As she struggled with the sudden loss, she attempted suicide on several occasions. Briege recalled: 'My mother was very dearly loved and has been very dearly missed. Losing her destroyed our family. Whilst coping without her has been hard for all of us what has made things worse were the media reports that she was a gunwoman and the rumours that followed us that we were the children of the gunwoman that was shot.'

Father Mullan, from Portaferry, had served a year in the Merchant Navy, before parishes in Belfast, County Antrim, County Down and finally Ballymurphy. His brother said he loved sailing on Strangford Lough and when he served in the Good Shepherd Convent in Belfast he would play guitar and sing to the children. On the fateful night his brother heard that a priest had been shot in Ballymurphy, 'I knew it would be him', he said. 'When I was later told that he was dead, I phoned our doctor and asked him to come to be with my mother as I didn't know how she would cope with this news. She was in a terrible state and had to be sedated.'[24]

Eddie Doherty had been a popular dustbin man, barman and golfer with friends across the Ulster Divide. On the day of his funeral, RUC officers lined the Falls Road and saluted as his coffin passed. It provided a rare ray of hope for the future. Six-footer John Laverty, the lad who shunned alcohol but enjoyed a flutter, had just passed his driving test and the photograph for his driving licence was the last ever taken of him alive. Joe Murphy, whose father had served in the British Army, worked as a rag and bone man. His daughter said he would often bring stray animals home with him, which was how she got her first pet – a kitten. She recalled: 'I remember my daddy going out on the day he was shot. We were all upstairs and I can remember running to the landing and shouting "Daddy where are you going?" and him saying "a wee message". I asked him to give me a kiss and stuck my head through the banister of our stairs and he kissed me.' John McKerr was a former British soldier who, despite losing his right hand in the Second World War, worked as a joiner. His eldest daughter Anne said the family had been brought up to 'live and let live', adding: 'The newspaper reports about Daddy being in the IRA were terrible lies which only made matters worse. As a family we were devastated by the untruths spoken about our father.' Her sister remembered an Army officer apologising to her mother before the funeral.

Noel Phillips' brother said that when trouble broke out on 9 August 1971 his brother was 'doing what kids do, you would go for a nosey that's all he was doing'. Other family members went to the local morgue and identified him, he said, adding: 'They came back in a terrible state; nothing was ever the same from that point. Nobody came to tell us Noel was dead; we just had to find out for ourselves.' He said, his mother, once a happy-go-lucky woman, 'went to pieces' and was never the same after losing her son. 'After his death everything just went black; everything changed for us. There was no laughing or messing about, the normal things six brothers would get up to, that all changed. We never spoke about our Noel's death and we never asked our older brother Robert about identifying his body. He never spoke about it right up until the day he died.' Daniel Teggart's daughter Alice later testified that when her father went missing, she went to the Henry Taggart army base to ask for information: 'I asked "did you arrest my father?" I was just asking different questions and they just said no we hadn't time for arrests, we only had time for killing and that was their words.' The Army later directed her to a morgue. 'After that, all of our lives changed completely and it affected our family in a big way,' she said. The IRA shot dead one of her brothers in 1973.

Eileen McKeown, the daughter of Shorts machinist Joseph Corr, got hate mail from his former colleagues after he was shot and after the Army had branded him a terrorist. The family had been in the process of emigrating to Australia when he was killed. She said: 'Daddy was in hospital for sixteen days before he died. At the beginning he was missing, we didn't know where he was, whether he was alive or dead before he was found in Musgrave military hospital. I remember thinking why did they take him there when the Royal Victoria Hospital is closer? When my daddy was in hospital, we were taken to a refugee camp somewhere in Dublin to a convent I think – mammy must have thought we would be safer there. The next memory I have is my uncle Paddy telling us that my daddy was dead.' She added: 'The soldiers who did this, they don't realise the after-effects. I mean, I used to have four brothers and now I've none. With all the boys they resented the fact that they lost their daddy and they never had a father figure around. Their dependence on alcohol and early deaths are as a direct result of losing my daddy.'[25]

John Laverty had been named after his uncle, who had fought in the Second World War. His younger brother Terry was sentenced to six months for riotous behaviour on the eyewitness testimony of a para private. In February 2015 the conviction was quashed by the Criminal Cases Review Commission after the private belatedly retracted his testimony.[26]

Ballymurphy, with eleven civilians dead and many more wounded and traumatised, was by far the biggest slaughter seen so far in the Troubles but for decades was largely forgotten outside the Province, overshadowed by the only marginally more bloody events in Derry a few months later. That may be because the shootings took place over three days rather than a few minutes. It was also because there is no video or photographic evidence of the killings or the violence that shook the residential neighbourhood. No journalists were present to record the events as they unfolded. The state's PR apparatus also proved effective in suggesting that soldiers were responding to clear and present danger. Captain Mike Jackson, at the time 1 Para's 'community relations and press officer' based at Palace Barracks in Holywood, reported a gun battle between soldiers and supposed terrorists that was widely believed.

It took a long time before it was generally accepted that there was no forensic evidence to suggest that any of the victims had fired a weapon themselves while there was plenty of evidence that victims had been abused and even finished off while in army custody. And, as we have seen, the grief of the families was exacerbated by claims that the dead somehow 'deserved it' because of the small community's support for nationalism or republicanism – potential terrorists, in other words.

The families' fight for justice continued through the Troubles and well beyond. In 2016 Northern Ireland's Lord Chief Justice, Sir Declan Morgan, recommended an inquest into the killings as one of a series of 'legacy inquests' covering fifty-six cases.[27] Those inquests were delayed, as funding had not been approved by the Northern Ireland Executive. Former Stormont first minister Arlene Foster of the Democratic Unionist Party (DUP) deferred a bid for extra funding for inquests into historic killings in Northern Ireland, a decision condemned by the human rights group Amnesty International.[28] The High Court said her decision to refuse to put a funding paper on the Executive basis was 'unlawful and procedurally flawed'.

The Ballymurphy inquest began at Laganside Courts in Belfast in November 2018 and over sixteen months heard almost 100 days of evidence from over 100 witnesses, including more than sixty former soldiers, more than thirty civilians, and experts in ballistics, pathology and civil engineering.[29] Those hearings showed that the prejudices, ongoing rage and self-delusions inherent in the military and the Establishment, and to some extent the republican community, had never died. A former para known as Witness M249 insisted he ran through gunfire to supply fellow soldiers with ammunition during the shootings, also claiming that during five tours he had never fired his own weapon. He told the court there had been sporadic gunfire and disorder around Henry Taggart Hall on the day of the killings as tensions escalated over British government policy which was seen as targeting Belfast's Catholic minority. He claimed two shots were fired at his patrol soon after he had supported soldiers carrying out an arrest at the Springfield Park area of Ballymurphy. Later while inside the Vere Foster School watching television to find out what was happening, a bullet came through a window which he assumed must have come from the Ballymurphy area. He recalled shots being fired as he made his way to his platoon to provide them ammunition. At no time did he recall seeing a gunman.[30]

A former Army major known as Soldier M45 described the shooting of Father Mullan as 'good press'. He was in command of B Company 2 Para at Vere Foster and Henry Taggart base on the Springfield Road, and asked to explain what that meant by his comment, he said the priest's death would have strong resonance with Catholic people and that 'they would make what they could of it'. Asked about the treatment of the wounded inside the base, he agreed that such behaviour would be 'quite unacceptable' if it happened but added: 'I don't honestly accept that it did happen. There may have been rough usage.'

M45 later described in detail how he climbed onto the roof of Vere Foster School and saw that his soldiers were under fire from the nearby Moyard flats. He ordered his men to return fire and that he believed two gunmen were 'taken down'. Early the next morning, he said, they could see the body of a man on the balcony. That version of events was challenged by a barrister for the next of kin, who explained that no civilian witness had seen a gunman or found a body. Journalists and television crews visiting the flat the following day had not seen any evidence either. The inquest had already heard from several witnesses who did enter the flat the next morning to rescue two sleeping infants, who had survived unharmed a few inches below the sustained gunfire. M45 told the court that 'Ballymurphy was just one of many little actions going on in Belfast that night … I thought that was accepted. Belfast had almost imploded on 9 August.' M45 explained that he had not immediately begun an investigation after his soldiers opened fire. 'It's quite frenetic when people are shooting at you and you are shooting back,' he said. 'You can't line up soldiers and ask them, "put up your hand, who did this and who did that?"'

Later a barrister for the Teggart and Phillips families asked if M45 knew if any of the people his soldiers shot had been on the list of internment suspects. 'No' said M45. 'How do you know?' asked the barrister. 'Well, we didn't shoot Gerry Adams and he was on the list,' said the former soldier, to some nervous laughter in the court. Adams lived opposite the Henry Taggart base at the time and his home was under surveillance. M45 also said during his evidence about his soldiers, 'the forbearance they showed that day was remarkable'.[31] Former soldier M506 denied having fired his weapon from the roof of Vere Foster School when civilians were shot and fatally wounded. Accused of being less than truthful with his evidence, he said: 'I should be commended for the lives I saved, and I took none.'[32]

Brian McLaughlin, a community and youth worker in the Moyard area, did not witness any killings but carried Father Mullan's body to a house where he and others took it upstairs. He testified: 'His blood ran down my arms. This has always stuck with me. I remember thinking, "Why is this happening?" It was a nightmare we lived. Nightmares, they don't fade that easily.' He also told the court he had seen one 'young fella' in the Moyard area with a revolver who appeared to be trying to hide.

At one point as he tried to help those who were injured, McLaughlin said he could hear the 'bullets zinging by'. Like several other witnesses to the inquest, he thought the shooting had come from Springmartin flats.[33]

One of the most eagerly awaited testimonies was that of the para press officer who had caused such offence by appearing to pin the blame on the victims. By now General Sir Mike Jackson, the former head of the British Army and Chief of the General Staff, was seventy-five and one of the best-known officers in the British Army after serving in Kosovo and as commander during the Iraq and Afghan wars. There was a heavy police presence outside the court and the general, weather-beaten from decades of overseas deployments, was whisked into the compound through the adjacent Musgrave PSNI station. Ostensibly that operation was for security reasons, but it also allowed him to avoid the bank of press photographers and camera crews outside. Both the press box and the public gallery were packed, with many seats in the latter filled by relatives of the Bloody Sunday victims who had last seen Sir Mike when he gave evidence at the Saville Inquiry. They stared at him with intensity, believing him to be the key man in 'starting the narrative that the victims were gunmen'.[34]

Michael Mansfield QC, counsel for the family of victim Joseph Corr, asked Jackson why soldiers involved in the shootings were not interviewed by the Royal Military Police at the time and suggested there had been an attempt to 'cover up' the shooting of Corr and John Laverty. Jackson responded: 'It is a preposterous accusation to make which would require a huge number of people to be part of. It simply does not add up. It may be there was a breakdown in procedure, it may be that the whole system was overwhelmed by the mayhem of that, I don't know. But I do know we (the British Army) don't do conspiracies.'

He recalled being part of an army movement down Whiterock Road towards Springfield Road in the early hours aimed at dismantling barricades. He recalled a gun battle between the Army and the IRA which he said lasted two to three hours and involved twenty gunmen. While he did not see the battle, he said he heard the shots, including the 'distinctive thumping noise of a Thompson submachine gun' – a weapon then associated with the IRA. Jackson described that type of gun as the weapon of the enemy. 'I have absolutely no doubt that the IRA were firing on soldiers and soldiers were firing on the IRA,' he said. A newspaper article published later on 11 August described Laverty and Corr as gunmen, although no guns were found when their bodies were recovered. Jackson told the inquest it was likely he was the captain quoted by the newspaper, although he did not recall giving the interview. Pressed on why the pair had been described as gunmen, Sir Mike said he would have been fed information from soldiers on the ground, by radio or face to face. 'In retrospect, of course I should have said "alleged",' he told the inquest. 'Let me say to the families who so long ago lost their loved ones: for me it's a tragedy. It's a tragedy which is hugely regrettable, but I would also say that anybody who loses their lives as a result of violent conflict is also a tragedy. I too have lost friends, so be it. My sympathies go to you and I'm sorry that it is only now after so long that you feel you can come to terms.'[35]

Kathleen McCarry had previously told the inquest of her brother Eddie Doherty: 'When you think about that one shot that killed Eddie and look at all those lives it affected, the ripple effect forty-seven years later and it will go on to their children and their children's children until there is some kind of acknowledgement, somebody holding their hands up and saying we are sorry.'[36] She and the other grieving families would have to wait even longer for that (*see Chapter 11*).

***

Every soldier serving in Northern Ireland was issued with the Yellow Card – Instructions by the Director of Operations for Opening Fire in Northern Ireland – dictating when he could shoot his weapon. It told soldiers that they should never use more force than the minimum necessary to enable them to carry out their duties and should always first try to handle the situation by means other than opening fire. The soldier should only fire aimed shots and a warning must be given. An exception was when hostile firing was taking place in his area and a warning was impracticable, or when any delay could lead to death or serious injury to people whom it was the soldier's duty to protect or to the soldier himself. In that case the soldier was only permitted to open fire against a person using a firearm – gun, grenade, nail bomb or gelignite-type explosive devices.[37] The instructions were clear and concise but, as we have seen, 1 Para's interpretation of them was, at the very least, wider than most.

Four days after Faulkner's march ban, on 22 January 1972, the Paras halted an anti-internment march to a new holding camp at Magilligan Strand near Derry. When it appeared that the marchers were going to go around the wire, the Army then fired rubber bullets and CS gas at close range into the crowd. A number of witnesses claimed that the Paras, who had been bussed from Belfast to police the march, severely beat protesters and had to be physically restrained by their own officers. The SDLP's John Hume accused the soldiers of 'beating, brutalising and terrorising the demonstrators'. It did not look good on TV and within the Army several senior officers privately complained that para 'brutality' was making the job of their regiments and other peacekeeping forces 'so much harder'.[38] NICRA intended, despite the ongoing ban on demonstration, to hold another anti-internment march in Derry on Sunday 30 January. NICRA, in an effort to avoid a repeat of the violence at Milligan Strand, placed 'special emphasis on the necessity for a peaceful incident-free day'.[39] That was repeatedly underlined by the chief organiser, Ivan Cooper.

Cooper, twenty-six, was an unusual firebrand for the time. A working-class Protestant, he was born in the village of Claudy, Co Derry, and was brought up for a while in nearby Killaloo, where his parents ran the local post office until the family moved to Derry in 1956. After school he worked as a shirt factory line manager. Moved by the poverty he saw among the workers, and by the anti-Catholic discrimination shown by the Unionist-dominated council, his first move into politics came in 1965, when he briefly joined the Claudy Young Unionist Association. Shortly afterwards he resigned, switching to the Northern Ireland Labour Party, which was trying to persuade working-class voters to join together on a non-sectarian basis. Cooper stood for election to the Stormont parliament in 1965, winning some cross-community support but failing to gain a seat.[40] As a strong advocate of non-violence, he speedily rose in the ranks of NICRA. In 1968, Cooper resigned from the Labour Party and founded the Derry Citizens' Action Committee (DCAC). That summer, at a protest meeting in the Guildhall he called on Catholics and Protestants to unite to fight for civil rights 'as the blacks in America were fighting'.[41] He passionately believed that the working classes of both groups shared the same greater interests, but his nationalism led many fellow Protestants to see him as a traitor.[42] While he continued to be loyal to the Anglican Church of Ireland, some worshippers refused to share a pew with him.

Cooper, having ignored a previous month-long ban imposed on marches in Derry in November 1968, organised the march in which up to 15,000 people took part and which many see as the start of the Troubles (*see Chapter 1*). Following violence resulting from numerous more illegal marches in the city, however, Cooper called for a halt to spontaneous marches. In the 1969 general election, Cooper was elected as an independent Stormont MP for Mid-Londonderry, defeating the sitting nationalist MP. During the Battle of the Bogside, Cooper tried to restrain Catholics protesting by linking arms with John Hume and Eddie McAteer, but they were swept aside, and Cooper was knocked unconscious by a brick.[43] In August 1970, Cooper co-founded the Social Democratic and Labour Party (SDLP) with Hume, Gerry Fitt and others.

Ahead of the forthcoming march, Cooper had obtained assurances from the IRA it would withdraw from the area for its duration.[44]

On the Monday before the march date, Frank Lagan, then Chief Superintendent of the Royal Ulster Constabulary (RUC), notified Brigadier Pat MacLellan, then Commander, 8 Infantry Brigade, of his contact with NICRA, and told him of their intention to hold a non-violent demonstration and asked that the march be allowed to take place without military intervention. MacLellan agreed to recommend this approach to General Ford, then Commander of Land Forces in Northern Ireland. However, Ford had placed Derek Wilford, Commander of 1st Battalion Parachute Regiment, in charge of the proposed arrest operation. The broad decision to carry out arrests if there was serious disruption was discussed by the Northern Ireland Committee of the UK Cabinet. Premier Edward Heath later confirmed that the plan was known to British government ministers. The next day the authorities agreed to allow the march in Catholic areas of the city, but to stop it from reaching Guildhall Square. A certain degree of disruption, short of a full-scale riot, was expected but contingency plans were drawn up to deliver a low-key but visible army presence.

Major General Ford decided that 1 Para was the best unit to deploy to arrest possible rioters in the operation codenamed Operation Forecast. Given Ballymurphy and other incidents, it is difficult to understand what he was thinking of – no other unit was more guaranteed to fire up the crowd and make violence certain. The Saville report criticised General Ford for choosing the Parachute Regiment for the operation, as it had 'a reputation for using excessive physical violence'. It added: 'In our view his decision to use 1 Para as the arrest force is open to criticism but he did not know his decision would result in soldiers firing unjustifiably.' However, in a secret memo to his superior, dated 7 January 1972, Ford said he was 'coming to the conclusion that the minimum force necessary to achieve a restoration of law and order is to shoot selected ringleaders amongst the DYH (Derry Young Hooligans), after clear warnings have been issued'.[45] The deployment was, then and now, seen by the nationalist community as a deliberate provocation. It is hard, with the weight of subsequent evidence, to disagree with the view that military commanders believed that protesting 'Fenians' needed to be taught a lesson and also believed they had a clear run to do just that. In the minds of many officers, the dogs of war had been unleashed.

Brigadier MacLellan was the operational commander. A Second World War veteran, his attitudes were forged during service in the Palestine Emergency. He issued orders from Ebrington Barracks to 1 Para's Colonel Wilford, who in turn issued orders to Major Ted Loden who commanded the company assigned to the arrest operation. Loden, like MacLellan, had experience putting down 'insurgents', having won the Military Cross for his actions during the 1967 Aden Emergency.[46] Wilford, Saville later concluded, 'wanted to demonstrate the way to deal with rioters in Derry was not for soldiers to shelter behind barricades like (as he put it) Aunt Sallies while being stoned, as he perceived the local troops had been doing, but instead to go aggressively after rioters, as he and his soldiers had been doing in Belfast'.[47]

Unwittingly or not, the scene was set for slaughter.

3

The Day

'the colour of death'

Willie McKinney, a twenty-seven-year-old printer on the *Derry Journal*, was a keen amateur cameraman and was last seen by his brother Mickey up a tree with his Super 8 cine camera, a cherished Christmas present from five weeks before. He considered it the best vantage point to film the start of the Derry civil rights march. According to his brother, he was 'inoffensive and a strong supporter of John Hume'. The oldest of ten siblings, he was engaged to be married in the spring.

Seventeen-year-old factory worker Jackie Duddy disobeyed his father and joined the march 'for the craic' with his friends. A keen boxer, Duddy had represented his club in bouts across Ireland and in Liverpool.

Another seventeen-year-old, Michael Kelly, had overslept and missed Sunday Mass with his family. He was also told by his kin not to go, but he too wanted to meet up with friends. His brother recalled: 'I remember saying to him "Look Michael, you've never been on a march before; if anything happens go home!" So I left him to his friends and he went his way, and I went my way…'[1]

Patrick Doherty, a thirty-two-year-old plumber, was a steward on the march and had tied a white handkerchief around his arm to identify himself as such. He accompanied his wife Eileen to the assembly point at Bishop's Field and left her there with her sisters, with instructions to stay safely at the rear. They planned to meet up for tea after the speeches.

He, and many others, would not be home for tea that day. Or any other day.

***

The scene set for slaughter was, and is, remarkably small – an area about a quarter of a mile square on the west bank of the River Foyle and overshadowed by the old City Wall. In 1972 the north-east corner of the Bogside district was bounded on the west by the Creggan, a largely new district built on rising ground. The flat area was criss-crossed by a mixture of ramshackle old terraced homes, some of them virtually derelict, and new blocks of flats and maisonettes interspersed with cleared areas full of rubble, concrete courtyards covered in lurid graffiti, and other open spaces. William Street, Eden Place and Pilot Row were urban wastelands, with most of the buildings demolished. All the flats, however – the Rossville, Glenfada Park, Kells Walk, Columbcille Court, Abbey Park and Joseph Place – were brutally modern slabs of glass and concrete. The Rossville Flats consisted of three ten-storey blocks.[2]

The original game plan of the anti-internment organisers was that the march would gather at Bishop's Field on the Creggan Estate and assemble behind a coal delivery lorry carrying the main speakers and bearing a NICRA banner. It would then make its way down to William Street on the edge of the Bogside, and on to the Guildhall in the city centre, where a rally would be held. Army commanders believed that if the march took place, whatever the intentions of NICRA might be, the 'hooligans backed up by the gunmen' would take control. They faced a real dilemma: any attempt to stop by force a crowd of 5,000 or more, perhaps as many as 20,000, might result in heavy casualties, but to allow such a well-publicised march to take place without opposition would bring the law into disrepute and make control of future events so much harder.

Various Provisional IRA witnesses gave figures for overall membership of the Provisional IRA in Derry that varied between twenty and sixty but the higher number is the likeliest. PIRA and Martin McGuinness, who as respectively Officer Commanding (OC) and Adjutant of the Brigade might be expected to have a greater overall knowledge of the membership than ordinary volunteers, gave figures that were at the higher end of the scale.[3] The paramilitary witness known as PIRA 8 said that a member of the Provisional IRA Command Staff told him that NICRA had been given an assurance that there would be 'no [paramilitary] activity in the area of the march'.[4] McGuinness' evidence was that the request for an assurance was 'no big deal' because the Provisional IRA would not in any event have thought of using the march to try to shoot at soldiers. 'I can never recall a civil rights march where the IRA had taken advantage of people on the street to attack the British Army. It was unthinkable,' he said.[5] That such action was 'unthinkable' was news to the security forces but was underscored by several paramilitary witnesses. PIRA 17 explained why a march would not be used as a cover for paramilitary activity: 'We could not have established Free Derry without massive popular support. We had that massive support, but we did not have many weapons and indeed did not have enough to go round the volunteers we had. I was proud that after the Battle of the Bogside the people of Derry got off their knees and said "enough was enough and no further". The massive public support which we had meant that I was confident that people would not seek to interfere with the (weapons) dumps or the orders which had been given by the Adjutant or the OC. Neither would we put this support at risk by taking any military operations during the march – hence the orders.'[6]

PIRA 24, Officer Commanding (OC) of the Derry Brigade, also gave evidence of the need not to alienate local support: 'The Provisionals had to be careful that they did nothing wrong and thereby alienate our support in the community. For example, we were careful not to steal a car which someone desperately needed for their work. We were very keen not to mount operations which exposed civilians to danger. I have been asked about whether marches or riots were used by the Provisional IRA as shooting opportunities. Marches were never used by us for those sorts of purposes, although it is possible that riots or their aftermath might be so used. What we used to do was to send a well-known volunteer down to a riot in order to clear the rioters from the street. There were a couple of our volunteers who were so well known so that you only had to see them on the streets for people to get off sides so an operation could commence. I have been asked whether we would use women, children or youngsters for cover, for example, but this never happened.'[7]

That was underlined by another witness, Sean Keenan Junior: 'At that time the Provisional IRA was trying hard to gain public support. Any military action on the day would have been pointless. With tens of thousands of people cramming into the streets on a peaceful march, people would not have tolerated any IRA action. We knew this and had no intention of alienating support. The march was being held to gain the basic rights which everybody else took for granted.'[8]

The IRA's alleged, new-found adherence to inaction was not known to police and army commanders although intelligence pointing towards it had filtered through in the days preceding the demonstration. The head of Derry RUC, Chief Superintendent Frank Lagan, advocated that no action should be taken against the marchers, save photographing the organisers with a view to prosecuting them later for defying the ban. His views were passed on to RUC Chief Constable Graham Shillington, and to Brigadier MacLellan, who in turn passed them on to Major General

Ford. The final decision was that the march would be allowed to go ahead but should be '(contained) within the general area of the Bogside and the Creggan Estate so as to prevent rioting in the City centre and damage to commercial premises and shops'. On 25 January Ford put MacLellan in charge of the operation and ordered him to prepare a detailed plan. The Operation Order he devised provided for the use of 1 PARA as the arrest force, but also made clear in express terms that any arrest operation was to be mounted only on the orders of the Brigadier.[9]

MacLellan's tactical plan envisaged containment by twenty-six sequentially numbered barriers cutting off all streets leading from the march route to the Guildhall. These would be erected in the late morning/ early afternoon, before the march began, and consist of wooden 'knife rests' reinforced with barbed wire and concrete slabs, backed by an army armoured personnel carrier (APC) on either side of the road to give the troops some cover from stone-throwing. Each barrier would be manned by locally garrisoned troops of 8 Brigade and RUC officers.[10] Further units and equipment were to be brought in as reinforcements and reserves: 1st Battalion Parachute Regiment, 1st Battalion Kings Own Border Regiment, two Companies of the 3rd Battalion Royal Regiment of Fusiliers, and two water cannon vehicles. The Operation Order provided that the march should be handled in as low a key as possible for as long as possible; if it was confined entirely within the Bogside and Creggan it should go unchallenged. No action was to be taken against the marchers unless they tried to breach the barriers or used violence against the security forces. CS gas was not to be used except as a last resort if troops were about to be overrun and the rioters could no longer be held off with water cannon and riot guns.[11] It was further stated: 'An arrest force is to be held centrally behind the checkpoints and launched in a scoop-up operation to arrest as many hooligans and rioters as possible. (1 Para will) maintain a Brigade Arrest Force...' The scoop-up operation was only to be launched on MacLellan's orders, when 'the rioters and the marchers were clearly separated'. 1 Para would also 'act as the second Brigade mobile reserve'. However, General Ford, in numerous verbal orders, had made it clear that he wanted a scoop of 'around 200' demonstrators who he regarded as 'hooligans' and troublemakers. Photo mugshots of scores of suspects were circulated to the soldiers.

1 Para arrived in Londonderry on the morning of Sunday 30 January 1972. Wilford organised the disposition of his men while the soldiers already stationed in the area erected barricades on the streets leading to Guildhall Square and manned those barriers by mid-lunchtime.[12] Colonel Wilford placed 1 Para's Support Company near the Presbyterian

church in Great James Street. His initial plan was to send soldiers from there directly south into William Street if rioting broke out in the area and if Brigadier MacLellan ordered an arrest operation. But Wilford then realised that street-side walls would make it hard for his men to move at any speed. He ordered one of his platoons to a derelict building, the former Abbey Taxis premises on the William Street side of the Presbyterian church. The Machine Gun Platoon was selected for this task and sent forward.[13]

Meanwhile, the marchers assembled on the Creggan Estate in carnival mood. It was a crisply sunny afternoon, and few expected any real trouble beyond what was considered 'normal' – stone-throwing by uncontrollable teenagers. Organisers and stewards toured the estate collecting additional numbers, which delayed the start; it was scheduled to start at 2 p.m. but left at 2.50 p.m. from Central Drive and took an indirect route towards the Bogside. People joined the march along its entire route, bringing the total to over 10,000 and maybe as many as 15,000. At 3.25 p.m. the march passed the Bogside Inn and turned up Westland Street before going down William Street. Behind the flag-decked lorry, the marchers did not move in any kind of military formation but walked as a crowd through the streets, occupying the entire width of the road, both carriageway and pavements. Even Lord Widgery, author of the subsequent inquiry report, conceded: 'The marchers, who included many women and some children, were orderly and in the main good humoured.'[14]

At the west end of William Street, it became obvious that their direct route to the Guildhall Square would take them face to face with army barrier 14. When the leaders of the march reached the junction of William Street and Rossville Street at 3.45 p.m. the lorry turned to its right to go along Rossville Street towards Free Derry Corner. The stewards made strenuous efforts to persuade the marchers to follow the lorry and thus avoid a head-on confrontation with the army barrier, but were greeted with jeers and catcalls from a section of the crowd. Although large numbers of non-violent marchers were successfully persuaded to turn to their right into Rossville Street, a substantial number, not all of them youths, continued into the cul-de-sac created by the William Street barrier. The crowd approached to within touching distance of the barrier itself. The pressure of the crowd from behind was heavy and a densely packed mass formed at the barrier, which was manned by men of the Royal Green Jackets. One middle-aged man tried to move the barrier but was stopped by a march steward. The front line at the barrier spat and shouted obscenities at the troops behind it. After a tense confrontation, the crowd in front of the barrier began to thin out as more marchers switched back and headed for Free Derry Corner as directed by Ivan Cooper.

Others, mainly young men, stayed and launched a barrage of stones at the soldiers, augmented by fire grates and metal rods used as lances. The troops responded with controlled volleys of rubber bullets, but the demonstrators brought forward an improvised shield of corrugated iron. A water cannon which had been held in reserve was brought up and drenched the crowd with water coloured with a purple dye. A pilfered canister of CS gas thrown by a member of the crowd exploded beneath the water cannon, briefly incapacitating its crew who were not wearing their gas masks. It was withdrawn for a few minutes and rubber bullets were fired again with little effect. When the gas had cleared from the water cannon it was brought forward a second time and used upon the crowd to better effect. At around 3.55 p.m. the troops appeared to be ready and able to disperse the rioters and relieve the pressure. It was at this point that the decision to go ahead with the arrest operation, for which 1 Para was earmarked, was made.[15]

After an earlier reconnaissance of the march route to determine the various points where 1 Para might launch their arrest operation, it had been thought that at barrier 14 it could be done over a wall on one side of William Street, just to the east of Little James Street, on the other side of which was the Presbyterian church. This would have allowed the paratroopers to outflank the rioters in a pincer movement, with other troops coming directly through barrier 14 itself. In full daylight, however, it was discovered that the top of the wall was covered in barbed wire, so a party of paratroopers was sent up ladders to cut it, while others covered them from the two lower floors of a three-storey derelict building on William Street, just to the west of open land. Shortly before 4 p.m., the paras were spotted by youths in William Street, who began to pelt them with stones and bottles. Corporal A fired two rounds and Soldier B fired three rounds and both soldiers hit their targets.

Damien Donaghey, fifteen, was known as 'Bubbles' because of his short, curly hair. Previously he had joined rioters in William Street, and was caught up in the relatively low-key rioting on waste ground near the Presbyterian church.[16] In a statement written when he was an adult, Donaghey gave a graphic, if inevitably biased in his own favour, account: 'Bloody Sunday was the first time that I had been on a march. At that time I was not particularly interested in civil rights. I went on the march with some friends of about my own age, as everyone else seemed to be going. We were all at school together. We met at the Creggan shops and went from there to join the beginning of the march. People of all ages and all walks of life had gathered to take part in the march. I was about a half to three quarters of the way back in the crowd of marchers as we set off. I walked with the crowd along the whole of the route of the march as far as William Street. The first sight that I had of any soldiers were those which were positioned at the junction of Francis Street and Great James Street. They were about 150 yards away. There was some catcalling from the crowd when they were noticed, but it was nothing venomous. There was no reaction from the soldiers. I saw another group of soldiers as the crowd moved further along William Street. There was some further catcalling from the crowd. I continued to walk along William Street with the rest of the crowd. Shortly afterwards, I noticed a number of soldiers on a flat roof at the back of the Presbyterian Church, to the north of William Street. I also noticed some other soldiers on the roof of the GPO sorting office close to the Presbyterian church.

'The next thing that I remember is that a group of young fellows near me noticed some other soldiers moving around in a derelict building next to the old bakery on the north side of William Street. The building was formerly used as an office by Abbey Taxis. I saw some of the soldiers moving between windows on the ground level... I watched as about five or six lads shouted abuse at the soldiers. The young lads then began to throw stones and bottles towards the derelict building where the soldiers were. This only lasted for about two minutes. I find it very difficult to say how many soldiers were in the building. They were moving back and forth between the windows. I would say there were three or so, but there may have been one or two more. I could see that they were armed with rifles and I think they were wearing tin helmets.

'People involved at the tail end of the march – approximately a couple of hundred – passed by as this was going on. Other people were cutting across to Free Derry Corner... I watched the young lads throwing stones for no more than a couple of minutes. The soldiers were taunting the young fellas. I am sure that during this period no petrol bombs or nail bombs were thrown, and I did not see anybody around me with any sort of weapon. I then recall that I heard two rubber bullets being fired from across the road from the direction of the derelict building next to the old bakery, the same building where I had seen the soldiers. There were two loud bangs, and one of the rubber bullets ricocheted off a wall not far from where I was standing. The rubber bullet fell onto the waste ground on my side of William Street. I saw it and decided to go and pick it up, as everybody collected them at the time and it was possible to sell them as a souvenir.

'I took about three steps towards the rubber bullet. I hadn't got within 20 feet of the rubber bullet when I felt a jab in my right leg. Initially, there was no strong sensation of pain, but I fell immediately onto my back.

I did not realise that I had been shot until I put my hand to my trousers. I looked at my hand and it was covered in blood. The bullet had hit me on the right side of my knee at a slight downward angle.'[17]

John Johnston, fifty-nine and the manager of a local drapery store, had been taking part in the march but on his way down William Street he saw clouds of CS gas ahead and decided to cut south across the waste ground in order to visit an elderly friend in Glenfada Park. He heard the sound of rubber bullets and saw soldiers in firing positions in a 'burnt-out house'. He had walked around two-thirds of the way across the waste ground when 'there was a big thump on the back of my right leg. I thought, my god, I've been whacked by a rubber bullet and went to hobble on, though I couldn't move well. Then a man shouted to me "Christ Mr Johnson [sic], you're shot, your trousers are soaking in blood".'[18] He went on: 'I can tell you with all truth, I never heard a shot nor any bomb before I was hit, not a solitary thing did I hear except the rubber bullets and the stones...' Johnston suffered a 'through and through' gunshot wound to his right leg, bruising to his left shoulder and a graze to his right hand.[19] The bullet was almost certainly the same one that had felled Donaghey.

After he was shot, Donaghey was dragged behind a wall and then carried by a number of people to Brigid 'Ma' Shiels' house in Columbcille Court. John Johnston was carried to the same house where they were treated by two doctors and volunteer members of the Order of Malta Ambulance Corps, a voluntary organisation of civilians trained in first aid and who attended public events to provide medical assistance.[20] Johnston was often described as both the first and last Bloody Sunday fatality – he died four-and-a-half months later – but subsequent inquiries ruled that he had not died from injuries sustained that day.

Evidence from civilians in the neighbourhood, including Johnston from his hospital bed, showed that although stones were being thrown, no firearms or bombs were being used against the soldiers in the derelict building. After the shooting, whilst some soldiers from the Mortar Platoon were cutting the wire, a single high-velocity round was fired from somewhere near the Rossville Flats and struck a rainwater pipe on the side of the church just above their heads. It is most likely that two Official IRA members had gone to a pre-arranged sniping position in order to fire at the soldiers; and probably did so when an opportunity presented itself rather than in revenge for the shooting of two civilians. Corporal A later gave evidence that he was on the middle floor of the building. From the window he saw some young men, who were hanging around after the main body of the march had passed, start throwing stones and bottles at the soldiers on the ground floor, some of whom replied with rubber bullets. He then allegedly saw two smoking objects, around the size of baked bean cans, go sailing past the window; and heard two explosions, louder than the explosion of the rubber bullet guns. As the two objects went past the window he shouted 'nail bombs' as a warning to the men on the ground floor. His Platoon Sergeant called back an order that he was to shoot any nail bombers. He testified that he then saw, around 50 yards away on the other side of the road, a man look round the corner and dart back again. Corporal A insisted that the man reappeared carrying an object in his right hand and made the actions of striking a fuse match against the wall with his left hand. When he brought his two hands together Corporal A took aim and fired at him. His first shot missed, so he quickly fired again and this time saw the man fall. Other people at once came out from the side of the building and dragged the man away. Soldier B told a similar story: he was on the ground floor of the building with his Platoon Sergeant and three other soldiers. A group of around fifty youths was throwing stones at them, undeterred by shots from the two baton guns. Some of the stones came through the window space. He heard two explosions on the waste ground to the left of the building but said he did not see them in flight because he was putting on his gas mask at the time. He noticed one man come out from the waste ground across William Street carrying in his right hand a black cylindrical object. Thinking that the man was about to light the nail bomb, and that there was no time to wait for orders from his Platoon Sergeant, Soldier B took aim and fired. As the first shot had no effect, he fired two more shots, whereupon the man fell back and was dragged away by two of his comrades. Under cross-examination Soldier B agreed that the wearing of a gas mask made it more difficult to take proper aim. The soldiers claimed Donaghey was the man holding a black cylindrical object,[21] but it was eventually established that those shot were unarmed. The soldiers had been at the very least economical with the truth.

The injured Damien Donaghey later admitted he had thrown three stones during disturbances but always insisted the British Army's claim that he and others hurled nail bombs was a 'cover-up and a lie'.[22] Although there were many IRA men – both Official and Provisional – at the protest, it was claimed they were all unarmed, apparently because it was anticipated that the paratroopers would attempt to 'draw them out'.[23]

A few minutes before 4 p.m., Wilford asked permission to 'deploy sub-unit through barricade 14 to pick up yobbos in William Street/Little James Street'.[24] MacLellan's reply was received at 4.09 p.m. and read: 'Orders given to 1 Para at 1607 hours for one sub-unit of 1 Para to do scoop-up op through barrier 14. NOT to conduct running battle down Rossville Street.' According to Brigadier MacLellan and his Brigade Major (Lieutenant Colonel Steele) the operation was authorised by the Brigadier personally. The order was passed on a secure wireless link, one which was not open to eavesdropping as it was known that normal military wireless traffic was not secure. Wilford confirmed that he received the order and all three officers agreed that it left the Commanding Officer free to employ all three Companies in the arrest operation.[25] They were A Company, C Company and Support Company, the latter being reinforced by a Composite Platoon from Administrative Company. The three Companies moved forward at the same time. A Company operated in the region of the Little Diamond and played no significant part in subsequent events. C Company went forward on foot through barrier 14 and along Chamberlain Street, while Support Company, having abandoned the idea of going over the wire-topped wall, drove in army vehicles through barrier 12 into Rossville Street to encircle those rioters either on the waste ground or being pursued by C Company along Chamberlain Street. The only Company of 1 Para to open fire that afternoon – other than with baton round guns – was Support Company.

Brigadier MacLellan had delayed giving an order for an arrest operation because he was correctly concerned that there should be separation between rioters and peaceful marchers before launching an operation to arrest the former. He maintained that he gave the order when he had reasonable grounds for believing that there was such separation in the area for the arrests that Colonel Wilford had previously identified. The order reflected MacLellan's anxiety that the soldiers should not become mixed up with the peaceful marchers further along Rossville Street. The arrest operation ordered by the Brigadier was accordingly limited to sending one company through barrier 14 in William Street, in an attempt to arrest rioters in the area of and to the north of Aggro Corner. Instead, Wilford deployed one company through barrier 14 as he was authorised to do, but in addition and without authority he deployed Support Company in vehicles through barrier 12 in Little James Street. The effect was that soldiers of Support Company did chase people down Rossville Street in line with the orders of their immediate superiors but against those from the top of the chain of command. There was no separation between peaceful marchers and those who had been rioting and no means whereby soldiers could identify and arrest only the latter.[26]

It was much later ruled that 'Colonel Wilford either deliberately disobeyed Brigadier MacLellan's order or failed for no good reason to appreciate the clear limits on what he had been authorised to do. He was disturbed by the delay in responding to his request to mount an arrest operation and had concluded that, by reason of the delay, the only way to effect a significant number of arrests was to deploy Support Company in vehicles into the Bogside. He did not inform Brigade of this conclusion. Had he done so, Brigadier MacLellan might well have called off the arrest operation altogether. Colonel Wilford did not pass on to Major Loden (the Commander of Support Company) the Brigadier's injunction on chasing people down Rossville Street, nor did he impose any limits on how far the soldiers of Support Company should go. Colonel Wilford's evidence was that it was not necessary to do either of these things, as he understood the injunction as prohibiting his soldiers from chasing rioters down to Free Derry Corner or beyond and because his soldiers already knew that they should not go further than about 200 or 250 yards from their starting point.'[27]

By the time 1 Para was unleashed, the pressure on barrier 14 had relaxed. Most of the marchers had either turned for home or were making their way down Rossville Street to the meeting at Free Derry Corner where several thousand were already assembled. On the waste ground between the Rossville Flats and William Street there was a mixed crowd of perhaps 200 which included some rioters together with marchers, local residents, newspapermen, camera crew and sightseers who were moving aimlessly about or chatting in groups. The Army had achieved its main purpose of containing the march and although some rioters were still active in William Street, they could have been dispersed without difficulty. If the Army had maintained its 'low-key' attitude the rest of the day would have passed off without further serious incident. On the other hand, the Army had been subjected to severe stoning for upwards of half an hour; and commanders regarded some arrests as a legitimate security objective. The presence of 1 Para provided just the opportunity to carry this out, but it had obvious risks. A large-scale scoop-up of rioters would inevitably see innocent people who were not rioters caught in the net and perhaps roughly handled; and if the troops were fired upon and returned fire, civilians might well be injured. Brigadier MacLellan had sought to minimise the first risk by withholding the order to launch the arrest operation until the rioters and the marchers were clearly separated. But this separation never happened. MacLellan, who could not see the area at all, relied mainly upon incomplete information from an officer in a helicopter. He later said that he had considered the possibility that if a shooting match developed there would be risk to innocent people but he described this risk as 'very bare'. He considered that the arrest operation was essential in the interests of security and gave the order accordingly.[28]

What he did not anticipate was that Wilford would either exceed or ignore his orders.

At 4.10 p.m., while C Company of 1 Para moved through barrier 14 on foot along William Street, a convoy of ten army vehicles carrying the battalion's Support Company (reinforced with a Composite Platoon known as 'Guinness Force' from Administrative Company) moved through barrier 12 and down Little James Street. In the lead was the Mortar Platoon commanded by Lieutenant N made up of eighteen all ranks and travelling in two armoured personnel carriers (APCs, colloquially known as 'Pigs'). Next came the Command APC of the Company Commander (Major 236) with a soft-top Ferret scout car, then two empty APCs belonging to the Machine Gun Platoon which had been deployed elsewhere, then two soft-skinned 4-ton lorries carrying the thirty-six all ranks of the Composite Platoon. The rear was brought up by two further APCs carrying the Anti-Tank Platoon, which consisted of Lieutenant 119 in command and seventeen other ranks.[29] According to Major 236 his orders were simply to go through barrier 12 and arrest as many rioters as possible. As the rioters retreated down Rossville Street he went after them.

The leading vehicle of Support Company careered along Rossville Street and then turned left onto an area of waste ground called Eden Place, where the soldiers disembarked. Beyond the waste ground were the three high blocks of the Rossville Flats partially surrounding a car park. The second vehicle, under the command of Sergeant O, the Platoon Sergeant of Mortar Platoon, went further along Rossville Street, stopped briefly on that street where some soldiers disembarked, and then turned left and stopped in the entrance to the car park of the Rossville Flats, where the remaining soldiers disembarked 230 yards from barrier 12.[30]

During that short but hectic drive, Sergeant O's vehicle accidently struck two people, eighteen-year-old Alana Burke and thirty-two-year-old Thomas Harkin.[31] Burke described how, drenched by water cannon and very scared, she was heading home: '...in hindsight I should have gone up Harvey Street to the Diamond and down Bishop Street, but I didn't, I cut through the alleyway that took you onto waste ground on William Street. I couldn't move; I was just glued to the spot in pure terror. Everybody was running for their lives. I didn't know where to run or what to do, and then I heard the roar of the army's engines revving up and I was afraid. People were running on either side of me and I could see a man lying against one of the old buildings at the back of Chamberlain Street – he was bleeding from his head. I could hear the engines and I could see the soldiers coming in on foot, and I was in the middle of this waste ground absolutely petrified. I couldn't move; I was just glued to the spot in pure terror. I can't explain how bad it was. Everybody was running for their lives. I could hear the shooting, and I could see the crowds coming from Rossville Street and the Saracens [armoured personnel carriers] coming behind, and I knew I wasn't going to make it. I crossed onto the tarmac of the flats and I started to run and that's really all I remember. I could see the Saracen coming towards me, and there was squealing and crying and horrendous panic all around me, and I just lay there. I thought he was going to come back over the top of me again, and I remember crawling on my hands and knees thinking I was going to die.' She was treated in a nearby home, then taken to hospital with a crushed pelvis. She added: 'I didn't think I was going to make it to the hospital. I thought, am I living or dead?'[32]

After the paratroopers disembarked, they began roughly seizing people. There were many claims of paratroopers beating people, clubbing them with rifle butts, firing rubber bullets at them from close range, making threats to kill, and hurling abuse. Excessive force outside their orders had seemingly become the norm. Lieutenant N later said: 'I'd never been in Londonderry on operations before and this area was unknown to me. I had the impression of large open spaces with the crowd standing round watching us. The crowd began to run away from us. We kept driving up the street to overtake some of them and caught up with the back people, and then I turned my pig left to somewhere between what I now know to be Eden Place and Pilot Row, cutting off around 100. My sergeant had followed the normal drill of pulling past me up the right and had halted towards the car park of the Rossville Flats.'[33] He went on: 'The aim in my mind was to cut as many off as we could so that we could debus in the middle of them.' He described the crowd as quite dense. Sergeant O described how people scattered to either side of Rossville Street as they drove down and how, after his Platoon Commander had turned left at Pilot Row, he continued and then swung left himself. 'In this way we cut off between us a group of about 200 people. These were intended as the people the snatch squads would go into. It was a Snatch operation initially at Aggro Corner.'[34]

Soldiers in their armoured vehicles ran a gauntlet of stones and bottles but, despite their testimony, no bombs or bullets. Protestor Neil McLaughlin was in the Rossville Flats car park when 'four or five army pigs approached the north-western entrance to the car park and stopped in a group at the north gable end of Block 1 of the Rossville Flats'. He continued: 'Together with about twenty other people ... I ran at the pigs, throwing stones at them. I am pretty sure that I hit one of them. Suddenly, soldiers jumped out of the back of the pigs.'[35]

Lieutenant N went towards an alleyway that led from the Eden Place waste ground into Chamberlain Street and fired three rounds from his rifle over the heads of people, some of whom had been attempting to rescue a man who had been arrested by one of his soldiers, while others had been throwing stones and other missiles at the soldiers. Those initial shots, the first since 1 Para entered the Bogside, appear only intended to frighten the crowd into submission.[36] Lieutenant N recorded that as he got out of the vehicle several people ran past and 'a man about 10 feet away began to throw lumps of concrete at me. I made straight for him. He turned and ran and then turned and threw another one. By which time I had closed with him. I started to try and grapple with him. My helmet strap broke and my helmet fell off over my eyes and during the confusion the man got away. As a result, I was somewhat behind the rest of the platoon who had pursued the crowd towards the high flats. I moved out of the open towards the backs of the houses in Chamberlain Street taking up position roughly at Eden Place with my radio operator and one man with a riot gun. The situation here was not comfortable.'[37] In his official statement to the Military Police some hours later he said: 'I had been in this position for about five minutes when I saw a man, aged about twenty-four years, dressed in a blue anorak, come around the corner of the wall at the rear of number 36 Chamberlain Street. The man vanished behind the wall and then reappeared holding something in his right hand. I saw smoke coming from the object he was holding and he drew his arm back to throw it at one of my vehicles which was about 20 yards north of his position. I assumed this object to be a nail bomb and fired one aimed shot 7.62 mm at the man. The man staggered, clutched at his right thigh and then fell back out of sight behind the wall from which he had originally appeared. Due to the situation I was unable to carry out any follow-up action to arrest the man.'

Lance Corporal V recorded that: 'As I debussed I heard the sound of shots. I cocked my weapon. I heard two explosions. Rioters also threw petrol and acid bombs... I heard the firing of single shots. I also saw the spurt of bullets hitting the ground somewhere to my right.'[38] Other soldiers gave evidence that they came under fire. Private Q was in an arrest group of three, two with an SLR and the other with a baton gun. He said that the people in the forecourt of the Rossville Flats were 'stopping, throwing at us and moving again... We took cover because the stoning became heavy.' He claimed that he and the soldier with the baton gun had run to the north end of the Rossville Flats and that it was at this stage that he heard four or five low-velocity shots, but he did not know where they landed or where they had come from. His testimony was later dismissed because of numerous contradictions.

Private 019 appears to have been more candid in his recollection. He took cover at the southern end of the Eden Place alleyway: 'I could see a crowd of civilians at the junction between Chamberlain Street and Harvey Street. I cannot remember what they were doing. I could hear the noise of the crowd at this stage and the bangs of baton rounds. I think I could hear rifle fire at this time too. I cannot remember hearing any pistol shots nor any automatic fire at this time or at any time. The rifle fire I could hear could have been hostile or it could have been ours. I simply did not know.' He added that: 'because no fire was directed at me and there was no immediate threat to me I was not concerned about it'. Another Para, Private 019, said that he was 'pretty sure' that the rifle fire that he heard came before the firing by Lieutenant N, but that he did not know whether or not it was hostile fire, but only that it was behind him and not coming his way.[39] The lack of any hard evidence of hostile fire suggests that the soldiers either mistook Lieutenant N's gunshots for hostile fire or used them as a convenient, post-action excuse.

The Paras were by then psyched up for action, as Rosemary Doyle learnt to her cost. She was a nineteen-year-old volunteer in the Order of Malta Ambulance Corps on duty on that day, wearing her bright white medical uniform and carrying an army issue gas mask in her kitbag. She and colleagues picked up a rubber bullet casualty to take him to safety. She recorded in her official incident report: 'We proceeded to walk across waste ground by the Rossville Flats when two Saracen tanks raced up the roadway and another across the waste ground. The leading Saracen passed within about 1ft 6 inches of us and we stood our ground to avoid injury. A paratrooper then jumped out of the back of the Saracen and fired a rubber bullet at my face... As I was still wearing my gas mask I was protected a good deal from the force of the rubber bullet which slightly damaged three teeth and I sustained bruising of the right jaw. We walked slowly away from the Saracen towards the Glenfada Park area and while doing so the paratroopers opened up with live machine-gun fire after issuing no warning and with absolutely no provocation from the marchers.' It is likely that the APC involved was Lieutenant N.[40] None of the four soldiers in Mortar Platoon armed with baton guns admitted firing the round that hit Rosemary Doyle. It remains uncertain whether the round was aimed at her or at someone else nearby, or was shot at the ground and bounced up into her face or was recklessly fired in her vague direction.[41]

As soon as the vehicles appeared in William Street the crowd on the waste ground began to run away to the south and was augmented by many other people driven out of Chamberlain Street by C Company. Some of the crowd ran along Rossville Street on the west side of Block

1 of the flats, whilst the remainder ran into the courtyard/car park on the north side of the flats. Many remained under cover in the doorways of the flats while others remained facing the vehicles to see how far they would come. The APCs of Mortar Platoon penetrated more deeply than was expected by the crowd, which caused some panic. They were surrounded by high-rise flats and the only means of escape were two alleyways between Blocks 1, 2 and 3, both of which rapidly became very congested. The courtyard was a ready-made killing ground. Within ten minutes the soldiers of Mortar Platoon had fired forty-two rounds of 762 mm ammunition, killing one and wounding six.[42] Although many people sought to flee from the soldiers through the gaps between the blocks, there is evidence from both soldiers and civilians that at this stage some stopped or paused to throw stones and bottles. More bottles, flowerpots, even cans of baked beans were hurled from the balconies of the blocks. Ten-year-old Sean Collins watched from his top-floor flat 'as milk bottles smashed down from Block 1 near where the soldiers were standing'.

Francis Dunne said that he ran first to the alley that gave access to Joseph Place, which was choked with people. He thought that he would head towards the Fahan Street exit from the courtyard. He could see a crowd there too. He turned and saw the soldiers along the wall at the back of the Chamberlain Street houses. At this point the shooting started. The soldier at the front had his rifle at his hip. The soldier behind him was kneeling and aiming. The third soldier's gun was pointed at the ground. Some of 'the boys towards the Fahan Street side' were throwing stones at the soldiers. One of these boys fell and was dragged back by two or three others. Jackie Duddy was standing with his arms high in the air, towards the centre of the courtyard, shouting 'They're killing, they're killing, they're shooting' and pointing towards the Fahan Street side of the flats, where a young man had fallen. The soldier at the front of the group at the back of Chamberlain Street fired from the hip at the man who was shouting, who fell.

Jackie Duddy was seventeen and lived in Central Drive, Creggan, with his father, his five brothers, and eight of his nine sisters, his mother having died of leukaemia in 1968, aged forty-four years. He was a weaver in the factory of Thomas French & Sons Ltd on the Springtown Industrial Estate. He was a keen and successful amateur boxer. He went on the march with some of his friends, telling siblings that he was going to listen to Bernadette Devlin speaking.[43]

Patrick McCrudden, visiting a friend at 37 Donagh Place on the top floor of Block 2, recalled: 'The people were fleeing in panic. While one soldier was attacking a middle-aged man, a member of the Order of

Malta attempted to intervene. The soldier turned and struck this first-aid man first with the butt of the rifle on both body and face and kicked him. The Order of Malta man collapsed and disappeared from view behind a wall. The middle-aged man was arrested. Others were being beaten up and arrested in the same manner in different parts of the waste ground.'[44]

Father Edward Daly, a Catholic priest in the area out of concern for some elderly local parishioners, having seen the Army carry out arrest operations on the waste ground, did not think that the vehicles would travel beyond Eden Place. He did not run away until he saw that they were coming further and he was accordingly at the back of the running crowd. He remembered a young boy beside him: 'I was running and he was running and looking back, and I overtook him. He laughed at me. He was amused to see me running. I am not an athlete myself. I do not think I am a very graceful runner. He looked at me at this point about the corner of the wire. That is why he stuck in my memory. I went in here and the Saracens came right up this way, and I remember that the first shot I heard, this young boy was about a few feet behind me and there was a shot, and simultaneously he gasped or grunted – something like that. I looked round and he just fell.'[45] Daly ran on, not realising that a live round had hit Jackie Duddy, and after a few yards he heard a 'fusillade of gunfire', a 'huge number' of shots which he recognised as live bullets, so he dived to the ground. He was convinced that all the shots came from behind. After a time, he looked over his shoulder and saw Duddy lying on his back. 'I thought the shot was a bit sharp for that of a rubber bullet gun,' he said. From his evidence it was clear that the teenager was shot very quickly after the Paras entered the area.[46] The bullet had struck the teenager in the shoulder and entered his chest. Three witnesses said they saw a soldier take deliberate aim at the youth as he ran.

Meanwhile, Charles Glenn, a Corporal in the Order of Malta Ambulance Corps, described how he was hit with a rifle butt and knocked to the ground after trying to intervene when a paratrooper grabbed middle-aged William John Doherty. In his NICRA statement he recorded that as he fell, he heard a shot. He was stunned, but when he recovered, he saw a man lying in a pool of blood in the car park with Daly bending over him. Celine Brolly saw from her second-floor flat a 'first-aid boy' running to the aid of a middle-aged man who was being punched and battered by three soldiers. The medic was thrown on the ground and 'was still lying on the ground and Father Daly called him'. Glenn then went to the aid of Duddy.[47] Photojournalist Fulvio Grimaldi saw first-aid men and priests around a body in the middle of the car park. He said that he watched them duck as they were being fired at from the direction of the army vehicles; he went back to the corner of Chamberlain Street and shouted at the soldiers to stop firing. The shooting continued; the first three shots went over his head.[48]

Father Daly recalled that when he reached the fallen Duddy there was more gunfire, and he and Charles Glenn lay down beside him. Daly gave Duddy the last rites. He then saw another man, later identified as Michael Bridge, fall shot. Parishioner Willy Barber and another man crawled over and offered to help to carry Duddy to a position where he could receive medical aid. They suggested that Daly should go in front, carrying a white handkerchief, and that they would carry the lad behind him. Just as they were about to stand up and make a dash to Chamberlain Street, a gunman appeared at the wall of the last house in Chamberlain Street and fired two or three shots at the soldiers. Daly shouted at the gunman to go away, which he did. Daly remained on the ground for a few more moments, and then rose onto his knees and was about to stand up when the Army opened fire again. He and the others with him lay down again.[49] When it appeared safe to do so, Daly and several other men proceeded up Harvey Street. A photograph of people carrying the dying teenager though the streets of Derry led by Father Daly waving a bloodied handkerchief was to become one of the enduring images of the Troubles.

They laid Duddy on the ground at the corner of Waterloo Street, on Willy Barber's coat. Soldiers further down the street ordered them to clear off. A woman came out of a house and screamed at the soldiers that Duddy was only a child and that they had shot him. Another woman called an ambulance. People came out of the houses. Daly and others knelt by Duddy and said a prayer. After a time the ambulance arrived and took him to Altnagelvin Hospital where he was pronounced dead on arrival.[50]

Private R of Mortar Platoon was probably the soldier who aimed at and shot Jackie Duddy. This soldier had disembarked from Sergeant O's APC in Rossville Street, but then ran after this vehicle as it continued into the entrance to the car park of the Rossville Flats.[51] An autopsy of the body of Jackie Duddy was conducted the following day by Dr Derek Carson, then the Deputy State Pathologist for Northern Ireland. Dr Carson summarised his conclusions: 'Death was due to a gunshot wound of the upper chest. The bullet had entered the outer part of the right shoulder and had passed behind the upper part of the arm bone and the right shoulder blade, notching the inner border of the shoulder blade, before passing through the inner end of the second right rib and the second thoracic vertebra. On striking the spine the bullet had been deflected slightly upwards and had then fractured the middle third of the left collarbone and the adjacent parts of the first and second left ribs before leaving the body through the upper part of the left chest. No bullet was recovered from the body. In its course through the upper chest the bullet had damaged the upper part of each lung and divided the windpipe, the gullet and the left common carotid and subclavian arteries. Bleeding from the damaged blood vessels and lungs would have caused rapid death, whilst breathing would also have been severely impaired by the injury to the windpipe. Death must have occurred within a few minutes.'[52]

Neil McLaughlin, a 'self-confessed aggro man' who admitted throwing stones, described Jackie Duddy as someone who usually went miles to avoid trouble.[53] McLaughlin saw an Order of Malta Ambulance Corps volunteer fall, not necessarily shot, 'by the back wall of the Chamberlain Street row – in other words the crowd running forward had just about cleared the gable end'; then Margaret Deery was shot on his right and McLaughlin flung himself to the ground, after which he saw a crowd 'up in the car park' clustered around another body; and then Michael Bridge ran past Neil McLaughlin and was shot.[54]

The casualties mounted rapidly, and despite McLaughlin's testimony, there remains some confusion about the order in which more people were shot. Margaret Deery, often known as Peggy, was a thirty-eight-year-old widow with fourteen children, her husband having died a few months earlier of cancer. She had been given a car lift from her Creggan home to the area with several of her children. She chatted briefly with Father Daly at the junction of Rossville Street and William Street and he told her to take care as 'there may be a lot of trouble'. She stated: 'At this point there was no stone-throwing or trouble that I could see, but again I was in the middle of the main crowd. The Army then fired coloured dye and I ran like hell towards Rossville Street at the back of the high flats. By this time my sister and I had got separated in the crowd. I was round the back of these high flats running towards the wee gate at the back of the flats whenever I tripped and fell. There were hundreds of people in this area running to get away from the Army who had driven into the back of the flats in Saracens. A man had fallen on top of me and he got up and ran around the corner. Whilst I was on the ground I was able to see the Army men in front of me and I saw and heard them shooting. I attempted to get up but I slipped and cut my head and nose. I then saw a soldier in front of me and he appeared to be taking aim at me and I then felt a blow to my left thigh. I called to a man to help me which he did and he took me to a house in Chamberlain Street where Mr Slingwing the chemist treated my wound.'[55]

Leo Deehan was heading towards Free Derry Corner when there was a shout that the Army was coming: 'Suddenly a couple of Saracens appeared on the roadway racing towards the flats. All around me people were shouting and trying to hide or run towards the back of the flats. I followed but one of the Saracens headed right up on the waste ground. There was a big pool of water near the middle and I thought I saw a girl go down right in the path of the tank. I raced on. The Saracen seemed to be going one way then the other after people. All of a sudden soldiers appeared – some had helmets some none – but I noticed they all carried rifles and not the usual shield and Baton. I ran close to one tank to avoid being seen; as I got level a soldier ran round from the other side. I ran at him and believe I pushed him more than punch him – he staggered, and looked like losing his gun. I ran on. I then saw one soldier beating an elderly man with the butt of his rifle. The old man fought gamely; he went down and the soldier tried to bash him with the rifle again. I had stopped and was edging back. I started to run towards the soldier shouting at him. I saw another appear and raise his gun. He seemed to point at me. I faltered and just then a woman ran across my path. She shouted he will shoot you and, I believe she pushed me; it was like a bad dream and I must have been all tensed up for I know I lost my balance. At that second I heard the same type of sharp shot I had heard earlier. It made me jump for it was much closer, and I just noticed the soldier's rifle move or something made me look at him, as I started to run in the opposite direction. Then I heard a fellow close by calling she is shot. It was then I noticed the woman that had pushed me was lying on the ground bleeding. I thought she had been hit by a rubber bullet. I ran back and grabbed her and pulled her toward the cover of the wall. Another fellow reached her and we two carried her across to Nelis's house on Chamberlain Street.'[56]

Lance Corporal V of Mortar Platoon, who had moved towards the car park of the Rossville Flats after disembarking from Lieutenant N's APC, was probably the soldier who shot Margaret Deery.[57] Mrs Deery suffered a severe gunshot wound which went through her left thigh, smashing her femur and damaging muscle. An ambulancewoman dressed her leg with dressings borrowed from the other Ambulance Corps volunteer in the house, and with pillowcases provided by the occupants, because a soldier outside the house had rifled through her kitbag.[58] Mrs Deery suffered serious complications following an operation at Altnagelvin Hospital that night, during which she received a transfusion of blood which was afterwards discovered to be rhesus incompatible. She developed acute renal failure and for a time it was thought that her leg might have to be amputated. She was not discharged until the end of May.[59] She died in 1988.

Taken to hospital in the same ambulance as Margaret Deery was twenty-five-year-old unemployed labourer Michael Bridge who lived in Tremone Gardens, Creggan.[60] After the march had begun, he was approached by a girl who asked him to act as a steward. He agreed and was given a white steward's armband. He and other stewards walked in front of the lorry at the head of the march, asking people to stay at the side of the road until the lorry had passed and then fall in behind it if they wished to join the march. He was separated from the main march when he vomited in an alley after the CS gas had been thrown at barricade 14.[61] He later admitted to having thrown stones at the barricade.

He testified: 'I ran along Chamberlain Street and cut into Eden Place. On waste ground in front of me I saw an armoured personnel carrier parked with the back doors towards me. These doors were open. I saw two soldiers jump out of this vehicle and they were firing their rifles. I ran back into Chamberlain Street and a man aged about thirty to forty years fell and I lifted him up. At this stage I saw a soldier standing with a rifle at the corner of the small shop at the rear of 12a Chamberlain Street. I heard a shot fairly close and I thought that this soldier had fired. I ran up Chamberlain Street towards the courtyard of the flats. There were about fifty other people running along Chamberlain Street as well. As I ran I heard a young lad say that there was a young fellow shot. His exact words were, "He's shot dead, he's shot dead". I ran into the courtyard and I saw a priest bending over a body. I had got to within 2 or 3 yards of the priest and I saw blood on the face of the person lying on the ground. I turned round, screamed at the soldiers and walked towards them. I saw a soldier about 20 yards from me with his rifle at his shoulder aiming at me. The next thing I felt was a thud on the left thigh. The soldier with the rifle at his shoulder could not have shot me but I was aware of another soldier at the bottom of Rossville Flats and to my left. I turned and walked a short distance and two fellows came running out and caught hold of me and told me I was shot. I felt the blood on my thigh and I was carried into the first house in Chamberlain Street.'[62] The bullet went through his left thigh.

Sam Gillespie photographed Jackie Duddy on the ground and later stated: 'While I was taking it a young fellow who seemed to be his friend turned and faced the soldiers shouting, "Shoot me, you bastards. Shoot me." He was waving his hands in the air, and as he was moving toward the soldier who was taking cover at a Saracen he was shot...'[63] Father Daly testified that as he gave Duddy the last rites, 'a young man dashed out past where we were lying towards the soldiers ... I screamed at him to get back. He danced up and down in front of the soldiers shouting something that I could not understand. He had his hands held up at full stretch over his head. I saw a soldier at the corner of the flats take aim and fire at this man ... he staggered and ran crazily around for a moment. I don't know where he went then ... I am certain that he was hit.'[64]

Unemployed painter Michael Bradley, twenty-two and newly married, went on the march with some of his brothers and friends.[65] He admitted taking part in the fracas at barrier 14. He went from William Street to the Eden Place waste ground where he heard that Duddy, who he knew personally, had been shot and turned towards the Rossville Flats car park. He testified: 'I was still on the waste ground, not yet having reached the courtyard, when I looked round and saw the Saracens driving along Rossville Street. There were several other people near me and when we saw the troops we began running and shouting "There's the Army." The crowd ran in all directions. I ran straight ahead across the courtyard towards the far top corner of the flats – that is, the corner that leads out to the steps towards Fahan Street and to Joseph Place. There was quite a few people running towards this corner also. After I went through the opening at the corner I stopped to catch my breath. I heard gunfire and ran back out through the opening towards the courtyard and it was then I saw a body lying on the ground about 5 to 10 yards away... I was standing there with my back towards the back of the shops and I was looking across the courtyard in the direction of the Army, whom I could quite clearly see at the Rossville Street end of the courtyard. There was also a Saracen just stopping in the courtyard. I could see soldiers jump out and take up firing positions at the front of the Saracen. All during this time I could hear the sound of gunfire. Suddenly, I felt a heavy pain in my right arm. I realised I had been shot but didn't know how serious the wound was. I pulled myself back over the small wall behind the shops. I was still on my feet. I hadn't lost consciousness. In a bent-over position I stumbled along towards the opening which leads out of the courtyard towards Joseph Place and which I had come through a few minutes earlier. As I came near the opening a few men reached forward, grabbed me and carried me through to a house. My main thought at the time was, would I live or die?'[66] A bullet had gone through his left forearm, scraped across his chest and entered his right forearm, to which it caused much more severe damage, probably because by that time it was spinning. Bradley insisted that he was not throwing stones, but in an interview twenty years later he said: 'I lost the head and looked around to see what I could pick up to throw at the soldiers who were pouring into the area. I grabbed two pieces of brick and was just about to throw them when I was shot.'[67]

A witness, Derrick Tucker, watching from a flat in Block 2, delivered an account which encompassed several shootings: 'Two Saracens turned into the car park of the flats from Rossville Street. In doing so, they drove through the crowd and the first Saracen knocked down one man, sending him spinning away. The Saracens stopped and soldiers deployed from the back of them. One soldier ran to the front nearside wheel and took up a firing position. Another ran to the wall at the backs of the Chamberlain Street houses and started pushing people with his rifle held in a port position. The soldier at the nearside front wheel of the Saracen started firing and I saw a man fall to the ground. Someone running in front of the man stopped, turned and went to his aid. The shot which that soldier fired was the first shot that I heard that day. Shooting continued and I saw two other men shot in the car park. The first of these was roughly in the middle of the car park with his hands raised in the air. He appeared to be shot in the leg as he suddenly grasped his right leg with his right arm and hopped into the top corner of the car park where the kiddies' play area is. The second man who was shot was crouching at the little wall dividing the service area of the shops from the car park. He got up from his crouching position. I saw him clutch his stomach and bend over.'[68] Michael Bridge was probably shot by Lieutenant N, while Michael Bradley was probably felled by Private Q of Mortar Platoon from a position near to the northern end of Block 1 of the Rossville Flats.[69]

Patrick McDaid, twenty-four, was an unmarried man living with his parents in Creggan, a plumber for the Londonderry Development Commission. He went on the march with his brother-in-law and saw people stoning the soldiers in the area of Sackville Street and Little James Street. He moved up Rossville Street to get away from the CS gas.[70] He saw some of the chaotic carnage around the Rossville Flats, included the wounded Mrs Deery being carried away, and during a spate of firing ducked down to take cover behind some steps and felt a heavy blow to his shoulder. He and the people around him assumed he had been shot, but that was ruled out after he was medically examined. The most likely explanation for his superficial wound was that he was hit by debris caused by a ricocheting bullet.[71]

Another ricochet round shattered concrete cladding in the gap between Blocks 2 and 3 of the Rossville Flats and a chunk hit thirty-year-old Pius McCarron in the head.[72] Details remain sketchy, but witness Patrick Clarke described running along Chamberlain Street towards the Rossville Flats and seeing, when he reached the car park area, someone lying flat on his back being tended by two people. He continued: 'At this particular point I was able to see British soldiers in firing positions and shooting over the head of the priest at other people who were taking cover behind a low wall at the rear of the steps in the high flats. I made my way round to the passage at the lower intersection of the two blocks of high flats and here I came upon a member of the Knights of Malta in attendance on another injured person. He asked for assistance. We were unable to determine there and then what was wrong with him as he did not seem to have any wounds. I knew the man to be Pius McCarran [sic]. Another fellow and myself started to carry him to one of the nearby houses, and while doing so some shots were also fired at us, hitting the wall above our heads. When we got him into a house we found out that he had been hit in the head by a piece of masonry from a ricochet. This he told us himself when he recovered. In that same house was a young girl who had been hit by a Saracen and was in great pain from back injuries.'[73] McCarron's wound was judged superficial but his family blamed it for a brain haemorrhage that developed a year and half later. His daughter Maureen later told BBC Radio Foyle: 'Everyone says daddy was left the way he was because of Bloody Sunday... he was bleeding that day from the ears and that indicates brain damage, a brain injury.'[74] Patrick McDaid and Pius McCarron were injured by debris from bullets fired by one or more of Sergeant O, Private R and Private S, all of Mortar Platoon.[75]

After taking part in the march, forty-year-old Patrick Brolly from the Creggan peeled off to visit a relative by marriage in Block 1 of the Rossville Flats. From the flat he watched Father Daly give the last rites to Duddy in the car park below. As he turned away from the window, he heard a loud bang and was hit by a bullet 'which came through the window and skimmed the left side of my head just above my forehead. I fell to the ground and was knocked out for a while.' His wife Celine testified that a small blond stout soldier directly behind an army vehicle 'aimed the gun and my husband threw me to the ground and they fired right in at the bedroom window'.[76] The bullet lodged in the top of a wardrobe in the sitting room. Brolly was unconscious for thirty minutes, but his wound proved superficial. The only soldier who admitted firing live rounds into the south-east side of Block 1 of the Rossville Flats was Private T, who claimed he had shot at an acid bomber. Although he did not aim at Patrick Brolly, he was probably responsible for the shot that directly or indirectly injured him.[77]

Journalist Simon Winchester testified that he was walking across the open ground to the north of Rossville Flats when he met a crowd of people moving away from the William Street area towards Free Derry Corner. He decided to go with the crowd. A very short time later a number of armoured vehicles swept in along Rossville Street and the crowd started running. Some ran along Rossville Street towards Free Derry Corner, others towards the exits between the three blocks of the

Rossville Flats. Winchester heard a number of shots, probably fewer than ten, coming from behind him. He dropped to the ground, as did everyone else. In the ensuing panic and confusion he saw an injured man bleeding profusely from the leg. Winchester did not see or hear any nail bombs or petrol bombs, nor see any weapons other than those carried by the Army. He did not hear firing other than that which he attributed to army rifles until after he had made his way through to the south side of the Rossville Flats.

Mrs Mary Bonnor, from her flat in the central Rossville block, saw a crowd running towards the flats from William Street followed by two armoured vehicles. Some soldiers jumped out. One of them knelt down and pointed his gun; another, firing from the waist, shot a boy, later identified as Duddy, in the back. Mrs Bonnor said that she heard no shots until the soldiers shot the lad. Another onlooker from the central block was English-born Derrick Tucker, veteran of both the Royal Navy and the Royal Air Force. From his flat he saw people start to run and shout as the armoured vehicles drove up Rossville Street. Soldiers at once jumped out and adopted firing positions beside their vehicle. One of them started firing towards the landings of the flats in Rossville Street. Tucker saw the shooting of John Duddy and of Michael Bridge. He estimated that the interval between the soldiers getting out of their vehicles and starting to fire was between thirty seconds and two minutes. During that time he heard no explosions nor any firing directed at the soldiers. The only firing he heard was of gas canisters and rubber bullets at the junction of William Street and Rossville Street. He felt sickened and degraded by the action of the British Army against unarmed civilians.

Francis Dunne, a Londonderry schoolteacher, said that he was drifting across the open ground in front of the Rossville Flats towards Free Derry Corner. He was just short of Eden Place when the large crowd began to run. He ran too, as far as the north end of Block 1 and from there he saw the armoured vehicles driving in. He made for the alleyway between Blocks 1 and 2 and found it jammed with people. Up to that stage he was not aware of any shots. He saw a tall, fair-haired young man slightly to his right, who was shouting 'They're killing, they're killing, they're shooting' and pointing towards the Fahan Street side of the flats, where a young man had fallen, probably hit by a baton round. A couple of boys seemed to be helping him and dragging him. The soldier at the front of the group at the back of Chamberlain Street fired from the hip at the man who was shouting, who fell, with his hands 'high in the air'. Dunne saw that the alleyway through the flats was no longer jammed and went through it. His impression was that shots were coming through the alleyway towards him from the direction of the soldiers and he realised that live bullets were being fired. He was certain that there was no firing at the soldiers from the Rossville Flats as he ran across the courtyard. Neither were there any nail bombs.[78]

The entire action took place in an area barely 100 yards square. The soldiers' testimony contradicted that of the civilian witnesses and followed a constant theme that they only fired when under direct attack themselves. Eventually much of their testimony was revealed to be a tissue of lies, but it is worth recording as evidence of collusion across all ranks.

Major 236 said he halted his command vehicle in Rossville Street and as he and his driver dismounted a burst of around fifteen rounds of low-velocity fire came towards them from the direction of Rossville Flats. They immediately moved the vehicle to a better-covered position at the north end of Block 1. There was, he said, continuous firing for the next ten minutes. He saw seven or eight members of the Mortar Platoon firing aimed shots towards the flats but he could not see what they were firing at. Lieutenant N reported that on leaving his vehicle he was faced by a man throwing stones whom he tried to arrest but failed as the strap of his helmet broke. He then moved towards Chamberlain Street where he was faced by a hostile crowd and fired a total of three shots above their heads and fired one further round at a man whom he thought was throwing a nail bomb in the direction of Sergeant O's vehicle. Sergeant O, with ten years' experience in the Parachute Regiment, had returned from a training course in Cyprus that morning. When his vehicle halted, he said that he and his men began to make arrests but were met with fire from the Rossville Flats; he thought that the fire came from four or five sources and possibly included some high-velocity weapons. He saw the strike of bullets 4 or 5 metres from one of the members of his platoon. He and his men returned to his APC to secure their prisoners and then spread out in firing positions to engage those who had fired upon them. Sergeant O fired three rounds at a man firing a pistol from behind a car parked in the courtyard. The man fell and was carried away. He fired a further three rounds at a man standing at first-floor level on the catwalk connecting Blocks 2 and 3, who was firing a fairly short weapon like an M1 carbine. The flashes at the muzzle were visible. Sergeant O caught a glimpse of Soldier S firing at a man with a similar weapon, but his view was obscured by people 'milling about'. The Sergeant returned to his vehicle, but later fired two more rounds at a man whom he said was firing an M1 carbine from an alleyway between Blocks 2 and 3. Sergeant O described the firing from the flats as the most intense that he had seen in Northern Ireland.

Private Q, after dismounting from his vehicle, said he was being stoned and so took cover at the end of Block 1 of the Rossville Flats. There he heard four or five low-velocity shots, though he could not say from what direction. Shortly afterwards he saw a man throwing nail bombs, two of which simply rolled away whilst another one exploded near to the houses backing onto Chamberlain Street. He shot at and hit the man as he was in the act of throwing another nail bomb. That bomb did not explode and the man's body was dragged away. Private R claimed to have heard one or two explosions like small bombs from the back of Rossville Flats, and the firing of high- and low-calibre weapons. He noticed a man around 30 yards along the eastern side of Block 1, who made as if to throw a smoking object, whereupon Private R fired at him. He thought he hit him high up on the shoulder but was not certain what happened to the man because he was at that moment himself struck on the leg by an acid bomb thrown from an upper window in the flats. A few moments later R saw a hand firing a pistol from the alleyway between Blocks 2 and 3. R fired three times but did not know whether he made a hit.

Private S said that he came under rapid, single-shot fire from the Rossville Flats as soon as he dismounted from his vehicle. He dodged across to the back of one of the houses in Chamberlain Street, from which position he saw a hail of bottles coming down from the flats onto one of the armoured vehicles and the soldiers around it. He fired a total of twelve shots at a gunman or gunmen who appeared, or reappeared, in front of the alleyway between Blocks 1 and 2 of the flats. The gunman was firing what he thought was an M1 carbine. He thought that he scored two hits. Private T also claimed to have heard a burst of fire, possibly from a semi-automatic rifle being fired very quickly, around thirty to forty-five seconds after dismounting from his vehicle. He was splashed on the legs by acid from an acid bomb and noticed a person throwing acid bombs around three storeys up in the flats. On the orders of Sergeant O he fired two rounds at the acid bomb thrower. He thought that he did not score a hit. Lance Corporal V said he heard two explosions, not baton rounds or rifle fire, before his vehicle stopped. As soon as he jumped out he heard rifle fire and saw several shots spurting into the ground to his right. He thought that this fire was coming from the alleyway between Blocks 1 and 2 of the Rossville Flats. He saw a crowd of around 100 towards the end of Chamberlain Street who were throwing stones and bricks. Lance Corporal V moved further forward and shot at and hit a man around 50 or 60 yards away from him in the act, he testified, of throwing a bottle with a fuse attached to it.[79]

The account of his firing given by Private S to the Royal Military Police was: 'I had been in my position for about five minutes when a gap appeared in the crowd. I saw a man standing in the gap between Blocks 1 and 2 of the flats. The man went down into a kneeling position facing towards me. I heard the sound of gunfire. About four single shots were fired in my direction. They passed about 5 to 10 metres from me and struck the walls of derelict houses behind me about 50 metres away. I saw the man move and I think he was attempting to stand up. As he moved I saw he was holding a long metallic object which appeared to be a rifle. I fired three aimed shots 7.62 mm at the man. I do not think I hit him but before I could fire again the crowd moved and closed the gap. I saw a man in a kneeling position in the gap between Blocks 1 and 2 of the flats. The man was facing my way and I saw two muzzle flashes coming from his shoulder position. I fired three aimed shots at the man and I saw his body jerk backwards. I believe I hit him. The crowd closed the gap again so I was unable to fire any more. The gap opened again after about thirty seconds and I saw a man in a kneeling position. I saw three muzzle flashes from his shoulder position. I fired three aimed shots at the man before the gap in the crowd closed again. I do not think I hit him. About thirty seconds later the gap opened again and once more I saw a man in a kneeling position. This time I saw four muzzle flashes come from his shoulder position. I saw these shots strike the water in a pond about 50 metres to my rear. I fired three aimed shots at the man and saw his body jerk backwards as if my rounds had hit him. I cannot say if it was the same man firing at me each time. Altogether I fired twelve rounds 7.62 mm.'[80]

Lance Corporal V was near the fence across the southern edge of the Eden Place waste ground when, he claimed, he observed a man with a petrol bomb quite close to the end of Chamberlain Street. He insisted in his oral evidence to this inquiry that his oral account to the Widgery Inquiry was to be preferred and that he had shot in accordance with the Yellow Card at a man who was posing a danger to life, though he agreed that he had shouted no warning. He believed that he had hit the man at whom he had fired.[81] According to Private Q, he was at the north-east corner of Block 1 of the Rossville Flats when he saw a man in the gap between Blocks 2 and 3 throwing a number of objects, which Private Q believed were nail bombs, towards soldiers in the area of the houses at the end of Chamberlain Street. One exploded around 10 yards from Sergeant O's APC. When the man reappeared and was about to throw again, Private Q fired a single shot at him. He said that he believed he had hit the man in the chest and had killed him.[82] According to Private R, he ran to where Sergeant O's APC had stopped in the Rossville Flats car park, from where he saw a man around halfway down the eastern side of Block 1 with a fizzing or smoking object in his hand. He fired one shot at this man and believed that he had hit him in the shoulder. After acid bombs had been dropped near him he saw a man's hand with a pistol appear from the gap between Blocks 2 and 3 of the Rossville Flats. Private R fired three shots at this man but did not know whether he had hit him.[83]

Sergeant O, said that while he was near his APC and soon after he had arrested William John Doherty, he fired three shots at a man holding a pistol who was behind a Cortina car on the south-east side of the car park; then three shots at a man holding an M1 carbine or similar weapon towards the south-west end of the lower balcony of Block 3 of the Rossville Flats; and finally two shots at a man holding an M1 carbine or similar weapon at ground level on the corner of the gap between Blocks 2 and 3. He said he was sure he had hit his first two targets, but said he thought that he had not hit his third. He estimated the time between firing at his first target and firing at his third as around three to four minutes.[84] Later, Sergeant O added: 'we were not faced with a sniping incident. My pig arrived in the courtyard of the Rossville Flats as a total surprise to the local people and I think that they took the view that they were being invaded by the army. I became aware that the IRA had agreed to stay out of the area well after the event when speaking with a television journalist, Peter Taylor. I think that it is probably true that the IRA had kept their hard men out of the area, up in the Creggan Estate, and I believe that "dicks" or second-rate men got hold of low-quality weapons which were in the Rossville Flats ready for use and disobeyed the IRA and opened fire on us. If experienced IRA snipers had been firing the weapons, there is no doubt that the paras [paratroopers] would have lost a number of men. If any of us had been killed, my guess is that there would have been no inquiry in 1972 or now.'[85]

On the basis of these accounts, the soldiers of Mortar Platoon fired thirty-two shots, hitting three nail or blast bombers, one petrol bomber, one man with a pistol, and two or three men with rifles or carbines, while missing an acid bomber, and probably missing another man with a pistol and another man with a carbine.[86] Again, according to the soldiers, they were fired on constantly after they disembarked and made arrests, as well as being subjected to an exploding nail bomb and a number of acid bombs. While two soldiers, Privates R and T, sustained minor injuries from acid or a similar corrosive substance contained in bottles thrown down from a balcony of Block 1 of the Rossville Flats, none of the soldiers of Mortar Platoon sustained any significant injury in what they described as in effect a close-quarter battle zone.[87] None of the soldiers of Mortar Platoon who fired admitted shooting Jackie Duddy, Margaret Deery, Michael Bridge and Michael Bradley. Private R believed that he had hit his intended target with his first shot but denied even the possibility that it was Jackie Duddy.[88] Even hardened military comrades who understood the confusion and complexity of urban 'warfare' found their accounts less than plausible.[89]

***

Meanwhile the remainder of Support Company vehicles had halted in Rossville Street. The Company Commander (Major 236) claimed that his command vehicle came under fire, so he moved it with his scout car in attendance to the north end of No. 1 Flats to obtain cover. The soft-skinned vehicles of the Composite Platoon halted under cover of buildings at the south-east corner of the junction of William Street and Rossville Street, where the troops dismounted. The Anti-Tank Platoon's vehicles halted behind the 4-ton lorries and the men of that platoon dismounted and moved to Kells Walk. The Composite Platoon Commander deployed half of his men to the east in support of the Mortar Platoon, the other half to the west in support of the Anti-Tank Platoon.[90] Most of the soldiers of Machine Gun Platoon remained at this stage in the derelict building on William Street.

As their comrades were engaged in the car park of the Rossville Flats, soldiers of Anti-Tank Platoon reached the low walls of a ramp at the southern end of a block of flats named Kells Walk, on the western side of Rossville Street. They found themselves facing a number of people on or around a rubble barricade around 80 yards away which had been cobbled together across Rossville Street to halt army vehicles. The paratroopers took up position behind a low wall. Some stones were thrown from the barricade, but the distance was too great for them to hit the soldiers. The paratroopers nevertheless opened fire. Within a few minutes seven men had been shot dead or fatally wounded.

Schoolteacher Brian Rainey described the run-up to the killings: 'I had just crossed the street barricade across Rossville Street, just in front of the high flats, and was approaching the small wall surrounding the block of maisonettes at Glenfada Park when I heard shouting and as I looked behind I could see Army Saracens rushing into Rossville Street. A number of young lads were running in all directions in front of them. One Saracen stopped about 15 to 20 yards of the William Street side of the street barricade in Rossville Street. Most of the young lads stopped level with the barricade. I stepped up onto the wall which runs along the front of the maisonettes at Glenfada Park so that I could see better what was happening. I saw a couple of young lads being captured by the Army and being led towards the Saracens. At this stage other soldiers were taking up positions. A number of the young lads began stoning the Army, and I saw and heard other young lads shout towards the people at the meeting to come and join them. Then I heard a burst of gunfire. I decided to get down from the wall and I stood close against the front of the maisonettes. There came another burst of gunfire and as I looked back towards the Army I saw a closely packed group of about four young lads fall lifelessly to the ground. Their position was directly behind the Rossville Street barricade on the Glenfada Park side of the road. At this burst of shooting I got down on my hands and knees and crawled along the base of the maisonettes at Glenfada Park. Just before I turned the corner I looked back to see if what I had seen had actually happened. From the way this small group had fallen – they seemed to be piled on top of one another – I was quite certain they had been shot. Again I must state I did not see any guns except those used by the Army, nor did I see any petrol bombs nor did I hear any nail bombs. The only weapons I saw being used by a number of young lads were stones.[91]

The barricade in Rossville Street running across from Glenfada Park to Block 1 of the Rossville Flats had fallen into disrepair and was only around 3 feet at its highest. There was a gap to allow a single line of traffic to go through but there were also reinforcements of barbed wire on wooden knife rests, hampering people fleeing in panic down Rossville Street. The soldiers at Kells Walk fired indiscriminately on the crowd as it tried to escape over the barricade.

A key witness to the atrocity was James Chapman, a civil servant who had previously been a regular soldier in the British Army with the rank of Warrant Officer Class 1, and who had lived in Derry for thirty-six years, thirty of them in the Bogside itself. His sitting room window at No. 6 Glenfada Park directly overlooked the Rossville Street barricade. He described how the main crowd of marchers had passed peacefully down Rossville Street before the soldiers' vehicles appeared. When the armoured personnel carriers appeared and the rest of the crowd began to run, soldiers deployed from their vehicles and immediately opened fire into the back of the crowd as it scrambled over the low barricade. Chapman, in a TV interview, recalled: 'I watched them shooting indiscriminately into a fleeing crowd of several thousand people, not just as some people say a few hundred hooligans.' He insisted that no firearms or bombs were being used against the soldiers at that time.[92] Three young men fell almost simultaneously with fatal wounds.

Michael Kelly, seventeen, lived at home with his family, kept racing pigeons, and worked as an apprentice sewing machine mechanic in the factory of Deyong Golding Ltd on the Maydown Industrial Estate.[93] He left for the march with a brother-in-law and several friends. Just before the Paras entered the Bogside, Kelly's mother shouted and beckoned to him from the first-floor walkway on the western side of Kells Walk, but he was too embarrassed to respond.[94] Kelly helped the wounded Margaret Deery before reaching the area of the rubble barricade. Differing eyewitness accounts ranged from Kelly being a passive bystander to an active rioter and stone-thrower, but most agreed that he was not throwing stones when he was shot. Instead, according to one account, he was dragging fencing 'to close the gap' in the rubble barricade.[95] Another account had him attempting to untangle himself from barbed wire on the barricade. Whatever his precise actions, Kelly was shot in the stomach and the copper-jacketed, lead core SLR bullet sliced through his small intestine and the artery and vein serving his left leg before it embedded itself in the middle of his pelvis.[96] Later forensics confirmed it had been fired by Lance Corporal F who admitted that he had shot Kelly – but said insisted he had only fired at people with bombs or weapons.[97]

As soon as Kelly dropped, another seventeen-year-old was promptly picked off by Private U's rifle. Hugh Gilmour, the baby of his family who lived with his parents in the Rossville Flats, was employed as a trainee fitter by Northern Ireland Tyre Services.[98] Gilmour was shot, possibly twice, in the arm and chest.[99] He managed to stumble over the rubble barricade and carry on a little further before he collapsed. A woman said she heard him cry 'I'm hit, I'm hit'. The teenager was pulled to safety but died shortly afterwards.[100]

Photographer Eamon Melaugh said: 'I was facing the Army and watching the members of the Security Forces fire their self-loading rifles. Most of the shots were being fired from waist level and they weren't deliberately aimed. Two shots rang out; the lad standing beside me who I now know to be Hugh Gilmore lurched forward from the waist. He said "I've been hit Eamon, I'm hit", meaning that he was shot. I looked at him; there was an expression of amazement, total amazement on his face. He turned round and ran up the street away from the barricade and from the soldiers. I ran after him. I wasn't able to catch up with him because I was lumbered down with two cameras and long lenses. He ran, after having been shot, to the gable end nearest to Free Derry Corner. He then slumped to the ground out of the line of fire and sometime later he died.'[101]

Hugh Patrick O'Donnell gave an account of running from the junction of Rossville Street and William Street towards the Eden Place waste ground and of armoured cars passing him. He continued: 'There was four or five of them and then the Ferret car behind that. Well I looked back and I saw my mate and he seemed to be c – he seemed to be caught though I wasn't sure. And I ran on and I ran into the waste ground and the army they were – and Saracens they were ploughing into the crowd. They were trying to ram the people … everything started to get confused then and we were surrounded by hundreds of soldiers; they were batoning people all round me and I was looking for a way out. There was a young – young bloke in front of me and the soldiers just at arm's reach away; don't know how he missed me but he did. And he hit me … head … his rifle butt and I got past him and as I passed the soldier I heard the rifle shots and I wasn't sure where they came from or anything else but then I saw a soldier outside a Saracen and I saw him shooting his rifle. So I ran up to the end of the Rossville Street Flats and I met another mate of mine and he told [me] that there was two young fellas lying dead around the back of the flats and nobody could get at them and he then started to cry and panicked and he led a few of us over a barricade at Rossville Street and we run down … the army and as we were running a black soldier stepped out of a Saracen and he started firing his rifle at us and the bullets were hitting the barricade behind us and hitting the wall beside us and I could feel the wind passing me. And I ran back to the corner of the flats and I looked back and saw that my mate was all right and as I turned the fella just at the corner of the flats fell beside me; he was shot; he was right beside me and I got over to look, someone pulled up his jumper and opened his shirt to see how he was. There was a hole in him and the blood was running out of his nose and mouth and a man says he's dead.'[102]

Michael McDaid, twenty, worked as a barman at the Celtic in Stanley's Walk. The high-velocity rifle bullet entered his left cheek, fracturing his jaw, passed through his mouth and neck, severed his spinal cord before entering the right chest cavity, fracturing the first two ribs, and cut through his right lung before leaving the body through the back of his chest. Mercifully, the injury to the spinal cord would have meant a rapid death.[103]

Witness James Begley gave another graphic account of the chaos and carnage as people scrambled away from the soldiers: 'I heard a roar and the Paras came up. And there was a wild scatter… I run down Chamberlain Street and run along as far as the bookies… There was a boy lying there. I went down on my knees to look at him and everybody else went past and he was coughing up blood and I knew I'd seen he was a goner; anyway when I looked at him, you know, he was a goner. I went down and went over and outside of the flats across Rossville Street and I run down and seen more soldiers and I run down there with a couple of other boys and they started shooting at us, so I went back over the barricade and hid in behind it when there was right up there a young man who was Will Nash known as Stiff he was lying there. Well I lay down and they were still firing at us, then the firing stopped and a – another boy came up, his name is Young, he come over to me and says "are you all right?" and I says "aye" and I was getting up and started firing again and I told him to get down and I looked up and I seen he got it right between the eyes just on there and er – he fell over the top of me and they kept on firing and then another boy came up; it was Mr Nash, I knew him by looking at him. I looked up and seen him and told him to get down but I was too late he got it too. And some other fella then came out to give us a hand over and er – I don't know what you call him but he got it as well and there was three or four all lying there at the barricade and me and another boy just creeped in from the corner and hid in behind the flats. They then stopped shooting and went back over the road. That's it.'[104]

Docker William Nash, sometimes known as 'Stiff', was nineteen and lived in Creggan with his parents, four of his seven brothers, and his five sisters. He was the brother of Olympic boxer Charlie Nash.[105] One of his other brothers had been married on the day before and the celebrations had continued late into the night. Their mother had missed the wedding, as she had suffered a heart attack a few days earlier and was recovering in Altnagelvin Hospital.[106] Nash was shot in the chest, the bullet piercing a lung and his heart. His father, Alexander, rushed to him as he died.

So too did John Young, a seventeen-year-old salesman in the men's clothing shop of John Temple Ltd in Waterloo Place, who lived with his parents and a sister in Creggan.[107] As speeches were about to start at Free Derry Corner, a friend pulled off his hat and ran off with it. Young chased after him and laughingly retrieved his headwear. The two friends were separated by the crowd and Young moved to the barricade around 30 yards away. There he suffered a fatal gunshot wound, shot in the face at the rubble barricade, apparently while crouching and going to the aid of William Nash.[108]

Matthew Connolly gave witness: 'I was standing near rubble at Ros[s]ville Street when a young fellow of sixteen or seventeen was shot and fell in front of me. He was shot fairly high up in his chest. The soldier who fired the shot was crouched behind the door of a Saracen. At this time the fellow was not dead. As we went forward to help him, automatic fire riddled the rubble. Everyone lay flat out on the ground; about four stayed on for about a minute and during this time the soldiers were still shooting and we could hear the bullets above our heads. The fellow was screaming. We retreated behind a wall. About a minute later John Young crawled with his head down towards the boy who had been hit. He got to within a yard of him when a single shot hit him; he was dead. A youth tried to move towards the two bodies but only got out into the open and was shot. He stumbled back towards the wall and was taken on to a house.'[109]

Meanwhile, Alexander Nash remained by his son. The fifty-two-year-old jobless painter had before the march been drinking since 11 a.m. in a pub where he consumed, by his own estimate, 'about seven or eight stouts and two whiskeys'.[110] But his later testimonies were remarkably lucid and consistent. In his statement to the RUC, he said: 'I then heard shooting although I thought it was rubber bullets or gas. I turned around and looked towards the wee barricade in Rossville Street and saw my son William lying on his stomach with his head looking towards me. I also saw two other bodies lying one on either side of him, on their backs. I ran over to the barricade and I put my right hand up to stop the Army from shooting. The next thing I heard was more shots and I fell to the ground for safety. I then realised that I had been hit in the left arm and on my left side. I fell just beside my son and the Army tank then came and soldiers lifted the three bodies into the tank. They didn't say anything to me or interfere with me. When the tank went away I got up and went around to the back of the Rossville high flats into a wee house there where the Knights of Malta men dressed my wound. They put me into their ambulance along with some other injured people and a dead body. They then brought us all up to Altnagelvin Hospital where I have been ever since.'[111]

Denis Patrick McLaughlin, sixteen at the time, recalled during an interview: 'I was down at the William Street to see what was happening and er – they started to shoot the gas and we came running up Rossville Street. To get away from the gas. I was hit with a rubber bullet and I fell and two men dragged me up... I was all right and er – ... I says "I'm ... going down, see what's happening down here again". And I went down and I seen a body over at the barricade and there was another fella along with me; he goes over at the body and I went over along with him and er – this other fella walked out and he was shot in the stomach and he fell, then another man came out again he was shot and he fell and a boy came out and he was shot in the head... They just came out to help with this body that was lying there. They thought we were – they thought we were shot too as we were lying beside him because we didn't want to get up, you know. And they shot him in the head and the – the blood spurted out of his head it came away in my hands, you know. And er – there was a – the oth – there was a boy then that came over and he dragged this boy by the feet, you know, to get him out of the road. He says for us to come over out of the road, you know, you don't want to get shot. We says "what about these bodies?" He says "you have to come over here in case you get shot", you know. So he dragged the first boy by the feet then he grabbed my hands and he dragged me across and we run in against the wall with Father Bradley, you know. And I grabbed Father Bradley down beside me, you know, as he's sort of like a little scared, you know. Some of the soldiers came around the corner and there was another man and he pulled off his coat and the steam was rising out of him and there was a hole in his shoulder and I knew he was shot.'[112]

Kevin McElhinney, seventeen, the third of five children, lived with his parents in Pennyburn. He was a shop assistant in Lipton's supermarket in Strand Road. He left home after lunch to go on the march with a few friends. One of them, Frank Hone, later admitted that he only went to throw stones, but he said that Kevin was not interested in rioting in the way that he was.[113] Another friend, Paul Coyle, testified that McElhinney was carrying a 'paint bomb' – a bottle containing paint – because he wanted 'to make his mark on a Saracen'. It is likely he took part in the rioting at barricade 14 before reaching the rubble barricade where he was shot while trying to crawl away to safety. A bullet was fired into his buttock which carried on through his pelvic cavity, lacerating muscle, artery, intestines and bladder. He died of internal bleeding,[114] the last person to be killed by army gunfire at or near to the rubble barricade. Sergeant K testified he saw two men crawling from the barricade in the direction of the door of the flats and fired one aimed shot, but could not say whether it hit.[115] Either Private L or Private M, members of Composite Platoon who had taken up positions at the low walls of the Kells Walk ramp, shot Kevin McElhinney as he was crawling south from the rubble barricade away from the soldiers. Both probably fired at him on the orders of one or perhaps two nearby non-commissioned officers, Colour Sergeant 002 and Corporal 039.[116]

Friend Alex Morrison said: 'When the soldiers entered Rossville Street I retreated and ran towards the entrance of the high flats. From there I saw a batch of soldiers getting out of a Saracen opposite. One of these soldiers ran towards a wall at the maisonettes opposite the high flats – he aimed the rifle at a group of young boys who were standing on the Free Derry Corner side of a barricade of rubble which is directly outside the main doors of the high flats. These boys had retreated to this point as the Army came along Rossville Street. I saw one of these boys fall just as a soldier fired from his position at the maisonettes. This was the first boy shot. Immediately I heard further shots which came from the soldiers and were directed at the other boys at the barricade of rubble. We retreated immediately to the doors of the flats. Kevin McElhinney was running alongside me. We were crouched and running at the same time – making for the main door of the flats. As I entered I heard Kevin – who was now just behind me – shout "I'm hit … I'm hit …" I dived on in the door and went up the stairs thinking that Kevin was behind me. I realised that no one was behind me so I ran back down and saw Kevin lying dead just inside the door. Others lifted him and took him upstairs."[117]

Witness Patrick O'Hagan recorded that he was in the doorway of the Rossville Flats at a time when six people crawled towards this area, under fire from the Army. The first five reached cover, but the sixth man was shot, was pulled into the flats, possibly by the person who preceded him, and was attended by a first-aid man.[118] He testified that the youths had been 'trapped' at the rubble barricade by army gunfire before they began crawling to the flats. Patrick O'Hagan here said that the youth who was shot had 'collapsed partially around the open door'. He had seen him several times during his crawl and was sure that he was not armed.

James Norris, an Order of Malta Ambulance Corps volunteer, was in the Rossville Flats treating Hugh Hegarty, who had been hit by a gas canister in William Street when the firing began. He stated in his official report that he left the flat to find another first-aid volunteer or a doctor to assist, and after brushing past numerous people who were taking cover, he began to descend the stairs. As he did so, he was told that someone had been shot 'around the corner from the flats doorway'. When Norris reached the bottom stair, he 'saw a cameraman and just at that a boy aged between sixteen to twenty years fell in the doorway'. This youth was bleeding profusely and one of his legs was shaking violently.[119]

Father Terence O'Keeffe gave consistent accounts of how, after he had seen the bodies on the rubble barricade, he saw a youth dragging himself towards the south-western entrance to the Rossville Flats. He formed the impression from the manner of the youth's movement – crawling more on his side and back than his front – that this man had been injured in the leg. The youth had nearly made it to the doorway when he hauled himself up – possibly on the first of the poles that supported the porch roof – in order to get over the step. At this point his body jerked and the priest assumed that a bullet had hit him.[120]

Sisters Helen and Margaret Johnston testified that they saw the youth jerk twice, once at a point between the rubble barricade and the doorway, and again when he was at the doorway. Another witness, Margaret Healy, testified: 'Looking out of the window of the flat where I was taking refuge, I saw a soldier in a kneeling position. He was approached by another soldier who seemed to be in a position of authority and his attention was drawn to a young boy who was crawling along the ground. The soldier who had been kneeling rose to his feet, took aim at the boy and pulled the trigger. I saw a red flash spurting from his rifle. The boy stopped moving and someone from the flats pulled him into the doorway.

The soldier who fired the shot followed the instructions given him by the other soldier and fired at targets as he was told.'[121]

As before, the testimony of soldiers was quite different. Private U suggested that Alexander Nash and his injured son had been shot by an IRA gunman: 'I saw the pistol jerk, observed the strike of the bullet. It hit about 5 metres short on the other side of the barricade, ricocheted and hit the man who had gone over to the youth in the right arm. Immediately after this shot, another was fired by the gunman at the doors. I saw the youth's head jerk and he slumped into the man's arms.'[122] Private U explained why he did not fire at the gunman: 'The target was too small and there were too many people around the area from which the man with a pistol was firing for me to fire at him. I might have hit one of them or possibly someone further in the distance near Free Derry Corner. The target was just too small, unlike the first target I had fired at. I knew, however, that the soldiers on the other side of the road by the wall would have a better angle so, when I saw the pistol appear, I shouted over to them "grey doors". I don't think they heard me. I did not see them firing at the target. In fact, I do not remember the soldiers by the wall firing at all.'[123] His testimony was challenged, not least because he had made no mention of the 'gunman' in his first statement to the military police. That said, however, other witnesses did testify to the presence of an Official IRA volunteer who may or may not have fired one shot with a revolver but who could hardly have shot both Nashes.

Robert Campbell, the Assistant Chief Constable of the Renfrew and Bute Constabulary, who was observing the scene from the City Wall, described how people streamed through the barricade on their way to the meeting at Free Derry Corner, but he also observed a group of demonstrators who detached themselves from the main crowd and remained close to the barricade from which they threw stones and other missiles in the direction of the army vehicles. He heard automatic fire from the direction of the Rossville Flats, followed by a single high-velocity shot which caused the demonstrators to take cover. Then came a cluster of ten or twelve high-velocity rounds which finally scattered them, leaving 'three or four bodies' lying at the barricade. Father O'Keefe, a lecturer in philosophy at the University of Ulster in Coleraine, said that when the armoured personnel carriers arrived the bulk of the marchers had already moved to Free Derry Corner. He held back to make contact with friends and when the soldiers arrived he was part of a group of twenty-five to thirty people standing near the barricade. Whilst he and others took cover behind the gable end of the Glenfada Park Flats, some five or six remained at the barricade and the soldiers opened fire. He saw one of them hit and three bodies on the ground.

During the fusillades near the rubble barricade, it is certain that Lance Corporal F shot Michael Kelly; and that Corporal P shot at least one of William Nash, John Young and Michael McDaid, although Lance Corporal J may have been responsible for one of the casualties and it is possible that Corporal E was responsible for another. It is also certain that Private U shot Hugh Gilmour; and that Private L or Private M shot Kevin McElhinney.[124]

***

Bernadette Devlin, then twenty-two and MP for Mid Ulster, was on the makeshift platform on the back of a lorry when paratroopers opened fire. Thirty years later she recalled: 'The only clear memory I have, which I have now as I speak of it, is terror,' she said. 'My mouth was dry. I think I could taste coal dust. There was a pain in the bottom of my back. My stomach was like lead and yet I couldn't feel anything at all.' In the panic, she found herself under the lorry, and she recalled thinking: 'There is nobody here, only me, dead people and the British Army coming down in front of me.'[125]

The line of fire from Kells Walk southward to the Rossville Street barricade came dangerously close to Free Derry Corner. When the soldiers began to fire at the barricade the crowd around the speakers' platform, though agitated by the sound of the shooting, did not immediately break up. A second burst however caused the crowd to fall flat on their faces and at the next lull in the firing they quickly dispersed. There is no evidence that any soldier deliberately fired at this crowd. Lord Brockway, who was attempting to address the meeting at the time, acknowledged as much. No one in this crowd was injured, though some of the shots aimed at the barricade which missed their mark may have come uncomfortably close.[126]

After the firing on the barricade had begun, soldiers of Anti-Tank Platoon moved forward from the low walls of the Kells Walk ramp and four of them – F and D closely followed by G and H – went into Glenfada Park North, a residential building complex that lay to the west of Rossville Street, where a number of civilians were seeking refuge from the soldiers by a gable end.[127] The civilians, including Father O'Keefe, moved en masse through the south-east gap between the blocks of Glenfada Park North and into its central courtyard, heading for the south-west entrance leading to Abbey Park. Within seconds there was another deadly fusillade.

Joseph Friel, known as Joe, twenty and single, lived with his family in the Rossville Flats, and worked as a tax inspector for the Inland Revenue, was the first to be shot.[128] He had watched the march from his seventh-floor flat and decided to go to Free Derry Corner to listen to the speeches. He was on his way there when he heard a lot of single shots being fired. He recalled: 'I then ran like mad towards my block of flats and when I reached the block nearest the Rossville Street end I stopped to get my breath. Shooting was fierce at this time although again I couldn't see who was doing the shooting. There were about five young chaps at the entry door of my block of flats and I walked quickly up towards them keeping in near to the flats. I got right up to these fellows, who were young fellows, none of whom I knew. I didn't say anything to these chaps and they didn't speak to me. I stood with my back towards the upper entry of our flats which is off the old Bogside Road. I then heard somebody shout, "Look out" or something like that and saw three or four soldiers appear at the entry between Rossville Street and the square where I was. They immediately opened fire and then I heard the shots and felt a thud on my chest. At first I thought I was hit by a rubber bullet but when I looked down I saw blood pouring out of my chest and mouth. I ran around the corner where I was assisted by some people.'[129]

In a later filmed interview, Friel described running into a square 'the minute the shooting started ... a group of other boys ran into it too. We thought that was the safe spot, where there was a confined square. There was no way to get into it except two wee alleys ... down at the foot of it. So we thought we were safe from the shooting and we were just standing ... and bullets were flying everywhere. We saw people panicking and running, hundreds of them. Next thing we saw is about four soldiers coming down that alley. Then they stepped out into the square and one of them opened fire from his hip. He couldn't have had time to take aim because the minute they appeared I heard a shot, looked, saw him, heard about three shots bang, bang, bang. I thought I was hit with a rubber bullet and I looked down and I saw blood gushing out of here, and ... I panicked I'm shouting "I'm shot, I'm shot" and I ran down the alley way and was carried out from there over into a house.'[130] He was then put in a car which was stopped at barrier 20 and one of the other occupants allegedly hit by a rubber bullet or a rifle butt. Friel was eventually taken to Altnagelvin Hospital in an army vehicle. Friel's gunshot wound to the chest was caused by the bullet passing through from right to left of his sternum. He was operated on that night and discharged eleven days later. His surgeon described him as 'an extremely lucky young man' as his injury had been caused by 'an almost near-miss bullet'.[131]

Michael Quinn, a seventeen-year-old schoolboy, was the next to be shot at the Glenfada Park flats. The bullet went through his right cheek and exited by his nose.[132] Wearing a rust-coloured windcheater, he was caught in a rush of people into the estate's car park when the Paras started shooting. He testified: 'After some hesitation, I decided to get out of Glenfada Park. I ran across towards the alleyway leading into Abbey Park and as I was nearing this entrance I felt myself being struck on the right cheek by a bullet. I stumbled but got up and ran on through the alleyway. As I was passing through I noticed the man who I had seen being shot earlier lying in the shadows of a nook in the alleyway. When I reached Abbey Park, someone grabbed me by the arm and we kept on running through Abbey Park and across the old Bogside towards Lisfannon Park.'[133] There he was given first aid and taken to hospital.

Daniel Gillespie, a thirty-two-year-old unemployed steel erector, was grazed on the forehead by either a ricocheting bullet or a fragment of brickwork detached by the same bullet. After moving to the centre of the courtyard, he had turned back and saw a group of boys coming through the south-west alleyway carrying broken flagstones that he assumed they intended to throw at the soldiers; he told the boys that live rounds had been fired and that they should go to a safe place. He recalled that he fell forwards suffering from a head wound, and that on regaining his senses he saw that two of the boys he had spoken to had come to his aid. As they lifted him up there was another shot from the soldier at the northern end of Glenfada Park and the taller of the two boys groaned, apparently shot.[134]

James Wray, known as Jim, was twenty-two years old, engaged to be married to an English girl he met during a work stint in England, and worked as a refrigeration inspector.[135] He was, according to friends, outgoing and popular. He also worked in a city bar and dancehall at weekends.[136] After joining the march with family members, he made his way to Glenfada Park North. He was leaving the estate through the south-west alleyway into Abbey Park when Joe Friel and Michael Quinn were shot in front of him. Wray was shot twice in the right side of his back and fell to the ground.[137] Whether he fell because he was shot and whether he was shot after he had fallen and was lying on the ground became matters of great controversy. Evidence from his autopsy showed that either wound would have been fatal without immediate medical attention, which he did not receive, and that the first shot would have resulted due to spinal damage in the loss of the use of his legs.[138] Indeed, witnesses stated that Wray was calling out that he could not move his legs before he was shot the second time.

Wray's family, supported by some but not all eyewitness and forensic evidence, insisted that he was 'executed' by being shot at close range while on the ground.[139] Eight civilians supported that view. Among them was William O'Reilly, forty, who described running to his house in Abbey Park with others after he had heard shooting. He said: 'I went to my front window and I saw a youth fall at Glenfada Park – his head was on the kerb and his body on the street. He moved slightly and just as I was going out to him more shots rang out, the youth's body jerked and lay still.'[140] Another was sixteen-year-old Malachy Coyle, who recalled how he had been pulled to cover in a yard in Glenfada Park North. He went on: 'We hid behind a dustbin and looked out to see if we could see the army. I could see three unarmed men lying on the ground in Glenfada Park. One of the men had his left eyebrow shot away. He was lying face down on the ground. I made a move towards this man but the man in the yard with me pulled me back. We then tried to get into this house, but the man said we should not as the door of the backyard was open and the army would be able to see us. We looked towards the wounded men on the ground and the man with the eye wound looked up at us and exchanged a few words with the man in the yard with me. I heard another shot coming from the direction of the soldiers and I then knew that the man had been shot again in the back of the left-hand shoulder. He gave a groan and I could then see that the man was dead.'[141] Wray's eyebrow wound was attributed to hitting the kerb when he fell, not a bullet. And John Porter, a thirty-three-year-old Quartermaster Sergeant in the Irish Army, testified: 'I saw the man lying on the ground that I had tried to rescue earlier on rise up again with his head and all off the ground and I saw the clothes on his back jump up and I knew that he had been shot at close range by a rifle – I saw the smoke at the back of his clothes. ... There was no doubt in my mind that the paratrooper shot a wounded man on the ground.'[142] The balance of probabilities is that Wray was shot before he fell and, paralysed from the waist down, spoke briefly to other civilians before being shot a second time.

Meanwhile, William McKinney, three days short of his twenty-seventh birthday and carrying his new cine camera, had filmed the start of the march and moved away from the tear gas. He spoke to his brother while taking more footage before heading towards Glenfada Park North. McKinney was shot, probably by Lance Corporal F, as he went from the southern end of the eastern block of Glenfada Park North towards the south-west alleyway into Abbey Park. Shortly before he had been standing among the crowd round the body of Michael Kelly.[143] His autopsy showed that he had been shot in the back with the bullet exiting his lower chest and going on through his left forearm, although it is possible he was shot twice.[144]

Legal representatives for the soldiers raised the unproven suggestion that McKinney may not have been attempting to flee but was rather 'standing his ground' when soldiers came into Glenfada Park North; and that his possession of both a cine camera and an ordinary camera might, with 'sudden movement with such a piece of photographic equipment', be mistaken for some kind of aggressive, armed behaviour. McKinney was known to take risks to get his pictures, but it is highly unlikely that anyone at that distance could mistake a cine camera for a firearm. And he was shot in the back.

Dr Raymond McLean, a local GP, civil rights activist and the first Catholic mayor of Derry, tried to give McKinney words of reassurance while he lay dying from his gunshot wounds. McKinney asked: 'Doctor, am I going to be OK?' Dr McLean later said: 'I told him that if I got him to hospital in time he should be OK.' Shortly after that exchange, McKinney passed into a coma and died half an hour later. 'Willie was not a stone-thrower, a bomber or a gunman. He had gone to the civil rights march in the role of amateur photographer,' said the *Derry Journal*'s tribute to him. Up to five more people were injured by the same group of soldiers.

Joseph Mahon, known as Joe, was sixteen, lived with his family in the Creggan, and had left school a few weeks earlier to begin an apprenticeship as a joiner. He was shot above the right hip, the bullet penetrating his abdomen. It has been suggested, but not proven, that it was the same bullet which killed William McKinney. The teenager, terrified he would be 'finished off' by a soldier, played dead as he lay on the ground. Mahon described the effect of the injury on his subsequent life: 'I have never fully recovered from the wound I received that day. I have to have regular check-ups and the damage to my intestines means I have to be careful about what I eat and drink. I am unable to drink strong spirits. I regularly get pain and cramp in my hips and suffer frequent bowel infections and some numbness in my leg. Before Bloody Sunday I was a very keen sportsman and played Gaelic football. I played football once for Derry Minors and had been captain of the school hurley team. After Bloody Sunday I did not dare take up these sports again because I did not believe that my hips were up to it. Whilst I was in hospital I had been told that I would suffer severe arthritis and would be in a wheelchair by the time I was forty-five. Mentally, my outlook on life changed. I became more withdrawn and introverted.'[145] He spent a month in hospital and as a result lost his apprenticeship.

Patrick O'Donnell, known as Patsy, was forty-one, married with six children, and employed as a roofing contractor. He ran towards Abbey Park because people were shouting and he had seen people lying at the rubble barricade. He said: 'As I started to run I saw somebody falling some distance in front of me across the Park. There were other ones running as well as me. As I ran along I could still hear shooting. I stopped for a second and across Glenfada Park in the direction of Columbcille Court and about 30 or 40 yards from me I saw a soldier with a rifle in his hands. He appeared to be aiming in the direction of where I stood. There was a woman just in front of me and we both dived down behind a wooden fence and I kept the woman pushed down as far as possible. I heard a crack and felt pieces of cement of the wall behind me hit me around the shoulders. I looked round and saw the right shoulder of my coat was torn and I also saw a mark on the wall just above my shoulder. I felt a pain in my right shoulder, like burning. The tear in my coat also looked burnt. The woman and I rolled round to the shelter of the gable of the flats.[146] He suffered a through and through bullet wound to his right shoulder.

The woman was forty-four-year-old Winifred O'Brien, who later testified that while taking shelter she was comforted by a teenager as the Paras opened up. She went on: 'Next thing, an older, heavier-built man came up and he sort of threw himself on top of me to protect me behind the fence. I can't remember how it happened but he suddenly said he was hit in the right shoulder. He was going to put his own hankie on the wound but I'd a brand-new one, never been used, with me and I said here, take this one, it will be cleaner. I opened his coat and put the folded hankie inside his shirt against the wound. There was quite a lot of blood and I got some on both hands. The next thing was five or six Paras rushing up and lifting everybody there. The young boy, the first one who helped me, was knocked around very rough and they were also shoving the man hit in the shoulder.'[147] Before being hospitalised, O'Donnell was arrested at the southern gable end of the western block of Glenfada Park North. As a result of his injuries he was unable to return to his work for almost eight months.[148]

It is probable that Corporal E shot and injured Patrick O'Donnell. It is not possible to identify which particular soldiers shot the other casualties. It is more likely than not that either Lance Corporal F or Private H fired the shot that mortally wounded William McKinney; that one or other of these soldiers was responsible for the shot that wounded Joe Mahon; that either Private G or Private H fired the shot that wounded Michael Quinn; that either Lance Corporal F or Private G fired the shot that wounded Joe Friel; and that either Private G or Private H fired the first shot to hit Jim Wray, and one of them also fired the second as he was lying on the ground. Joe Mahon was probably wounded by the shot that had first hit William McKinney. It is not clear whether Joe Friel and Michael Quinn were specifically targeted or were hit by shots fired indiscriminately at the people who were in the south-west corner of

Glenfada Park North. All these shots were fired from the northern side of Glenfada Park North within a very short time of each other. All the casualties were on the southern side of Glenfada Park North, around 40 yards from the soldiers.[149]

Subsequent inquiries found that, with the exception of the second shot to hit Jim Wray, the gunshot injuries were as the result of the initial burst of firing by the soldiers who had come into Glenfada Park North. Michael Quinn, Joe Friel and Jim Wray were shot when close to the south-west alleyway leading into Abbey Park, within a very short time of each other. William McKinney and Joe Mahon were shot further to the east. Patrick O'Donnell was probably shot slightly later, as he turned back from running to the south-west exit of Glenfada Park North after seeing someone fall in front of him. The timing and circumstances of Daniel Gillespie's wound remains problematic.[150] What is clear, however, is that none of the casualties were armed or posing a threat to soldiers who opened fire with no warning. Private G separated from his three comrades and entered Abbey Park, another residential area which lies to the west of Glenfada Park North,[151] and added to the rising death toll.

Father of seven Gerard McKinney, often known as Gerry, thirty-five, lived in the Waterside area of Londonderry. His wife, Ita, was eight days off birthing their eighth child.[152] McKinney managed a junior soccer team and ran the city's Ritz roller-skating rink.[153] He attended the civil rights march with his brother-in-law, John O'Kane.

O'Kane recorded that the shooting 'started in earnest' near to Columbcille Court and was carried out by the Army who concentrated on a retreating crowd. He and Gerard McKinney saw a youth of around sixteen who had been shot in the side, probably Michael Kelly. Along with a couple of others they tried to carry the youth out of danger, but the crowd soon knocked him from their grasp.[154] The shooting continued and: 'We lay with our backs to the wall on one side of the Court in the company of some six others, afraid to move for a time. Gunfire was heavy when I suggested that we try to cross the court in the direction of Blutcher St. [sic] one at a time. However as gunfire got heavier I decided not to risk it. Gerry decided after a few minutes to take a chance and accompanied by a youth, whom I don't know, he led us out across the court. As we went forward, I was some yards behind Gerry. At a stage when I can only assume he was visible from the other side of the entrance. Gerry turned, shouted "No, no" and put his hands in the air. A shot rang out which caught Gerry about the chest and he fell forward. A second shot rang out and the youth who was leading the way along with him fell to the ground. We retreated back to the wall of the court. I cannot state emphatically enough that Gerry, the youth, and everybody else in the courtyard at the time were completely unarmed and defenceless.'[155]

Forensic evidence confirmed that McKinney, no relation to Willie, was shot with his hands in the air. The bullet entered below his left armpit, hit his vertebrae and exited his back.[156] He joined his hands together, made the sign of the cross and blessed himself after he had fallen, according to two witnesses. He died within minutes.

The other young man, Gerald Donaghey, who fell at the same moment, was hit probably but not certainly by the same bullet despite O'Kane's hearing of another shot. The seventeen-year-old known as Gerry lived with his sister and her husband and son in the Bogside, his adoptive father having died in December 1965 and his adoptive mother four weeks later.[157] A member of the IRA's youth wing, *Fianna na Éireann*, he had worked at Carlin's Brewery in the Waterside but was jailed for six months for disorderly behaviour in a riot the year before and was not re-employed after his release in December.[158] He was shot in the abdomen, the bullet grazing his spine and causing internal injuries to his stomach, duodenum, aorta and inferior vena cava.[159] The wounded Joe Mahon recalled 'seeing a single soldier on the opposite side of the court from the others, looking towards the passageway and firing two or three shots from under his arm and at the same time shouting to the other soldiers "I've got another one [of] them, Dave." The soldier then pulled back towards the van.'[160] Although two soldiers of Anti-Tank Platoon were called Dave, Private G was probably addressing his 'pair', Lance Corporal F.[161]

Maureen Doherty, watching events from the scullery window of a friend's house in Abbey Park, saw two men, one young and the other middle-aged, walking towards a soldier who had a gun trained on them. She said: 'The two men were walking, with their hands on the crown of their heads, from Abbey Park out towards Glenfada Park (had they continued walking they would have reached Rossville Street). Just outside Mrs O'Reilly's window the soldier fired his rifle; he had his rifle against his chest, and the two men fell. The older man, who was also the tallest of the two, fell first, then almost immediately the younger man fell. They both fell on their backs.'[162]

Several members of the Order of Malta Ambulance Corps and at least one other civilian bravely ran towards the two dying men. Two of them, Eibhlin Lafferty and Hugh Leo Young, ran from Lisfannon Park and were themselves fired upon, causing them to either duck or dive down. Neither was injured, and they continued to move to the two dying men.[163] Hugh Leo Young, twenty-six, was the older brother of earlier fatality John Young. Eibhlin Lafferty, described by her boss as committed, bright and bubbly, later recalled that she just had time to see that one of the fallen men was still alive when a burst of shooting forced her to dive down: 'I shouted "don't shoot, don't shoot, red cross" but they didn't stop firing. Robert Cadman, Malta man, came out to help with the first two bodies...'[164] In much later evidence, she said: 'There was shooting going on as I ran past the front of the houses in Abbey Park and bullets were bouncing around me. I was shouting, "Don't shoot, first aid" but the shooting was continuous, shot after shot. I did not see where the shooting came from but I thought it was coming straight towards me ... I could hear the "ping" of bullets.' She described one shot hitting the side of her trousers and stated that she dived down just before she reached the body of Gerard McKinney. She recalled saying the Act of Contrition in his ear.[165] Gerald McCauley, the civilian who also went to aid the men, recalled: 'I became aware of soldiers at the corner block of houses beside the wooden palings. I froze on the spot and a girl in a white overall (Lafferty in her uniform) come on the scene. The soldiers fired at her but the bullet hit the pathway about 2 feet in front of her. The soldier shouted "Get back" and the girl threw herself on the ground and started to crawl over to the man in the brown coat. Afterwards I was told he was McKinney.'[166] The gunshot wounds to Gerard McKinney's body were not immediately apparent even to those attending him, and it was initially thought that he had suffered a heart attack.

In a later statement, O'Kane said: 'I could not move; I just stood there frozen to the spot. I heard voices all round shouting "come back, come back". I just don't know how I got back but some other men who were standing in the [flats] pulled me out the garden so eventually they got me into one of the flats through the window and they pulled me by the shoulders into a room. By this time they were lying there and no one could get near them. A while after this, I cannot say how long, people started to appear with their arms above their heads. The first one I saw beside my brother-in-law was a Knights of Malta girl in uniform. By the time I reached him there was three male Knights of Malta treating him as a cardiac case. I told him he was shot but I could not convince them that this was the case. They asked me to get a cardiac ambulance. I respected their efforts and what they were trying to do so an onlooker and myself went to call an ambulance. This we succeeded in doing and we returned to the scene. By this time the ambulance arrived. We helped to lift him onto the stretcher and into the ambulance.'[167] The ambulance rushed McKinney to Altnagelvin Hospital.

Patrick Campbell, fifty-three, was a casual docker at shipping merchants Pinkertons and lived in the Creggan with his wife and nine children. He had been on the civil rights march from its start. Like many others he was driven away by CS gas and was already on the south side of the rubble barricade when the vehicles of Support Company entered the Bogside.[168]

He recalled: 'I stood for some time beyond the wee barricade which is outside the Rossville Flats looking down towards William Street, where they were throwing the gas. The Army tanks then came into Rossville Street and the soldiers jumped out and at this I turned and ran towards the gable end of the Rossville Flats. I stood there for a few minutes and I then ran across the waste ground towards Free Derry Corner. I then felt like a thud in my lower back and fell onto my knees. I put my hand to my hip and I saw there was blood on it. I then put my hand up and called that I was shot. Some men then came and took me into a house near Free Derry Corner, and I was kept waiting there for a car to take me to hospital.'[169] In a later note for enquiring journalists, he said: 'I saw soldiers jumping out and when the shooting began I made a dive for cover behind a small gable near the telephone box. From there I could see soldiers milling about in Glenfada Park. I then made a dash for Joseph Place and was shot in the back.'

The army bullet – which astonishingly was not found in two medical operations – entered close to his left kidney and damaged his colon, bladder and ureter. He was unable to return to work and died in the mid-1980s.

Daniel McGowan, thirty-seven, lived with his family in the Creggan and his wife was expecting their ninth child. For thirteen years he had worked as a maintenance serviceman at the DuPont plant.[170] In a written statement, McGowan described events after leaving his brother-in-law's house at St Columb's Wells to listen to speeches at Free Derry corner: 'I had proceeded about 20 yards along the rear of these houses when I heard what I thought was either a rubber bullet or gas gun being fired. I proceeded on and was about 15 yards from the northern end of the houses at Joseph Place when I heard a large volley of shots. I got to the end of the houses and went out into the forecourt facing the row of shops at Joseph Place. I looked down to my left in the direction of Rossville Street and I noticed a young man lying on the ground near the telephone kiosk at the gable wall of the flats on Rossville Street. I also noticed a young girl who was in a hysterical state just outside the chemist's shop at the western end of the row of shops. I also noticed two soldiers on their knees in firing positions at Glenfada Park. Then I noticed a man whom I now know as Patrick Campbell staggering in a drunken fashion about 20 yards from me just above the butcher's shop at Joseph Place. He shouted to me "I'm shot son, I'm shot". I ran over and caught him by the arm and helped him along towards the rear of the houses on Joseph

Place. Just as I had pushed him round the corner of the rear of the houses my right leg folded underneath me and I realised then that I was shot. I went unconscious for a very short while. When I came to, I dragged myself round the corner of the houses and proceeded along for about 15 yards. While I was doing so I heard another burst of gunfire but I can't say where it came from. Two men came and dragged me along by the arms and put me into a car at St Columb's Wells. I was eventually taken home and subsequently taken to hospital in an ambulance.'[171] In a later deposition he said that as he fell, he locked eyes with a soldier lying prone on a wall by Glenfada Park, and had the impression he was the one who had shot him.

He was shot through the left leg, the bullet fracturing his tibia and fibula. A metal pin was inserted and three months of traction and physiotherapy followed before his discharge in April. Left with a shortened leg, McGowan never worked again. Years later he described the impact that Bloody Sunday had had on him: 'My life fell apart after Bloody Sunday. I had worked throughout my adult life until Bloody Sunday ... My personality also changed as a result of the events of Bloody Sunday. I became very strict with my children, particularly my sons, and started drinking heavily. I was strict with my children simply because I feared for them; I did not want them to get into any sort of trouble ... Whilst I agree with the aims of the civil rights movement I do not condone paramilitary activity. I do not believe in violence and my being shot has not changed that.'[172] He died almost exactly thirty-two years after being shot.

***

Soon after the shootings in Rossville Street, Glenfada Park North and Abbey Park, some of the soldiers who had been in Glenfada Park North, including the ubiquitous Lance Corporal F, went to its south-east corner, where there was a road entrance to Rossville Street. From this position they fired across Rossville Street into a pedestrianised area between the Joseph Place flats and the front (southern) side of Block 2 of the Rossville Flats.[173]

March steward Patrick Doherty, a thirty-two-year-old plumber at the DuPont plant where he was known as Skelper, lived with his wife and six children in the Brandywell. In the six previous months he had become increasingly involved in the civil rights campaign and had joined the local civil rights association. He had attended a number of protests against internment, including the demonstration at Magilligan Strand a week before.[174] He was an active member of the Northern Ireland Civil

Rights Association. George McKinney, a brother of the fatally wounded William McKinney, saw Docherty pushed up against a wall with his white handkerchief rolled under his chin. Later Docherty, having fled water cannon and CS gas, was seen with Bernard McGuigan outside the 720 Bar on the corner of Harvey Street and Chamberlain Street.[175] He then, during a lull in the firing, made his way towards the gap between Blocks 2 and 3 of the Rossville Flats.

Wearing a black leather jacket and three-quarter-length black tweed car coat, Doherty cut a distinctive figure – and made an easy target. He was most likely shot as he bent forward on his hands and knees facing away from the soldiers, according to forensic evidence. The bullet that killed him clipped his leather belt, entered his right buttock and exited on the left side of his chest, having lacerated the two main blood vessels in the abdomen, his left lung, his colon and bowels.[176] His death was not instant. Witness Joe Nicholas described seeing Doherty shot as he 'was crawling across the courtyard in front of the flats towards the alleyway at Joseph Place. He was two thirds of the way across when he was shot.' Later he told the *Sunday Times* Insight team that moment before 'I shouted to get up and run, there was no point crawling as he was right out on his own. I then heard a burst of three or four shots and saw them striking the wall directly behind the crawling man. Then, as I watched, one shot hit him, I saw his coat jump and sort of puff out, he jerked once and stopped dead, his head lifted a couple of times and then he seemed to stop moving. I knew he was badly hurt.'[177]

Twelve-year-old Derrick Tucker Junior, who watched events unfold from the window of his family's flat in Block 2 of the Rossville Flats, described seeing the last of three men crawling under fire into the Joseph Place alleyway: 'a shot rang out and he fell. He lay still but there was no sign of a wound. A man of between forty or fifty, slightly bald, crawled out and asked for his hand. There was no response so he pulled him in by the head but he had to retreat into the alleyway as more shots rang out. Some other men came out to try and see where he was wounded but they too had to retreat.'[178] The 'slightly bald man' was identified as Patrick Walsh.

Derrick's older brother Martin stated: 'I went to the living room window. Outside I saw people running in all directions looking for shelter. I saw a small group of men who tried to run to laneway behind maisonettes. Then I saw a man trying to crawl across the same area. He was wearing a grey checked coat with fur collar and had black hair and a moustache. He crawled a few yards when a few shots rang out, he groaned and his legs shot out. He lay still. Then a few men who had already got to the safety of the laneway attempted to come out and drag him to safety, as soon as they appeared the army fired at them. They tried a few times but without success.'[179]

Their father, Derrick Tucker Senior, watched from the same living room window: 'From there, I could see into the Fahan Street car park, the maisonettes and Joseph Place. The first thing that struck me there was that everyone was lying down. I saw two men lying in the alleyway which connects the shops with the back of the maisonettes. These two men appeared to be shot in the leg. At this stage a man started to crawl from right beneath my window across to the alleyway. He reached halfway, when a shot rang out, and his right leg kicked out and he lay still. This man I now know to be Patrick Doherty. From the alleyway another man crawled out to meet him. Another shot rang out, didn't seem to hit anyone and the second man stopped crawling and lay still. After about five minutes he started crawling again, reached the first man and tried to pull him into the alleyway. He then turned him over onto his back and appeared to try to revive him.'[180]

Patrick Walsh described in a media interview how he saw the shot man outside the alleyway lying on his face. He saw slight movements and heard an occasional groan. He shouted: 'Are you all right, mate?' When he got no reply, he crawled out and turned him over. Walsh said: 'Do you know, I just didn't recognise him as Paddy Doherty. I knew Paddy well enough, I used to see him waiting for his lift to work and around town, you know, but I hadn't seen him for quite a long time, over a year or more I suppose, and he had grown his moustache, you know?' There was more shooting and bullets hit the wall by the steps. A girl in the flats shouted down to be careful and Walsh crawled back to the alleyway.[181]

The fallen man continued groaning softly. Walsh waited until the shooting stopped again and then crawled out again. He recalled: 'I could see he was going, his face was a terrible colour, it was almost yellow. I've never seen a man die until then, but that was the colour of death. I started to say a rosary but I just couldn't finish, I had to turn away. It took me very bad.' Walsh saw no wound or blood but began feeling for Doherty's heart under his clothing. He said: 'I found it all right, it must have been hanging out of him with a whole lot more.' Sickened, Walsh crawled back to the alleyway. He saw other people in the passageway opposite waving and shouting, and one young man stepped out towards the dying man but had to 'go to ground' when the Army resumed shooting as an ambulance arrived. When that stopped and the medics reached the scene, Walsh knelt by the person he had tried twice to save. 'I think somebody recognised him and said, "God, that's Paddy Doherty from Hamilton Street, he's got five youngsters" and I knew it was him then.' He stayed with him until he helped carry Doherty into the ambulance.[182]

Lance Corporal F claimed he had shot a man holding a pistol, but that was disproved by French journalist Gilles Peress who photographed Doherty moments before and after he died.[183]

Creggan resident Bernard 'Barney' McGuigan, forty-one, married with six children, had two years earlier been made redundant as a maintenance foreman with Monarch Electrics. Since then he had worked as a casual painter and decorator and became more active in his local community as treasurer of the Bligh's Lane Tenants Association. Interested in youth welfare, he was seeking to establish a community centre which would provide a focus for local children and so keep them out of trouble.[184] That Sunday he and his family attended Mass at the local church; he had then gone to the funeral of a family friend before returning home for Sunday lunch. He left the house at around 2.30 p.m. to attend the march. His wife Bridget gave him a piece of orange towelling she had soaked in vinegar in case he was caught by CS gas. According to Liam Lynch – a friend since their teens – McGuigan had not attended a march before because he had a brother-in-law serving in the Royal Air Force and so 'did not want to get mixed up in such matters'.[185]

Both friends were among the first half of the marchers and saw, but did not participate in, the rioting at barrier 14 and the Army's use of water cannon. The two got separated. Lynch saw army vehicles enter the Bogside and, feeling trapped, ran towards Free Derry Corner. He ran into McGuigan again near the Rossville Street entrance to Glenfada Park North. As the shooting had momentarily stopped, they chatted for a few moments and watched three or four soldiers taking position near Kells Walk and other soldiers in Eden Place. They heard live shots and Lynch told his friend: 'Let's get out of here.' Lynch then took shelter behind a low wall in the area of the south gable end of the eastern block of Glenfada Park North. He thought McGuigan had followed him but did not see the latter again.[186]

McGuigan stepped out a few yards south of the south end of Block 1 of the Rossville Flats and waved a white handkerchief a few yards south of the south end of Block 1 of the Rossville Flats. Witness evidence suggests he was trying to attract attention, possibly for personal safety reasons as he moved or, more generally, to alert soldiers to the presence of civilians at the gable end of Block 1. Other witnesses remain convinced he was going to the aid of Doherty. All such explanations may be true, but whatever his reasoning, he was killed instantly by a rifle shot that hit the side of his head behind his left ear. The vinegar-soaked cloth given to him by his wife remained clutched in his dead hand. Soldier F, who was still in Glenfada Park, testified to having fired in the direction of where McGuigan died.[187]

McGuigan fell to the ground beside a nineteen-year-old paramedic who later said: 'He raised his hand in the air and shouted "Don't shoot, don't shoot". And seconds later he was just shot and landed in my lap.'[188] The pathologist found that the bullet had fragmented during its passage through the skull, leaving some forty-two pieces within the cranial cavity.[189] The massive damage led to speculation, later generally dismissed, that some soldiers had fired modified 'dum-dum' bullets. The impact of regular army issue, high-velocity rounds would have been much the same.

In a written statement, press photographer Fulvio Grimaldi recorded going through the passageway towards Joseph Place: 'The other side of the building I saw a body I now know to be Doherty's. Further down, in front of the telephone box, I saw out of the corner of my eye a man spin round and fall. I now know this was Barney McGuigan. I then took photographs. Doherty was dying. I saw no blood. I photographed McGuigan.'[190] Later, in a media interview, Grimaldi said: 'A crowd of us waving handkerchiefs ran up the steps between the flats and out onto the Joseph Place side. I saw another six or seven bodies lying on the ground there, but it appeared that only three were dead.' They were identified as Gilmour, Doherty and McGuigan.[191] Decades later Grimaldi described photographing Doherty and Walsh's attempts to rescue him. He went on: 'I then saw a man, to my right, moving towards the body. He moved out diagonally from the area of the shops at the bottom of Block 2 of the Rossville Flats. I think he took three to four steps diagonally towards Doherty. He was walking carefully and after a couple of steps I saw he was hesitant. His head jerked back, his face whipped round to the left, his body spun around and he collapsed. He was looking towards the body of Patrick Doherty when he was shot. The man fell in the position parallel to Patrick Doherty, also on his back. His right eye had been shot out and there was a hole where his eye should have been. I have since found out that the man's name was Barney McGuigan. I was not aware of hearing the actual shot that hit him. There was shooting generally going on in this area at the time.'[192]

Another witness, Joe Nicholas, later testified that he saw two Paras, one kneeling and the other squatting, both with rifles at their shoulders, with the prone Doherty directly in their line of fire.[193] He also saw McGuigan lying in a 'huge' pool of blood.

Columba McLaughlin described seeking shelter from gunfire: 'I moved in the direction of the first house in Glenfada Park, collected my wife on the way and went into the house of Mrs. Mackey, a friend of my wife and myself. My wife and I entered the front room which faces the multi-story flats' entrance. On looking out the window I saw a number of people, of some seven to ten, sheltering in the corner beside the telephone kiosk. There was a body lying on the ground with two people trying to attend to him. Two people were sheltering behind a tree and a lamp post. I ducked down beneath the window-sill, realising that the shooting was coming from the William St. end of Rossville Street. A few seconds later there was a lull in the shooting – I looked out of the window and saw three bodies. Two were in the vicinity of the telephone kiosk. One of these, the nearer of the two, was a young person hit in the region of the chest. The second person was an elderly man with receding hair lying on his back with his head facing towards Derry Walls. The third person was lying on his stomach opposite Harley's Fish and Chip Shop in the centre of an open space... None of these three people moved and I could see a would-be rescuer crawling towards the third body. When he reached the body, the person lying moved his head as if in response to some question. The rescuer then tried to drag the body away. During this period sporadic shooting was continuing. To me this was quite clearly high-velocity gun fire. The injured man jerked and the rescuer retreated. I moved under cover again beneath the window-sill. I waited there till the shooting died down. When I next looked up, about thirty seconds later, people were starting to move towards the bodies, waving white handkerchiefs and holding their hands in the air.'[194]

Bystander Patrick Clarke used his own sheepskin coat to cover McGuigan's body, and a woman threw a blanket from a window in Block 2 to do the same, but it became stuck in the canopy over the block's line of shops. Two more women appeared with a replacement blanket. Someone else covered the dead man's bloodied face with a college scarf. An ambulance responded to an emergency call at 4.38 p.m., left Altnagelvin Hospital at 4.39 p.m., reached the scene at 4.51 p.m. and arrived back at the hospital at 5.15 p.m., carrying '2 DOA 2 injured'.[195] Their speedy action was admirable, but for Doherty and McGuigan it was too late. Lance Corporal F certainly shot Bernard McGuigan and Patrick Doherty and it is highly probable that he was also responsible for shooting the other two casualties: Patrick Campbell and Daniel McGowan.[196]

Soldiers continued to shoot across the car park until a ceasefire was called. Around twenty minutes had elapsed between the time soldiers drove into the Bogside and the time the last of the civilians, Barney McGuigan, was shot.

Respected journalist Simon Winchester, a war zone veteran, filed his newspaper copy that night: 'The tragic and inevitable doomsday situation which has been universally forecast for Northern Ireland arrived in Londonderry yesterday afternoon when soldiers firing into a large crowd of civil rights demonstrators, shot and killed thirteen civilians... After the shooting, in and around the Rossville Flats area of Bogside, the streets had all the appearance of the aftermath of Sharpeville. Where, only moments before, thousands of men and women had been milling around, drifting slowly towards a protest meeting to be held at Free Derry Corner, there was only a handful of bleeding bodies, some lying still, others still moving with pain, on the white concrete of the square.

The Army's official explanation for the killing was that their troops had fired in response to a number of snipers who had opened up on them from below the flats. But those of us at the meeting heard only one shot before the soldiers opened up with their high velocity rifles. And while it is impossible to be absolutely sure, one came away with the firm impression, reinforced by dozens of eyewitnesses, that the soldiers, men of the 1st Battalion, The Parachute Regiment, flown in specially from Belfast, may have fired needlessly into the huge crowd.

Shortly before 4.15 p.m. Mr Kevin McCorry, the civil rights organiser, began to walk through the crowd, telling them through a megaphone that a meeting was starting at Free Derry Corner and that Miss Devlin, Mr Cooper, and Lord Brockway were to speak. Just as this meeting was getting underway four or five armoured cars appeared in William Street and raced into the Rossville Street square, and several thousand people began to run away. The move had been expected and it is a tactic we have all seen before - nothing, not even gas, breaks up a crowd more effectively than several huge armoured cars careering through the streets.

But it was then that the situation changed tragically. Paratroops piled out of their vehicles, many ran forward to make arrests, but others rushed to the street corners. It was these men, perhaps twenty in all, who opened fire with their rifles. I saw three men fall to the ground. One was still obviously alive, with blood pumping from his leg. The others, both apparently in their teens, seemed dead. The meeting at Free Derry Corner broke up in hysteria as thousands of people either ran or dived for the ground. Army snipers could be seen firing continuously towards the central Bogside streets and at one stage a lone army sniper on a street corner fired two shots towards me as I peered around a corner. One shot chipped a large chunk of masonry from a wall behind me.

Then people could be seen moving forward in Fahan Street, their hands above their heads. One man was carrying a white handkerchief. Gunfire was directed even at them and they fled or fell to the ground. There was certainly some firing from the IRA. I heard one submachine-gun open up from inside the flats and heard a number of small-calibre weapons being fired intermittently, but the sound which predominated was the heavy, hard banging of the British SLRs, and this continued for about ten or fifteen minutes.

Weeping men and women in the Bogside spent the next half hour in Lecky Road, pushing bodies of dead and injured people into cars and driving them to hospital. I saw seven such cars drive away with some of the bleeding bodies on the back seats, inert and lifeless. By 5.30 p.m. it was all over. A full moon was rising over a shocked and still numbed Londonderry, and heavily armed soldiers were still keeping Bogside and the Creggan cordoned off.[197]

That night Bernadette Devlin said it was 'bloody cold-blooded murder', while John Hume said it was 'another Sharpeville', and demanded the immediate withdrawal of all these 'uniformed murderers'. Michael Canavan of the Derry Citizens' Central Council said 'It was impossible to say who fired first. Personally I am sure it was the army, but it doesn't really matter. What was so terrible and so tragic was that the soldiers fired into a huge crowd of people, and fired indiscriminately at that. The death toll must show us that their firing was indiscriminate.' An Army statement at 7.30 p.m. said that after an hour of heavy stoning, men of the 1st Battalion, The Parachute Regiment moved into the William Street and Rossville Street areas from behind the units who were manning barricades. 'They went in to arrest people in the crowd and chased and caught several men who were running away,' the statement said. 'While this operation was in progress, gunmen opened up from rubble at the base of the Rossville Flats and soldiers returned the fire. Casualty returns are still coming in.' Finbar O'Kane, one of the civil rights organisers, said he had never thought that the Ulster crisis would ever get as bad as this. 'It was a shocking, terrible thing,' he went on. 'Those soldiers shot into a crowd and shot down innocent men. What on earth will happen to us all now?'[198]

An ammunition check on return to barracks showed that Support Company of 1 Para had fired 108 rounds of 7.62 mm ammunition used in the SLR rifle, with which all ranks in the Company were armed, except three who had sub-machine guns. Some of the men carried, in addition to their SLR, a baton gun. The only other weapon with which the Company was equipped that day was the Browning machine gun on a Ferret scout car.[199] No soldiers were injured in the operation; no guns or bombs were recovered at the scene of the killing.[200]

Some of those shot were given first aid by civilian volunteers, either on the scene or after being carried into nearby homes. They were then driven to hospital, either in civilian cars or in ambulances which began arriving at 4.28 p.m. The three younger men killed at the rubble barricade were driven to hospital by the paratroopers who, according to witnesses, lifted the bodies by the hands and feet and dumped them in the back of their APC as if they were 'pieces of meat'.

The wounded Gerald Donaghy had been taken from Glenfada Park into a nearby house, where he was treated by a civilian doctor, while others present searched him for any identification, before being driven by car to hospital. En route the car was stopped at an army checkpoint; the driver and Hugh Leo Young were arrested and taken away. A soldier then drove the vehicle to the Regimental Aid Post at Craigavon Bridge.[201] The car was driven to an army first-aid post, where Donaghy was examined by a Royal Army Medical Corps doctor and pronounced dead. Sometime later, an RUC officer reported that four bulky nail bombs had been found in the pockets of Donaghy's denim jacket and jeans. The civilians who initially searched him, the soldier who drove him to the army post, and the Army medical officer all said that they did not see any bombs, leading to claims that soldiers planted the bombs on Donaghy to justify the killings. Decades later, however, police informer Paddy Ward claimed he had given two nail bombs to Donaghy as he was a member of an IRA-linked republican youth movement, *Fianna Eireann*, several hours before he was shot. The subsequent Saville Inquiry concluded that the bombs were probably in Donaghy's pockets when he was shot but that he was not about to throw one when he was shot and was not shot because he had bombs but because he was trying to escape from the soldiers. That verdict remains hotly contested by the relatives and the supposed discovery was heaven-sent for soldiers just beginning to realise the enormity of what had been done. Sorry to say, the planting of weapons and explosives was fast becoming almost routine as the war got dirtier and dirtier.

The soldiers of Support Company gathered in their barracks to get their individual stories straight for interviews with the Royal Military Police in which they would be asked to justify each shot and the precise direction it was fired. The adrenalin would have still been pumping through their veins. They told themselves that they had taught the 'Yobboes' a lesson they would never forget. But the enormity of their actions may well have begun to sink in, which made it all the more important that the NCOs and officers ensured that they were all singing from the same hymn sheet. That was particularly true of Lance Corporal F. Just as he was denying ever firing at anyone on the rubble barricade, a 7.62mm calibre bullet was being dug out of the spine of Michael Kelly's body. A Belfast laboratory matched it to F's rifle, whereupon he suddenly remembered firing at a 'bomber' on the barricade.

In all, twenty-six people were shot by the paratroopers; thirteen died on the day. All the soldiers responsible insisted that they had shot at, and hit, gunmen or bomb-throwers only. No soldier said he missed his target and hit someone else by mistake. No warnings were given before soldiers opened fire. One paratrooper who gave evidence at the later tribunal testified that they were told by an officer to expect a gunfight and 'We want some kills.' Ivan Cooper said: 'I want to say this to the British government ... You know what you've just done, don't you? You've destroyed the civil rights movement, and you've given the IRA the biggest victory it will ever have. All over this city tonight, young men, boys, will be joining the IRA and you will reap a whirlwind.'[202]

Willie McKinney's grainy footage of the start of the demonstration has been replayed in news reports and documentaries ever since Bloody Sunday.

4

Interlude: Martin McGuinness

'... it was just a mass of confusion.'

That night, by his own admission, PIRA's Martin McGuinness authorised the firing of 'symbolic' shots in or near the Bogside as families mourned and the injured were treated. It was a gesture of defiance.

Although there were many IRA men—both Official and Provisional— at the protest, it is claimed they were all unarmed, apparently because it was anticipated that the paratroopers would attempt to 'draw them out'.[1] One man was witnessed by Father Edward Daly and others haphazardly firing a revolver in the direction of the paratroopers. Later identified as a member of the Official IRA, this man was also photographed in the act of drawing his weapon but was apparently not seen or targeted by the soldiers.

At the time McGuinness was Adjutant of the Derry Brigade of the Provisional IRA and, as we have seen, had supposedly given orders that the march should not be used as a cover for terrorist acts and attacks on the Army. But second-hand rumours emerged at the time, and have persisted since, that he was involved in plots to plant and use bombs, that he was armed with a Thompson sub-machine gun, and that he could have fired the first shot.[2] Given his prominence both paramilitarily and politically through the Troubles and its aftermath, it is worth looking at the evidence.

McGuinness was born in the Bogside area of Derry, the second of seven children of deeply religious Roman Catholic parents.

He supported Manchester United from the age of eight, and Derry City FC where his younger brother Paul played for the Candystripes. His father William was a foundry worker. Unlike Gerry Adams, McGuinness did not come from a republican background, but grew up seeing evidence of the stranglehold Derry's Protestant bosses held over jobs, pay and housing. He failed his eleven-plus, and on leaving the Christian Brothers' technical college aged fifteen he was turned down for a job as a car mechanic because he was a Catholic. He became a butcher's assistant instead.

He was still a teenager when he was outraged at the 1968 images of Gerry Fitt splashed with blood after being hit by police batons as he led a civil rights march. McGuinness took to the streets just as the IRA was rearming. IRA leaders saw him as capable of providing organisation in Derry to mirror what which Adams was developing in Belfast. Within months McGuinness was second in command of the IRA Derry Brigade, aged twenty-one. McGuinness always justified the 'armed struggle' of those early days, saying that a 'little boy' from the Catholic Bogside was no more culpable than a little black boy from Soweto.[3]

His PIRA unit proved particularly effective, pulverising so many premises that the city 'looked as though it had been bombed from the air'. During the two years when he was in command or second-in-command either side of Bloody Sunday, PIRA killed twenty-nine members of the security forces, twenty-four of them regular soldiers. He recalled: 'There was a state of war between the IRA and British military forces. This was a war area.' On the morning of Bloody Sunday, according to his account, he arose at around 9 a.m., went to Mass and locked away his guns and bombs. 'Certainly, the IRA had nail bombs, but not in that area,' he said. 'It would have been lunacy of the worst kind for anyone to have nail bombs when 30,000 people were on the street.' He went unarmed to the march on what turned out to be 'the worst day that I had ever experienced in my life'. It was, he said, 'devastating – I was in a daze'. The IRA did not engage the Army, he insisted. He said: 'I felt helpless, angry and disgusted that there was nothing I could do. I wanted to get a rifle, find other Volunteers and try to do something.'[4]

In both written and oral statements, and in reply to questions, McGuinness consistently insisted that he took part in the march and little more until authorising the symbolic gunshots in the evening. He went to the assembly point at Bishop's Field with his friend Colm Keenan at around 2.30 p.m., but they quickly lost each other in the swelling crowd. He followed the route of the march until it reached the junction of William Street and Rossville Street.[5] At that junction 'I could see that the main body of the march had turned right towards Free Derry Corner and that a large group numbering several hundred had proceeded on down William Street towards the City Centre. I walked on towards William Street and stood with the crowd in front of the British Army's blockade at William Street ... It was clear to me that a riot would soon begin. Shortly after this the protesters began throwing stones and bottles at the British Army who were blocking William Street.' He was at the barrier for around five minutes before leaving, fearing that he might be caught by a snatch squad and interned.[6]

He walked down Chamberlain Street and heard people running behind him and so assumed that the Army had sent in such a snatch squad. He did not see any soldiers while other marchers ran past him, so continued to walk in the direction of Free Derry Corner. As he crossed the Rossville Flats car park he saw a woman being carried away. At this stage he had not heard a shot or seen either a soldier or an army vehicle in the Bogside. He walked on through the gap between Blocks 1 and 2 and, near Joseph Place, he heard self-loading rifle (SLR) shots for the first time and also heard army APCs coming down Rossville Street.[7] He moved back to Lisfannon Park and then Abbey Park. He assumed that the firing was coming from William Street because he knew that there were soldiers there. In Abbey Park he was told that people had been shot. The shooting was still continuing. He moved back to the Westland Street area near the Bogside Inn and there met other PRA volunteers. One told him that people had been shot at the Rossville Flats and he realised that the situation was becoming increasingly serious. He initially urged the volunteers to arm themselves. They went to a safe house close to PIRA's weapons cache and there met other volunteers, sympathisers and the brigade's commanding officer (OC). There they received reports that all was quiet in the Creggan and the Brandywell and that the violence was confined to a narrow strip of the Bogside. According to McGuinness, he, the OC and a small number of volunteers decided that PIRA should not go into the Bogside with weapons, giving the British Army an excuse to fire. They thought it better to let the journalists present report that the British Army had opened fire on innocent civil rights marchers. The order was duly passed to volunteers that there was to be no retaliation and McGuinness was certain that it was obeyed. In any event, no one other than the men in two cars patrolling the Brandywell and the Creggan had access to a weapon.[8] Stocks of guns, ammunition and explosive material in the Derry 'arms dump' were so low that only older and experienced volunteers were allowed to use them for training denied to the more volatile youth wing.[9]

Army counsel later pointed to an alleged twenty-minute gap in his timings, suggesting that period was used for paramilitary activities and in the subsequent months and years more contradictory – and self-conflicting – evidence emerged.

In April 1984 an IRA double-agent codenamed *Infliction* provided a Security Services agent known as Officer A with information concerning McGuiness' alleged activities on Bloody Sunday.[10] The officer's written account of the conversation suggested that McGuinness 'seemed to have it on his conscience that he fired the first shot' on 30 January 1972. It went on: 'He (Mr McGuinness) fired the first shot and nobody knows this. This seems to be on McGuinness's conscience. He has spoken to Infliction about it several times.' Infliction's notes and a tape recording of the debriefing were the subject of a Public Interest Immunity Certificate issued by the Home Office alleging that full disclosure of the contents of Security Service documents could cause real harm to the work of the service. Infliction was described in the certificate as an agent resettled outside the UK. The application covers another informant, Observer B, said by the Home Office to be a former agent. However, a section was released: 'Martin McGuinness had admitted to *Infliction* that he had personally fired the shot (from a Thompson machine gun on single shot) from the Rossville Flats in Bogside that had precipitated the Bloody Sunday episode.' Observer B was alleged to have witnessed IRA auxiliaries drilling at the Rossville Flats in the days leading up to Bloody Sunday and to have been told afterwards that the IRA opened fire first. He had already been granted anonymity.[11] In November 1984 Infliction repeated the allegation to a different Security Service officer, Officer B, in a taped conversation. Officer B said he asked Infliction about whether or not McGuinness had a 'conflict [with republicanism] because of his Catholicism'. He replied: 'Well, you know, McGuinness found himself in a certain position. Er, really didn't manipulate it. Er, he found himself as overseeing Derry and first spokesman and, er, I think the one thing that bothers (him) is, er the Bloody Sunday thing, that he fired the first shot... he talked to me a few times about it...'[12]

Officer A was Infliction's handler for several months in 1984 before rising to a high rank in the Security Service. He testified: '... for the most part, Infliction's reporting was reliable and, in [the Security Service's] view, honest. However, there were some areas where he was not prepared to provide information and there were a small number of occasions on which, we believe, that he did not tell the truth.' On the occasions on which Infliction did lie, he did so in order to protect his security. Officer A went on: 'Infliction produced an enormous amount of information on which he had direct knowledge, either by talking directly to people or by seeing an event or whatever. Now, with that information – on those areas he was very rarely, if ever, mistaken and most of that material, we are confident, was truthful and subsequently much of it was corroborated.'[13] Infliction was paid between £15,000 and £25,000 a year for his work for the Security Service. He was not given payment in return for specific pieces of information but received bonuses when he had worked particularly hard to obtain information in a difficult subject area. His payment was at the top end of the informant scale to reflect his level of access to the IRA, the potential of the information and the risks that he ran to obtain information.[14] McGuinness's legal team suggested that Infliction had invented the allegation in order to make himself more attractive to his handlers as a high-ranking IRA insider.[15]

In 2003, by which time McGuiness had been education minister in the Stormont government, renegade ex-MI5 officer David Shayler gave evidence that Infliction was a 'bullshitter' – a term he used twenty-six times. Shayler had been jailed for leaking MI5 material to the media before making the claim. In 1992 Shayler had joined 'T2', the MI5 department tasked with countering the IRA threat to mainland Britain, and was tasked with investigating a potential terrorism 'target'. He had never heard of Infliction, never read his secret file and was not investigating McGuinness. But among the 'intel' on his desk, there was information from a source of the same name. The report stood out because it claimed his suspect was rather more important than at first appeared. Intrigued at the contradictions, the bored desk-bound agent asked a more glamorous 'agent runner' from section T8 for his opinion. 'He actually said to me "this guy is a bullshitter",' Shayler said. 'I remember him very clearly saying the word "bullshitter". When I went to discuss informally with any colleagues Infliction's reporting, that was the opinion they gave. Within the service, it is usual for officers to discuss matters they come across on their deck informally over lunch in the canteen or having a cup of coffee. Much the same from other people I had heard was that he was a bullshitter. People tended to use that word.'

Asked whether, given Infliction's alleged report was now in part in the public domain, McGuinness knew the identity of the alleged IRA mole, Shayler replied: 'Well, if Martin McGuinness genuinely did tell Infliction he fired the first shot, he would therefore know who Infliction was. If he had told the same piece of information to several people, and he now realises this has been reported back to the British government, he would have a list of people, one of whom must be Infliction. If Infliction is telling the truth, there would be no need to protect his identity because Martin McGuinness would already know who he is.'[16]

Authors Liam Clarke and Kathryn Johnston claimed that McGuinness and others broke into Duffy's bookmakers with the intention of planting a bomb that would, when detonated, kill or maim soldiers manning barrier 14. They wrote: 'Around 3.45 p.m., Daly warned Patrick "Barman" Duffy, one of the civil rights stewards, that he had seen some young people behaving suspiciously at the back of some nearby shops. One of them was Martin McGuinness. McGuinness and his fellow IRA men looked like all the other young rioters as they mingled with the crowd on Chamberlain Street. As the firing intensified, they began to kick in the door of Duffy's Bookmakers. One of the youths who helped McGuinness was Des Clinton, (the pseudonym of) an IRA sympathiser although never a member. "The army barrier was across the road, just where the old picture house used to be, and the crowd was not that many yards away. I went round the back of the bookies, the High Street entrance, and I put the back door in, me and another fella. Then McGuinness and the rest of us went into the bookies." Clinton had been on the civil rights march since the start, where he had met up with another friend who was in the IRA, who told him that weapons were on their way down to the city centre. As he looked around the bookies, Clinton believes he knew what McGuinness planned to do. "It was an ideal place for a bomb. The window upstairs looked on to William Street and we were actually looking down on the soldiers, they were only a few yards from us. You could do a lot of damage to the troops, but the crowd would have been safe because there was a gap between them and the soldiers. You could have blown every one of them up and still have got away. Then McGuinness got word that the army was coming in – I think from a walkietalkie – and there was no time to put a bomb there. We all ran out the back." Just before McGuinness and the others escaped from the back of the bookies, a shot was heard. One person who was there alleges that, just before McGuinness left, and as he heard that the soldiers were coming, McGuinness had fired a shot from the Thompson at the door."[17]

The Saville report ruled that such reports should be treated 'with caution' given the anonymity of the sources. One young man later gave evidence that he and another had broken into the bookmakers to 'suss out the place for future reference'. He stated that he and his companion were not going to do anything because they were 'not tooled up'.[18]

Some evidence emerged that McGuinness was in possession of a Thompson sub-machine gun. In a heavily redacted RUC interview, a witness said: 'I was in Chamberlain Street just before the shooting started... I saw Martin McGuinness had a Thompson S.M.G. under his coat. I don't know if any of the others were armed or not as I didn't notice any guns. Neither do I know if McGuinness fired the Thompson or not. I didn't see him firing.'[19]

Witness Sheila McLoughlin sheltered south of Free Derry Corner until she thought, wrongly, that the army shooting had stopped. She testified: 'The next thing I remember as we made our way down the Lecky Road is seeing Martin McGuinness and a couple of other men I did not know coming towards us from a little walkway which ran between the shopping precinct in Meenan Park and the Lecky Road. I do not think they were running, but they were certainly walking quite quickly and they were moving towards where we had come from. It was apparent from their faces that they [were] wondering what on earth was happening and I think one of them must have shouted "what's happening?" I distinctly remember shouting "so much for your protection then, they are killing people down there". I knew by that time that the army was killing people – you didn't need to see it to know what was happening. I have always assumed since that moment that Martin McGuinness and his friends must not have been on the march that day.'[20] Lawyers for the soldiers said that her evidence was at least inconsistent with McGuinness's own account of his movements. On the other hand, it gelled with his claim that initially he did not know what was happening.

In a Q & A session, McGuinness said: '... And a lot of people, hundreds of people went down to where the British Army was, and there was a state of if you like confrontation, you know verbal abuse and things like that going on. And I would have been there with that group, but I mean it quickly became clear to people that nobody was gonna get through. The snatch squad started to come out of the lower end of William Street and I ended up in Chamberlain Street over here, right, and this is where Peggy, right just here where Peggie Dearie [sic] was shot.' You ran down there, all the way down? 'We didn't run we walked originally because the soldiers were coming so far.' Somebody had shouted they're coming out? 'There was all sorts of shouting, state of confusion at that stage.' Did you see Dearie shot? 'I didn't see her being shot but I seen her shortly after she was shot.' As she was being carried into the house? 'She was bleeding profusely from a thigh wound.' And there were some people carrying her? 'She was carried, there were all sorts of people around her.' And then where did you go then? 'I ended up over here towards the front of the flats where, it was just a state of chaos at this stage because they were firing right left and centre and it was a matter of people surviving. Feeling that they were gonna be shot because this woman had been shot. And there was reports from all round this immediate area and this area here that the people were shot and were seriously wounded. Nobody at that stage knew that anybody was dead and at that stage it was just a mass of confusion. We ended up walking aimlessly round the place lifting people who'd been wounded and getting people out of the road who were frightened and scared. There was women crying and old men.' Any shots over your head when you were running down? 'No I dont remember shots over my head no.'[21]

The subsequent Saville Inquiry found inconsistencies in his evidence and little to explain his allegedly 'missing' twenty minutes, however. It concluded that 'here is no evidence that suggests to us that any member of the Provisional IRA used or intended to use the march itself for the purpose of engaging the security forces with guns or bombs. Nevertheless, we consider it likely that Martin McGuinness was armed with a Thompson sub-machine gun on Bloody Sunday and we cannot eliminate the possibility that he fired this weapon after the soldiers had come into the Bogside. Furthermore, we are unable, notwithstanding their evidence, to exclude the possibility that other members of the Provisional IRA may also have carried arms.'[22]

After Bloody Sunday, McGuinness's stock rose both on the political and paramilitary fronts. He was convicted in Dublin in 1973 after being caught in a car containing 250 lb of explosives and nearly 5,000 rounds of ammunition and was sentenced to six months. McGuinness always claimed that he left the IRA in 1974 to focus on his rising political profile in Sinn Féin. It was alleged – and strenuously denied – that he authorised the bombings on the same day in August 1979 that killed Lord Mountbatten, his grandson and other members of his family party in Sligo, and eighteen British soldiers at Warrenpoint, County Down, as well as authorising subsequent IRA attacks. McGuinness dismissed the allegations as provocation by people hostile to the peace process.

In 2005, Irish *Tanaiste* Michael McDowell claimed that McGuinness remained a member of the seven-man IRA Army Council, which he again strongly denied.[23] Experienced journalist Peter Taylor, in a BBC documentary shown in April 2008, alleged that McGuinness, as the head of the IRA's Northern Command, had advance knowledge of the 1987 Enniskillen bombing which left eleven civilians dead.[24]

Whatever the truth of such claims, McGuinness's pivotal role as Sinn Féin's chief negotiator in long-running peace discussions was widely acknowledged. Jonathan Powell, chief negotiator for Tony Blair as prime minister, noted McGuinness's careful preparation. The Unionist politicians he was negotiating with included David Trimble and Peter Robinson, who said: 'We came from polar opposite backgrounds but built up a relationship based on doing the best we could for all our people. We shared the hardships of taking risks for progress and the joy of seeing so many improvements in the lives of our fellow citizens.'[25] He was certainly one of the main architects of the 1998 Good Friday Agreement, his credentials as a former IRA 'hard man' helping rather than hindering the process. Enemies found they could trust him. US President Bill Clinton noted that McGuinness was the one who personally oversaw the arms decommissioning phase. Prime Minister Tony Blair also acknowledged the leading role which McGuinness had in ensuring the Agreement would be enforced.[26]

During the decades-long and tortuous negotiations, McGuinness was often wrongly described as Adams' deputy; instead they were a double act who gradually dismantled the Sinn Féin policy of boycotting all constitutional elections, standing eventually for Westminster. At a Dublin rally in October 2002, McGuinness said: 'They would love the IRA to go back to war. I'm delighted that we have not fallen into this trap. I'm delighted that we have an organisation which understands the political dynamics [of the peace process] … It's a … fool that believes that we will not succeed in achieving a sovereign independent Ireland.'[27] McGuinness was the abstentionist MP for Mid Ulster from 1997 until 2013 and came third as the Sinn Féin candidate in the Irish presidential election of 2011. He shook hands with the Queen and developed an unlikely friendship and comic double act with old enemy the Reverend Ian Paisley; at Stormont they were known as the 'Chuckle Brothers'.

In January 2017, McGuinness resigned as Deputy First Minister in the power-sharing Stormont government which had been created after the Good Friday accord in protest at a Unionist scandal over payments under the renewable heat incentive.[28] McGuinness died aged sixty-six of an unspecified genetic illness on 6 March 2017 in Altnagelvin Hospital, where the Bloody Sunday injured had been treated.[29]

5

Aftermath

'a fresh start'

The following day journalist Simon Hoggart quoted a man in the Rossville flats saying: 'That is it: there isn't any solution now.' Hoggart went on: 'He stared across at the crowds milling around the familiar debris of Londonderry – hundreds of them, scarcely talking to each other as they shuffled their feet in the biting wind. Some of them say they expected Sunday's events to occur sooner or later: now it has happened…

'The Army is presenting its case in Belfast and London: here the people are certain about what happened to them. Every single Bogsider, and every person who took part in Sunday's march, says there were no shots at the Army, no nail bombs, and no petrol bombs. They maintain the absolute innocence of all the dead, and say the soldiers came in firing at anything that moved. The whole Roman Catholic section of the city was virtually at a standstill yesterday after a three-day strike had been called. All shops west of the river Foyle were closed, except for the occasional kiosk and food shop, and virtually all Roman Catholic workers in the city stayed away from work, or returned home soon after going. In the daylight, police and troops kept clear of the Bogside, and police in the town centre patrolled in small groups after the IRA warning that it would avenge the thirteen dead. A group of seven Catholic priests said in a statement that they accused the Colonel of the Parachute Regiment of "wilful murder" and General Ford, Commander of Land Forces, of being an accessory before the fact. "We accuse the soldiers of shooting indiscriminately into a fleeing crowd, of gloating over casualties, and of preventing medical and spiritual aid from reaching some of the dying," they said. The priests called the paratroopers "trained criminals who differ from terrorists only in the air of respectability that a uniform gives them'.

In a community hall in the Bogside, members of eleven of the families who lost sons, brothers, or fathers on Sunday described their experiences. Most said they had left the march to go home before the shooting started, and some did not know their relatives were dead until they saw their bodies in the morgue.

Hoggart reported: 'The Bogsiders now accuse the Army of certain specific atrocities: they say men were shot as they ran with their hands in the air seeking shelter; they say people who were tending wounded men were fired upon and they say that in some cases men were shot after they had been arrested. They add that they believe soldiers tried to prevent ambulances from getting into the area of the fighting, and that the ambulances were fired on as they arrived. The meeting of relatives was tense and bitter. Occasionally, one of the people began to weep. They applauded loudly the most militant statements. They made it clear that they would not cooperate with any "British" inquiry, which they said would be designed to whitewash the Army. They said they would only cooperate with an inquiry set up under the United Nations or another international body from which both British and Irish representatives had been excluded.

'Mr Tony Martin, a ship rigger from Manchester who now lives in Derry, said soldiers had fired on himself and a group of about fifteen other men who had gone to tend the wounded near Abbey Park. "We saw four wounded people lying at the end of a patch of waste ground," he said. "We put our hands in the air to show we were unarmed and waved white handkerchiefs. We managed to walk as far as where the people were lying. Then a soldier opened up with a machine gun. One man was shot in the leg, and another had a scalp wound. We had to lie on top of the bodies of the wounded."

John McDaid said at the same meeting: "I went to the morgue because my brother had not come home. The police told me his name was not on the list, but when I got home a priest came to the front door. When I went back to the morgue, I saw my brother. There was a triangular wound on his cheek, and the back of his head was matted with blood. I have been round to Rossville Flats to talk to people who saw him shot. They said he was shot from 5 yards away with his hands in the air."

But Colonel Wilford, the paratroopers commanding officer, gave his own version: "We moved very quickly when the firing started. Their shots were highly inaccurate. I believe in fact they lost their nerve when they saw us coming in. Nail bombs were thrown and one man who was shot was seen to be lighting a bomb as he was shot. This is open to conjecture, but I personally saw a man with an M1 carbine rifle on the balcony of a flat. I don't believe people were shot in the back while they were running away. A lot of us do think that some of the people were shot by their own indiscriminate firing."[1]

For Edward Heath, relaxing at his Chequers country retreat, it should have been a time for quiet self-congratulation. True, the miners had gone out of strike on 9 January and were threatening to bring the country to a standstill, while unemployment was fast approaching the one million mark. And Uganda's Idi Amin seemed hell-bent on expelling 57,000 Asians, most of whom held British passports. But the prime minister had just fulfilled his lifelong ambition by signing the treaty taking Britain into the Common Market, the precursor to the European Union, despite fierce cross-party opposition. His early evening reverie was shattered when a flunkey brought him a telegram from No. 10 Downing Street written by the diplomat Lord Bridges headed 'Londonderry Riot'. It read: 'Latest confirmed reports received in Ministry of Defence are that about five people killed in Londonderry this afternoon and a further twelve in hospital. They are not able to confirm report carried by agencies that twelve were killed: this is based on a statement made by a spokesman for a Londonderry hospital, who said that the twelve had been brought in dead with gunshot wounds and all were in their early 20s.'[2] It was the first of a flurry of such messages which gradually, as more accurate figures came in, spelled out the full horror of Bloody Sunday. Within minutes it was clear that an instant response was vital.

The following day, Home Secretary Reginald Maudling told the House of Commons that the paratroopers had reacted to gun and nail bomb attacks from suspected IRA members.[3] The government's official response included the ministerial line 'We must also recognise that the IRA is waging a war, not only of bullets and bombs but of words... If the IRA is allowed to win this war I shudder to think what will be the future of the people living in Northern Ireland.' The Ministry of Defence also issued a detailed account of the British Army's version of events which stated that 'Throughout the fighting that ensued, the Army fired only at identified targets – at attacking gunmen and bombers. At all times the soldiers obeyed their standing instructions to fire only in self-defence or in defence of others threatened.'[4] That enraged many as, apart from the soldiers involved, all eyewitnesses – including marchers, local residents, and British and Irish journalists present – maintained that soldiers fired into an unarmed crowd or were aiming at fleeing people and those tending the wounded, whereas the soldiers themselves were not fired upon. It was stressed that no British soldier was wounded by gunfire or reported any injuries, nor were any bullets or nail bombs recovered to back up their claims. Within forty-eight hours Maudling was forced to concede an inquiry into the event (*see following chapter*).

In the Irish Republic, initial disbelief turned to anger as details of the massacre in Derry reached southern homes by teatime on Sunday 30 January 1972. Along with descriptions of what had happened, news bulletins also carried a call from Derry's James Connolly Republican Club that those angered by 'the murder tactics of the British Army' should 'go on immediate general strike and bring the country to a standstill'. That night just fifty people picketed the British embassy in Dublin. Memorial services were held in Catholic and Protestant churches, as well as synagogues, throughout the Republic. But on Monday morning walkouts took place at factories in the Shannon industrial estate and on Cork docks. By lunchtime thousands of workers in Shannon, Limerick, Cork, Galway, Dundalk and Waterford had struck and joined impromptu protest marches. In Cork city, so many marches were taking place that at times columns of protesting workers passed each other in the streets going in opposite directions. Protesters converged on Cork City Hall, where they were met by the lord mayor, who was widely quoted as telling the cheering marchers that 'if they want murder, they'll have murder – one of theirs will go for each of ours'. The older marchers remembered the 1916 Easter Uprising not so much for the street battles – the rebels initially had lukewarm public support – but for the military executions by British military firing squads that followed them. More than one speaker made a direct comparison with Bloody Sunday.

In Dublin a natural focal point for protest was the British embassy at No. 39 Merrion Square. Throughout the day, workers, students and schoolboys, socialists, republicans and people of no particular group converged on the impressive building. A report in the *Connaught Tribune* summed up the mood: 'In O'Connell Street and Merrion Square ... hundreds of people offered the Sinn Féin and IRA organisations whatever help they could. It was an emotional scene as people queued to have their names taken, committing themselves to whatever task the militant republican organisations gave them ... they abandoned their offices, shops, and factories and took to the streets ... not since the hectic general election period of the thirties were so many militants on the streets demanding drastic action.'[5]

In early evening, following an Official Sinn Féin rally during which it was announced that 'notice to quit' was being served, petrol bombs and flares were thrown at the embassy. Later that night a Provisional Sinn Féin march arrived and there was another attempt to storm the building, but Gardaí successfully dispersed the crowd after baton charges.

By then the government had withdrawn the Irish ambassador from London and announced that the following day, when the funerals of eleven of the victims were to take place in Derry, would be a national day of mourning. All schools were to close and RTÉ would provide live coverage of the funeral services. Most trade unions asked their members to take between one and three hours off work to attend memorial events and employers' organisations agreed. Many workers also agreed to donate wages to a fund for the Derry victims. Some businesses announced that they would close for the entire day. The Irish Farmers' Association also called for its members to cease work for at least an hour on Wednesday. Protests continued with 10,000 people marching in Sligo and rallies in Tralee, Wexford, Dungarvan, Maynooth and Ballyshannon. Over 150 local women, described as 'Foxrock housewives', marched on the British ambassador's residence in Sandyford. Airport workers refused to service British aircraft or to unload their cargo. Dockers blacked British shipping, and in Galway they boarded a British vessel and forced it to take down its ensign. Bus workers in Cork announced that they would strike for twenty-four hours on the national day of mourning. In Dublin, protests continued outside the embassy.

By Wednesday morning the state had come to a standstill. Despite fierce wind and driving rain, marches and memorial services took place in almost every town and village. In Ardee, County Louth, 5,000 marched. There were 'duffle-coated, rain-soaked clergy, nuns in black headscarves, youths wearing black berets, Ardee ITGWU, Ardee Order of Malta, Ardee Band, Ardee Bread Co., businessmen, men in green berets, children in duffles and little girls wearing plastic rainhats and bewildered looks, old men, old women moving their lips slowly .... one Garda marching in plain-clothes, another on duty eyeing up the crowd, his collar turned up against the rain'. In most areas a Requiem Mass was celebrated before or after the protest rally. In many places Protestant memorial services also took place. The rally platforms typically included politicians from all parties, clergy and trade unionists. Members of the IRA (Provisional and Official) appeared at several demonstrations, sometimes carrying arms. In all areas black flags were displayed, black coffins bearing the number '13' carried, and Union flags and effigies of British prime minister Edward Heath burnt.[6]

Many politicians and local councillors travelled to Derry for the funerals, but Taoiseach Jack Lynch and most of the Fianna Fáil cabinet attended a memorial service in Dublin's Pro-Cathedral. The Táiniste, Erskine Childers, took part in a similar service in St Patrick's Cathedral, while Dublin's Methodist, Presbyterian and Jewish places of worship all marked the day with special ceremonies. Many people in Dublin attended early morning Mass before making their way to the city centre. Some went directly to the embassy, where protesters had gathered well before noon waiting for something to happen. Others joined the Dublin Council of Trade Unions march from Parnell Square. There were perhaps 100,000 people in the city centre by afternoon, with observers noting both sadness and apprehension and 'a hint of anarchy in the air' amid the closed shops, bars, restaurants, theatres ... and the boarded-over frontages of British firms.

At first the protest was peaceful, with women telephonists kneeling on the embassy steps and saying the rosary, while most people, including the Gardaí, joined in. Dozens of the marchers carried rain-soaked black flags and tricolours – others had placards and banners with slogans attacking the British, Ted Heath, and the British Army – as the procession was led by four men carrying black, furled flags, and a drum band of the Irish Transport Union played the 'Dead March' as it reached the embassy. There was soon a mighty crush in Merrion Square, with people climbing trees or hanging onto lamp posts overlooking the embassy. Railings were torn up and crowds spilled into the park. Three coffins draped in black were placed on the embassy steps, two Union Jacks were burned, and an effigy of a British soldier was set on fire.

Grief-fuelled anger swelled into naked, ugly fury. By 4 p.m. the first petrol bombs began to hit the building having been lobbed over the heads of around 200 Gardai, some wearing white helmets, who were powerless to intervene. The bombers were encouraged by the crowd, who cheered when a bomb hit its target, 'almost as if they were at Croke Park'. Then at least three men scaled across balconies, making their way slowly to the embassy. With the 'deftness of a cat burglar', one raised the tricolour to half-mast on the embassy flagpole. Then hatchets were used to smash the upper windows. To cheers and the sound of 'For he's a jolly good fellow' petrol bombs were thrown through the broken windows. The three together then managed to kick in the shutters on three of the first-floor windows.[7]

By 7 p.m. the embassy was ablaze but came under renewed siege from stones, other projectiles and more petrol bombs. A gelignite bomb blew the door off. The crowd cheered as the interior of the embassy blazed fiercely. 'Burn, burn, burn,' they shouted as chunks of masonry and woodwork fell onto the street. They redoubled their cheering whenever they saw the fire breaking through into new parts of the building. They stopped fire engines from getting through, cut fire hoses, and attacked firefighters. The firemen managed to reach the embassy three hours after the attack began, but then became targets themselves. Ambulances were allowed through, however, as both Gardaí and members of the crowd had been injured. Thousands stayed to watch the embassy burn, but gradually the Gardaí started to regain control, carrying out several baton charges. Cars were overturned and dozens of windows smashed in Grafton Street before order was restored in the early hours of Thursday morning.

Simon Hoggart reported how he walked through the charred remains the following morning: 'The building was open to the sky, with only black twisted wrecks of filing cabinets and burned timbers visible. A fireman complained bitterly about the treatment of his colleagues earlier in the night. "They had no need to hit us, we were only doing our jobs," he said. Policemen on the spot reported that rioters had thrown petrol bombs at a maternity hospital 50 yards from the embassy, but there had been no damage. "We didn't know what was happening in the North until this lot attacked us," said one policeman.'[8] An embassy spokesman said that all the staff would remain in their homes for the time being. 'Sensitive' documents had been removed and the embassy's work would continue in another building whose whereabouts are being kept secret. He added that staff had expected the attack since Sunday.

Other buildings with British connections were also attacked. One of the worst incidents was at the port of Dun Laoghaire, just south of Dublin, where a British-owned insurance office was burned down. Hoggart reported: 'Irish police baton-charged demonstrators outside the British passport office in Merrion Square, Dublin, last night after a day in which anti-British hatred reached a hysterical pitch. About thirty people were injured, some of them seriously. The charges were made as the demonstrators, supporters of the Official IRA, moved towards the office. Lines of policemen had been on guard there since the main British Embassy building had been destroyed by petrol bombers earlier in the evening. Then, as the mob, estimated at 5,000, closed on the passport office, the police charged. The crowd scattered, but not fast enough. At least thirty people were lying on the street after the police had passed and most of them were last night being given hospital treatment. Demonstrators attacked an estate agent's premises with stones and petrol bombs, and, as the police charged, hurled petrol bombs at them, too. It was estimated that there were fewer than 200 police to cope with the rioting mob.'[9] The British government, which contemplated evacuating all diplomatic staff, made a formal protest over the attack and the Irish government expressed regret, and agreed to pay compensation for the damage. Taoiseach Jack Lynch declared that the people who had burnt down the British embassy were dangerous enough to pose a serious threat to his state.[10]

There were smaller-scale protests over the following days, but nothing on the scale already witnessed. On Sunday 6 February, however, perhaps as many as 15,000 people from the Republic travelled to Newry to take part in what was to be the last great civil rights march involving around 40,000 people.

Anglo-Irish relations hit rock bottom with Irish foreign affairs minister Patrick Hillery going to the United Nations Security Council in New York to demand that a UN peacekeeping force be sent to Northern Irelandt.[11] Opposition Leader Harold Wilson reiterated his belief that a united Ireland was the only possible solution to Northern Ireland's Troubles. William Craig, then Stormont Home Affairs Minister, suggested that the west bank of Derry should be ceded to the Republic of Ireland.[12]

In the immediate aftermath of Bloody Sunday, the *Sligo Champion* thundered: 'The South is in the mood for violence ... there is a growing feeling that the only language Britain understands is through a gun barrel.' Academic Brian Hanley, research fellow at the Institute of Irish Studies, Liverpool, wrote: 'After the destruction of the embassy, however, the tone began to change. There was widespread condemnation of arson attacks on British property and of threats against both British citizens living in Ireland and Irish Protestants. The Irish Press warned that "this is not a time to fritter away our energies and resources in internal savagery and disorder", and asserted that, while "the embassy burning was serious enough, what followed was appalling". Jack Lynch warned that a "small minority of men" were trying to use anger at Britain to overthrow the southern state. Others warned of the damage being done to an already ailing tourist industry and raised fears of British businesses fleeing the Republic. The Fianna Fáil *Ard Fheis*, held in late February, was notable for the lack of anti-British rhetoric. Some thought that Bloody Sunday had created a "completely new atmosphere .... after two and a half years of apathetic detachment, the emotions of the South have at last spilt over." By mid-1972, however, others were discerning a change in mood. Fears that the violence was "coming down here" were prevalent, as was growing indifference and even hostility to Northern nationalists.

Belfast's Bogside neighbourhood today, in a picture taken from the city walls. The Bogside provided the backdrop for many of the flashpoints that took place during the Troubles. (Courtesy of Nigel Hoult under Creative Commons 2.0)

An artist's rendition of 'Free Derry Corner', at the intersection of Lecky Road, Rossville Street and Fahan Street in the Bogside, as it would have appeared at the time of Bloody Sunday. The famous graffiti appeared in 1969 and marked the self-declared autonomous zone of the same name. The surrounding streets were host to the Battle of the Bogside in 1969 and the Bloody Sunday massacre of 1972. (Courtesy of Adreanna Robson under Creative Commons 3.0)

On Saturday 22 January 1972, eight days before Bloody Sunday, the Northern Ireland Civil Rights Association (NICRA) organised an anti-internment protest at Magilligan Internee Camp at Magilligan Strand on the north coast of County Derry. Elements of the British Army's Parachute Regiment were transported from their base in Belfast to deal with the protest, and broke it up. Organisers of the protest, including John Hume, claimed that soldiers had used excessive violence and some had to be physically restrained by their officers. In this photograph one officer is remonstrating with his troops about their behaviour. A similar arrangement was in operation on Sunday 30 January 1972, with paratroopers being transported from Belfast to Derry to deal with the planned anti-internment march. (© Eamon Melaugh)

The scene at 'barrier 14' before the protest parade reached the area. Just to the left and above of the 'NEWSAGENT' sign is a British Army sniper. This soldier was one of a large number of snipers that were positioned in vantage points around the perimeter of the Bogside area. During the shooting that followed some eyewitnesses claimed that soldiers positioned on the city walls overlooking Rossville Street had fired on the crowd. (© Eamon Melaugh)

This photograph was taken at 'barrier 15' in lower Waterloo Street before the anti-internment parade on Bloody Sunday reached the area. At this barrier the photographer was threatened by the soldier on the left of the picture. The soldier had threatened to shoot if the photographer did not stop taking photographs. At this point a friend of the photographer, Barney McGuigan, pulled him away and said, 'You're going to get youself into trouble.' Barney McGuigan was shot dead approximately thirty minutes later. (© Eamon Melaugh)

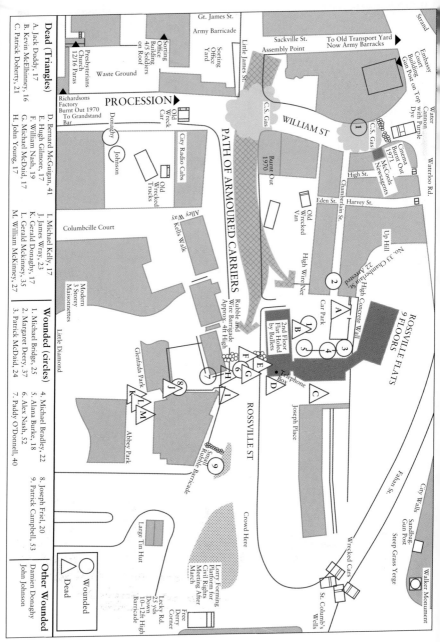

A map detailing the events of Bloody Sunday. (Drawn by SJmagic)

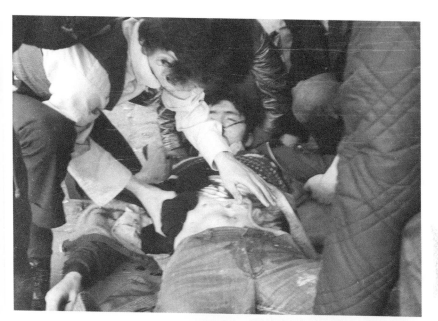

Above: This photograph shows the futile attempts that were made to treat Hugh Gilmour after he had been shot by a member of the Parachute Regiment of the British Army. As the paratroopers entered Rossville Street and began firing at the crowd, Gilmour and a few others tried to run for cover. Gilmour was shot as he was running away from the paratroopers. (© Eamon Melaugh)

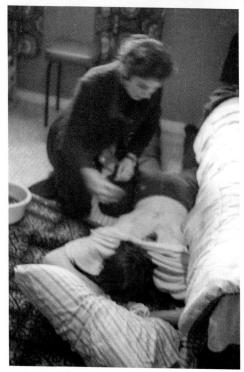

Right: Photograph of Patrick McDaid in the bedroom of a house in Joseph Place, Derry, shortly after he had been shot by a paratrooper. McDaid was shot as he was running for cover across the car park in Rossville Flats. He was helped into a house in Joseph Place where the householder tried to treat his wounds. (© Eamon Melaugh)

Mr and Mrs Wray at the grave of their son, James, one of the victims of Bloody Sunday. (© Eamon Melaugh)

Caoimhghín Ó Caoláin, Martin McGuinness and Gerry Adams (left to right) at the annual Wolfe Tone commemoration in Bodenstown in 1997. (Courtesy of Sinn Féin under Creative Commons 2.0)

Free Derry Corner still stands today, though the buildings around it have been demolished and replaced. (Courtesy of Nigel Hoult under Creative Commons 2.0)

One of the murals by 'the Bogside Artists', commemorating the fourteen killed in the Bloody Sunday massacre: John 'Jackie' Duddy, Michael Kelly, Hugh Gilmour, William Nash, John Young, Michael McDaid, Kevin McElhinney, James 'Jim' Wray, William McKinney, Gerard 'Gerry' McKinney, Gerard 'Gerry' Donaghy, Patrick Doherty, Bernard 'Barney' McGuigan and John Johnston. (Courtesy of Finn Terman Frederiksen under Creative Commons 2.0)

How and why this occurred remains for historians to explore and explain, but what is certain is that no event north of the border was ever again to have the same impact on popular mobilisation in the south as Bloody Sunday.'[13]

In London, journalist Roy Greenslade, who later outed himself as a supporter of armed insurrection, wrote: 'As for so many in Ireland, Bloody Sunday was a turning point for me.' He and his future wife Noreen 'joined a demonstration in Whitehall the following Saturday with the ambition of embarrassing the prime minister, Ted Heath, by placing thirteen coffins on the doorstep of No 10. Although there were no gates to Downing Street in those days, the authorities were not going to allow it and a riot broke out. We got right up to the police lines and Noreen's glasses were broken by a wayward blow from a truncheon.'[14]

At Westminster, Bernadette Devlin, the ferociously independent Irish nationalist MP for Mid Ulster, was furious at what she saw as British government attempts to stifle first-hand accounts of the shootings. Having witnessed the events herself, she complained that Commons Speaker Selwyn Lloyd consistently denied her the chance to speak in the Chamber about the shootings, although parliamentary convention decreed that any MP witnessing an incident under discussion would be granted an opportunity to speak about it.[15] Devlin publicly slapped Maudling when he claimed that the British Army had fired only in self-defence and was temporarily suspended from Parliament.

Throughout February the violence was again ratcheted up. Two IRA members were killed when a bomb they were planting exploded prematurely. A man died from injuries received in an explosion six days earlier. Two British soldiers were killed in a landmine attack near Cullyhanna, County Armagh. An IRA member was shot dead during an exchange of gunfire with RUC officers. Four IRA members died when a bomb they were transporting in a car exploded prematurely on the Knockbreda Road, Belfast. On 22 February, the Official IRA bombed Aldershot Barracks on the British mainland, in retaliation for Bloody Sunday; among the seven killed was a Catholic priest. Three days later Stormont home affairs minister John Taylor survived an assassination attempt in Armagh; his Official IRA attackers wrongly believed he was a chief architect of internment.[16]

Bloody Sunday, the storm of international condemnation that followed it, and the escalating violence, spelt the death of the Stormont administration. The UK government decided that London had to assume control of all security forces and when Stormont rejected that, premier Ted Heath announced the suspension of Stormont. That would continue, he said, 'until a political solution to the problems of the province can be worked out'.[17] Later, in a TV broadcast, Heath claimed that the introduction of direct rule from London could allow a 'fresh start'. He told Northern Ireland: 'Now is your chance. A chance for fairness, a chance for prosperity, a chance for peace, a chance at last to bring the bombings and killings to an end.' There was little hope of that – 1972 would prove the bloodiest year of the Troubles with over 500 killed. The decision was controversial within Heath's Cabinet. In a private letter to Heath not released for thirty years, Foreign Secretary Sir Alec Douglas-Home wrote: 'I really dislike direct rule for Northern Ireland because I do not believe that they are like the Scots or the Welsh and doubt they ever will be. The real British interest would, I think, be served best by pushing them towards a united Ireland rather than tying closer to the UK.'[18]

The Unionist parties were incandescent, having ruled themselves for fifty years. They organised a forty-eight-hour strike in protest at the abolition of Stormont which stopped public transport, power supplies and most large industrial plants. The strike and a 100,000-strong rally outside Stormont may have helped relieve immediate tensions 'by giving Protestants an opportunity to express their opposition to the British government's action'.[19]

The murders and maimings carried on regardless through March. Two Catholic teenagers were shot dead by RUC while joyriding a stolen car in Belfast. The Abercorn Restaurant in Belfast was bombed without warning and two Catholic civilians were killed and over 130 people injured. Four IRA members died in a premature explosion at a house in Clonard Street, Lower Falls, Belfast, and two more were shot dead by British soldiers in the Bogside. Two British soldiers were killed when attempting to defuse a bomb in Belfast. An RUC officer was killed in an IRA attack in Coalisland, County Tyrone. The IRA exploded a car bomb in Lower Donegall Street, Belfast, which killed six people, mortally wounded one person who died later, and injured around 100 others. Two of those killed were RUC officers who were trying to evacuate people from the area. Another was a member of the Ulster Defence Regiment (UDR) and the rest were Protestant civilians. Two people were killed in a bomb attack on the RUC station in Limavady.[20]

On 14 April the Provisional IRA set off twenty-four bombs and a week later an eleven-year-old boy, Francis Rowntree, became the first of seventeen people to die from rubber bullets during the Troubles. In May seven people were killed during two days of gunfights in Springmartin, Belfast, but at the end of the month the Official IRA declared a ceasefire.

PIRA, however, promised an escalation in its military actions against British and Loyalist targets.[21]

Bloody Sunday resulted in a recruitment surge for PIRA and the Official IRA's high command, rightly fearing that they were being side-lined, planned a violent response on the mainland. Their target was the 'open' and undefended Aldershot HQ of the 16th Parachute Brigade which included element present on Bloody Sunday. A time bomb in a Ford Cortina left in the garrison car park outside the officers' mess exploded but the target soldiers were either deployed abroad or working in offices elsewhere on the complex. Seven people were killed – five female kitchen staff, a gardener, and Roman Catholic British Army chaplain, Father Gerard Weston – and nineteen other civilians were wounded. The Official IRA claimed that it had carried out the attack in revenge for Bloody Sunday, adding: 'Any civilian casualties would be very much regretted as our target was the officers responsible for the Derry outrages' and saying that it would be the first of many such attacks on the headquarters of British Army regiments serving in Northern Ireland. Instead, the Officials faced widespread condemnation as their bomb had killed only civilian staff, and stung by such criticism within their own community, in May 1972 they called a permanent ceasefire. That in turn led to another recruitment boost for PIRA.

An inquest into the Bloody Sunday deaths was held in August 1973. The city's coroner, Hubert O'Neill, was a retired British Army major but proved to be no Establishment stooge. At the end of the inquest he declared: 'This Sunday became known as Bloody Sunday and bloody it was. It was quite unnecessary. It strikes me that the Army ran amok that day and shot without thinking what they were doing. They were shooting innocent people. These people may have been taking part in a march that was banned but that does not justify the troops coming in and firing live rounds indiscriminately. I would say without hesitation that it was sheer, unadulterated murder. It was murder.'[22]

Several months after Bloody Sunday, the 1st Battalion Parachute Regiment – again under Lieutenant Colonel Derek Wilford – were involved in another controversial shooting incident. On 7 September, 1 Para raided houses and the headquarters of the Ulster Defence Association (UDA) in the Protestant Shankill area of Belfast. Two Protestant civilians were shot dead and others wounded by the paratroopers, who claimed they were returning fire at Loyalist gunmen. This sparked angry demonstrations by local Protestants, and the UDA declared: 'Never has Ulster witnessed such licensed sadists and such blatant liars as the 1st Paras. These gun-happy louts must be removed from the streets.'

A unit of the British Army's Ulster Defence Regiment refused to carry out duties until 1 Para was withdrawn from the Shankill.[23]

In October 1972, Wilford, who by then was known as the 'Butcher of the Bogside', was awarded the Order of the British Empire by Queen Elizabeth on the advice of Heath.[24] The *Independent* editorialised: 'This was perhaps the greatest insult to the victims' relatives. There are many honourable units in the British army and many honourable soldiers also. The behaviour of members of the 1 Para in Derry, and elsewhere, indicates underlying disciplinary problems. While it is unlikely that any of the soldiers involved in the shootings will be punished for these crimes, at the very least the decision to award the OBE to Lt Col Wilford should be rescinded.'[25] It never was.

With the Official IRA and Official Sinn Féin having moved away from mainstream Irish republicanism towards Marxism, the Provisional IRA began to win the support of newly radicalised, disaffected young people.[26] In the following quarter of a century, PIRA and other smaller republican groups such as the Irish National Liberation Army (INLA) stepped up their armed campaigns against the state and those seen as being in service to it. Rival paramilitary organisations in the Unionist/Loyalist communities such as the UDA and the Ulster Volunteer Force (UVF) added to the rocketing death toll with bombs and bullets and enforced reigns of terror which mirrored those of their enemies. Unionist extremists did their bit to ensure that hate-fuelled venom would encourage more violence while pretending to be a force for 'law and order'. The newly formed Ulster Vanguard movement, a ragbag of Loyalist paramilitaries and rabble-rousers, held a rally in Ormeau Park, Belfast, attended by an estimated 60,000 people. Founder William Craig warned that, 'if and when the politicians fail us, it may be our job to liquidate the enemy'.

The British ambassador to Dublin, Sir John Peck, later wrote: 'Bloody Sunday had unleashed a wave of fury and exasperation the like of which I had never encountered in my life, in Egypt or Cyprus or anywhere else. Hatred of the British was intense. Someone had summed it up: we are all IRA now.'

6

The Widgery Cover-up

'There was no general breakdown in discipline.'

The day after the massacre, the government of Ted Heath, fighting other battles on the industrial front, swiftly decided that an inquiry was necessary to defuse the crisis – a tried-and-tested governmental formula. Within hours Home Secretary Maudling announced its remit. From the off, many Irish nationalists were sceptical that a British tribunal would be impartial. Such doubts were magnified by the appointment of the new Lord Chief Justice, Lord Widgery, to lead it. The tribunal was to sit for just three weeks in February and March 1972, with the final report published on 18 April.[1] Although given his role at the top of the legal profession Widgery was an obvious choice, Heath and Maudling could not have picked a more Establishment-orientated 'safe pair of hands'. Many witnesses threatened to boycott the inquiry due to doubts about Widgery's impartiality but were persuaded to take part.

John Passmore Widgery, sixty-one, was the descendent of a West Country gaoler, an enthusiastic Freemason[2] and had been head prefect at Queen's College, Taunton. He became a solicitor in 1933 and pre-war worked for a well-known firm of law tutors. During the Second World War he was initially a searchlight officer but transferred to the Royal Artillery. He was undoubtedly brave and efficient, taking part in the D-Day Normandy landings and winning the *Croix de Guerre* and the Belgian Order of Leopold. At the war's end, he was a brigadier. After demobilization Widgery gained a solid reputation specialising in town planning disputes which required a methodical approach, and in 1958 he was made a Queen's Counsel.[3] As a High Court judge from 1961 Widgery rarely rattled the rafters with his rhetoric or judgements and was generally regarded as fair and humane. The unexpected retirement of Lord Parker of Waddington saw Widgery replacing him in April 1971 as Lord Chief Justice; although he was the most junior option, his perceived administrative qualities landed him the job. He was created a life peer and his crest motto was 'God My Guide'.[4]

His choice of location for the inquiry was immediately controversial. For 'reasons of security and convenience' he chose the Protestant-dominated Coleraine, an unaffordable 30-mile train journey away for many Derry people, in the county council chamber which had an 'adequate' public gallery for families and the press.[5] He admitted: 'Initially there was some doubt as to whether the residents of Londonderry would be prepared to come and give evidence at the Tribunal at all. This was a matter of some concern. As the Army was to be represented by leading Counsel it was highly desirable that other interests should be represented on the same level so that cross-examination of the Army witnesses should not devolve on Counsel for the Tribunal alone. In the event this need was met by my granting legal representation to the relatives of the deceased and to those injured in the shooting, whose interest in the matter embraced that of the citizens of Londonderry generally.'[6]

Widgery's report, based on just three weeks of hearings, took the Army's side on almost everything. Under cross-examination, however, senior Army officers, and particularly General Ford, were severely attacked on the grounds that they did not genuinely intend to use 1 Para as merely an arrest squad. It was suggested that 1 Para had been specially sent in because they were known to be the roughest and toughest unit in Northern Ireland, and it was intended to use them in one of two ways: either to flush out any IRA gunmen in the Bogside and destroy them by superior training and firepower, or to send a punitive force into the Bogside to give the residents a rough handling and discourage them from making or supporting further attacks on the troops. Widgery wrote: 'There is not a shred of evidence to support these suggestions and they have been denied by all the officers concerned.'[7]

It was also said that when heavy firing began and it became apparent that the operation had taken an unexpected course, General Ford made no attempt to discover the cause of the shooting but instead washed his hands of the affair and walked away. Widgery ruled that such criticism was based on 'a failure to understand the structure of command in the Army'. The officer commanding the operation was the Commander 8 Brigade, who was in his Operations Room and was the only senior officer who had any general picture of what was going on. General Ford was present on the streets as an observer only. Although he had wireless equipment in his vehicle he was not accompanied by a wireless operator when on foot. The report said: 'When the serious shooting began the General was on foot in the neighbourhood of Chamberlain Street and had no means of knowing what was going on. Nothing would have been more likely to create chaos than for him to assume command or even to interfere with radio traffic by asking for information. Instead, he did the only possible thing by going at once to an observation post from which he could observe the scene for himself.'

Widgery conceded that the wisdom of sending in snatch arrest squads was 'debateable' with hindsight as the Army had achieved its main purpose of containing the march and although some rioters were still active in William Street, they could have been dispersed without difficulty. 'On the other hand, the Army had been subjected to severe stoning for upwards of half an hour; and the future threat to law and order posed by the hard core of hooligans in Londonderry made the arrest of some of them a legitimate security objective,' he wrote. 'The presence of 1 Para provided just the opportunity to carry this out. In view of the large numbers of people about in the area the arrest operation presented two particular risks: first, that in a large-scale scoop-up of rioters a number of people who were not rioters would be caught in the net and perhaps roughly handled; secondly, that if the troops were fired upon and returned fire innocent civilians might well be injured. Commander 8 Brigade sought to minimise the first risk by withholding the order to launch the arrest operation until the rioters and the marchers were clearly separated. But this separation never really happened.'

When 1 Para was ordered forward a substantial crowd remained on the waste ground between the bulk of the rioters who were in William Street and the bulk of the marchers who had either reached Free Derry Corner or gone home. The Brigade Commander, who could not see the area at all, relied mainly upon information from an officer in a helicopter, which information may have been incomplete. Widgery wrote: 'The Brigade Commander in giving evidence told me that he had considered the possibility that if a shooting match developed there would be risk to innocent people but he described this risk as "very bare". He considered that the arrest operation was essential in the interests of security and gave the order accordingly. Whether the Brigade Commander was guilty of an error of judgment in giving orders for the arrest operation to proceed is a question which others can judge as well or better than I can. It was a decision made in good faith by an experienced officer on the information available to him, but he underestimated the dangers involved."[8]

On the key question of who fired the first shots that afternoon, Widgery wrote: 'I am entirely satisfied that the first firing ... was directed at the soldiers. Such a conclusion is not reached by counting heads or by selecting one particular witness as truthful in preference to another. It is a conclusion gradually built up over many days of listening to evidence and watching the demeanour of witnesses under cross-examination. It does not mean that witnesses who spoke in the opposite sense were not doing their best to be truthful. On the contrary, I was much impressed by the care with which many of them, particularly the newspaper reporters, television men and photographers, gave evidence. The soldiers' response was immediate and members of the crowd running away in fear at the soldiers' presence understandably might fail to appreciate that the initial bursts had come from the direction of the Flats. If the soldiers are wrong they were parties in a lying conspiracy which must have come to light in the rigorous cross-examination to which they were subjected.'[9] Later, Widgery in effect spelt out whose side he was on: 'Those accustomed to listening to witnesses could not fail to be impressed by the demeanour of the soldiers of 1 Para. They gave their evidence with confidence and without hesitation or prevarication and withstood a rigorous cross-examination without contradicting themselves or each other. With one or two exceptions I accept that they were telling the truth as they remembered it.'[10]

Among the evidence presented to the tribunal were the results of paraffin tests, used to identify lead residues from firing weapons, and that nail bombs had been found on the body of one of those killed. Tests for traces of explosives on the clothes of eleven of the dead proved negative, while those of the remaining man could not be tested as they had already been washed. It has been argued that firearms residue on some deceased may have come from contact with the soldiers who themselves moved some of the bodies, or that the presence of lead on the hands of James Wray was easily explained by the fact that his occupation regularly involved the use of lead-based solder. Widgery ignored such expert evidence.

Widgery also dismissed multiple testimony that soldiers had fired into the backs of a panic-stricken crowd trying to clamber over the Rossville Street barricade to escape the violence. He said: 'I am entirely satisfied that when the soldiers first fired at the barricade, they did not do so on the backs of a fleeing crowd but at a time when some thirty people, many of whom were young men who were or had been throwing missiles, were standing in the vicinity of the barricade.'[11]

In his summary of conclusions, Widgery ruled that there would have been no deaths 'if those who organised the illegal march had not thereby created a highly dangerous situation in which a clash between demonstrators and the security forces was almost inevitable'. And in a rare instance of even-handedness, contradicting the above, that 'if the Army had persisted in its "low-key" attitude and had not launched a large-scale operation to arrest hooligans the day might have passed off without serious incident'.

The intention of the senior Army officers to use 1 Para as an arrest force and not for other offensive purposes was sincere, he ruled. Widgery conceded that Commander 8 Brigade may have underestimated the 'hazard to civilians' inherent in an arrest operation carried out in battalion strength in circumstances in which the troops were likely to come under fire. The tactical details were properly left to CO 1 Para who 'did not exceed his orders'. Widgery accepted pretty much all the evidence from soldiers claiming that they only fired back when fired upon. He wrote: 'When the vehicles and soldiers of Support Company appeared in Rossville Street they came under fire. Arrests were made; but in a very short time the arrest operation took second place and the soldiers turned to engage their assailants. There is no reason to suppose that the soldiers would have opened fire if they had not been fired upon first.'

Widgery went on: 'Soldiers who identified armed gunmen fired upon them in accordance with the standing orders in the Yellow Card. Each soldier was his own judge of whether he had identified a gunman. Their training made them aggressive and quick in decision and some showed more restraint in opening fire than others. At one end of the scale some soldiers showed a high degree of responsibility; at the other, notably in Glenfada Park, firing bordered on the reckless. These distinctions reflect differences in the character and temperament of the soldiers concerned.'

Lawyers from the start knew what side Widgery was on. When an opposing barrister raised a point of order, James Hutton, acting for the soldiers, said: 'It is not for you or the jury to express such wide-ranging views, particularly when a most eminent judge has spent twenty days hearing evidence and come to a very different conclusion.' The deeply Presbyterian Hutton was later ennobled, became the lord chief justice of Northern Ireland and a lord of appeal, and presided over the inquiry which cleared Tony Blair's government of wrongdoing over the 'dodgy dossier' on Saddam Hussein's alleged weapons of mass destruction.[12] His inquiry was denounced as a 'whitewash', but then Hutton was a veteran of Widgery.

On the victims, Widgery said: 'None of the deceased or wounded is proved to have been shot whilst handling a firearm or bomb. Some are wholly acquitted of complicity in such action; but there is a strong suspicion that some others had been firing weapons or handling bombs in the course of the afternoon and that yet others had been closely supporting them.' Even more controversially, he concluded: 'There was no general breakdown in discipline. For the most part the soldiers acted as they did because they thought their orders required it. No order and no training can ensure that a soldier will always act wisely, as well as bravely and with initiative. The individual soldier ought not to have to bear the burden of deciding whether to open fire in confusion such as prevailed on 30 January. In the conditions prevailing in Northern Ireland, however, this is often inescapable.'[13]

Widgery said: 'I have heard a great deal of evidence from civilians, including pressmen, who were in the crowd in the courtyard, almost all to the effect that the troops did not come under attack but opened fire without provocation. The Army case is that as soon as they began to make arrests they themselves came under fire and their own shooting consisted of aimed shots at gunmen and bomb throwers who were attacking them.'[14] For Widgery, there was no doubt which side was to be believed. Throughout, he fully accepted testimony from paratroopers who claimed they had been shot at, while downgrading that of marchers who insisted that no one on their side was armed, and pinned most of the blame on the march organisers. It later emerged that Widgery failed to take evidence from those wounded and did not personally read eyewitness accounts.[15] It was a whitewash, and it is hard now to understand how the Establishment thought that they could get away with it.

The Widgery report was accepted by the government but no formal action was contemplated either to modify the instructions on the soldiers' Yellow Cards or to reprimand individuals such as the anonymous Private H, who fired twenty-two shots, nineteen of which were 'wholly unaccounted for'. Defence Secretary Lord Carrington said that on the whole the Army had reason to be proud of itself and expressed the forlorn hope that the events of 30 January could now be forgotten.[16]

The report was understandably accepted by Unionists but immediately denounced by Irish nationalist politicians, while people in the Bogside and Creggan areas were sickened by his findings. Heath's government had garnered some goodwill because of its suspension of the Stormont parliament but that vanished when the conclusions were published.[17] The slogan 'Widgery washes whiter' – a play on the contemporary advertisement for Daz soap powder – appeared on walls all over Derry.[18]

The BBC later highlighted inconsistencies in the report: the investigation found no conclusive proof that the dead or wounded were shot while handling a firearm, yet Lord Widgery concluded the soldiers had been fired on first. Many important witnesses were not called to give evidence, and testimony was not taken from wounded survivors. The interpretation of the forensic evidence was flawed. Widgery concluded from firearms residue found on swabs taken from the bodies of the deceased that they had been in close contact with firearms. He dismissed any other explanations, including the possibility that the residue was due to transfer from soldiers or their vehicles. The possibility that victims were hit with gunfire directed into the Bogside from soldiers on the city walls was not given proper consideration.[19]

As with the previous probe into Ballymurphy, the relatives of the Bloody Sunday dead felt that Widgery had smeared them by following the Army line that most shot had been terrorists, snipers, or bombers. John Duddy's brother Gerry said: 'Widgery destroyed our loved ones' good name.' The report contained no expressions of regret for any of the deaths. Veteran Troubles correspondent David McKittrick wrote of Widgery's 'strong suspicion' that some had been firing weapons or handling bombs: 'The anger and indignation generated by these comments among the relatives of the dead and wounded helped keep Bloody Sunday as a potent issue through the decades. Widgery must have known the truth, is their refrain: he must have known it but he pretended otherwise. One of the most common criticisms of him was that he did not clear those shot of being active terrorists, although their families and neighbours knew they were not. In stark contrast he applied only light criticism to the Paras... Widgery did more to damage to the country's reputation in Ireland than almost any other single act during the history of the Troubles.'[20]

Tellingly, in an earlier case, Widgery had focused on the duty of the Crown to prosecute, saying: 'A and B are alleged to have committed a crime. A is charged with the crime, convicted and sentenced. B is not charged. At the trial of A there is evidence which suggests that B may have committed or been a participant to the crime. Can the prosecution be compelled to prosecute B?'[21] Historical prosecutions must 'indisputably be a matter of discretion'. Later, in 1974 he said that misidentification was 'the most serious chink in our armour when we say British justice is the best in the world'. But two years later he dismissed the first appeal by the Birmingham Six, wrongly convicted of that city's pub bombings. His dementia was becoming clear to all those present in his courts through the rest of the 1970s. The satirical magazine *Private Eye* claimed that 'he sits hunched and scowling, squinting into his books from a range of 3 inches, his wig awry. He keeps up a muttered commentary of bad-tempered and irrelevant questions – "What d'you say?", "Speak up", "Don't shout", "Whipper-snapper", etc.' He regularly fell asleep in court but resisted attempts to get him to resign until 1980. For at least eighteen months previously he had not been in control of either his administrative work or his legal pronouncements.[22] He died two days after his seventieth birthday in 1981. By then relatives of the victims and nationalists had campaigned for almost a decade for a new inquiry, unaware that they faced a much longer wait.

7

The Long Road to Calvary

'the sheer waste of children taught to hate'

The abolition of Stormont failed to stem the bloody onrush of violence – the nationalists/republicans wanted the British out, pure and simple, while the Unionists/Loyalists wanted their parliament back so they could take back control.

At the end of July 1972, the Army launched Operation Motorman to break down the barricades that Catholics had set up around their neighbourhoods and end 'no-go' areas. An extra 4,000 troops were drafted in, bringing the Army total to 12,000 and making it the biggest British military operation since the 1956 Suez Crisis. The troops, supported by tanks and bulldozers, smashed through the barricades. In the Derry part of the operation four people were killed, including a fifteen-year-old boy and an unarmed IRA man. On the same day the IRA exploded three car bombs in Claudy, County Derry, killing six people instantly while a further three people died of their injuries over the next twelve days.[1]

The shadow of Bloody Sunday hung over such events, usually as a justification for barbarous actions. It emerged in August that a file sent to the Director of Public Prosecutions for Northern Ireland by the RUC concluded that there would be no prosecution of any member of the security forces as a result of the 30 January killings, and that charges of riotous behaviour against some civilians were also dropped.[2] The first commemoration march and rally organised by the Northern Ireland Civil Rights Association was held a year after Bloody Sunday and became an annual fixture. But after a while, and with so much else happening during decades of violence, the event did not generate much more than a ripple outside the immediate area.[3]

Meanwhile, the Army covertly ratcheted up tensions with its deployment of the Military Reaction Force, active between 1971 and 1973, set up to kill IRA members in covert drive-by shootings. Many of its victims were unarmed and some had nothing to do with the IRA. The killings were blamed on Loyalist terrorists at the time and the truth did not emerge until many years later following investigations by journalists and others. One of the Force's members, coincidentally referred to as Soldier F, later told BBC journalists: 'We were not there to act like an army unit, we were there to act like a terror group.'[4] MRF operatives dressed like civilians and were given fake identities and unmarked cars equipped with two-way radios. Armed with Browning pistols and Sterling sub-machine guns, they motored around the streets in teams of two to four, tracking down and arresting or killing suspected IRA members. Former MRF members admitted that the unit shot unarmed people without warning, both IRA members and civilians, knowingly breaking the British Army's rules of engagement. They also claimed they had a list of targets they were ordered to 'shoot on sight', the aim being to 'beat them at their own game' and to 'terrorise' the republican movement.[5] According to one ex-member, the unit was told that these tactics had British government backing, 'as part of a deeper political game'. He said his section shot at least twenty people: 'We opened fire at any small group in hard areas [...] armed or not – it didn't matter. We targeted specific groups that were always up to no good. These types were sympathisers and supporters, assisting the IRA movement. As far as we were concerned, they were guilty by association and party to terrorist activities, leaving themselves wide open to the ultimate punishment from us.'[6] Another said that their role was to 'draw out the IRA and to minimise their activities'. They fired on groups of people manning defensive barricades, on the assumption that some might be armed.[7] The unit's role was one of 'repression through fear, terror and violence'. Such operational attitudes, it can be argued, mirrored those of Bloody Sunday.

At the same time, there were repeated allegations that the Army colluded with Loyalist terrorist groups, providing them weapons and intelligence enabling them to target and kill nationalists. There were further allegations that the Army took no action against Loyalist paramilitaries and obstructed police investigations against them. In 2012, an independent inquiry concluded that British agents had colluded with Loyalists over the murder of the Belfast solicitor, Pat Finucane, who had represented members of the IRA and the families of shoot-to-kill victims. The activities of Loyalist paramilitaries were stepped up, with or without collusion, during the rest of 1972. They raided an Ulster Defence Regiment/Territorial Army base in Lurgan, County Armagh, and stole eighty-five British Army issue self-loading rifles (SLRs) and twenty-one Sterling sub-machine guns (SMGs). The camp guard claimed that they were 'overpowered' by the Loyalists. One of the SMGs was recovered in the possession of Loyalist paramilitaries in Belfast. A confidential report indicated that this weapon alone had been used in at least twelve Loyalist attacks.

In another murky incident, two Catholic men were found dead at a farm at Aughinahinch, near Newtownbutler, County Fermanagh, in what became known as 'the pitchfork killings'. It was initially thought to have been carried out by Loyalists, but it was later discovered that a patrol of British soldiers were the killers. Nine years later two serving Argyll and Sutherland Highlanders were jailed for the murders. A third defendant, a former soldier, was jailed for manslaughter. A fourth defendant, a captain, was given a one-year suspended sentence for withholding information about the killings.[8]

In London, Prime Minister Edward Heath and new Northern Ireland Secretary Willie Whitelaw briefly considered moving towards a united Ireland but dismissed it for fear of a sure-fire violent backlash from the Unionist majority, although they both agreed that the Irish government should be given a role in any new settlement. Unknown at the time, as early as June 1972 officials from Whitelaw's office secretly met PIRA representatives in a country house in Ballyarnett, close to the Derry/Donegal border. The PIRA representatives included Gerry Adams, while one of the officials was an MI6 operative. The meeting laid the groundwork for a PIRA ceasefire and a direct but still secret meeting between PIRA and the British government on 7 July 1972. Adams, who had been released from detention for the purpose, was part of a delegation who went to London for talks with Whitelaw and other Northern Ireland Office ministers in the Chelsea home of Paul Channon, then minister of state. The IRA delegation also included Séamus Twomey, Seán MacStiofáin, Dáithí Ó Conaill, Ivor Bell, and Martin McGuinness. The talks failed, and so did the ceasefire, but first contact had been made.[9]

After more negotiations with the main parties in Northern Ireland, Heath and Whitelaw came up with the Sunningdale agreement which genuinely tried to treat both sides of the community equally. It provided for a new Northern Ireland Assembly made up from all political persuasions, elected by proportional representation. There would also be a Council of Ireland involving representatives from the Republic.

Unionists were outraged as not only would they have to share power with nationalist parties, but they would also have to stomach some input from the Republic. The IRA and its political wing, Sinn Féin, were also opposed because they felt it cemented British involvement in Northern Ireland and they wanted the British out altogether. The issue split the Unionist party but nevertheless, elections took place and the new assembly did convene, made up of Faulkner and his mainstream Unionists on one side and Social Democratic Labour Party (SDLP) members led by Gerry Fitt and John Hume on the other. If Sunningdale was a new dawn, it was short-lived. In May 1974 Northern Ireland was brought to a standstill by a Loyalist strike which was brutally enforced by violent thugs. Within weeks the Sunningdale power-sharing experiment collapsed and it was back to direct rule. Hope seemed extinguished and it was hard to imagine a solution that would work given the entrenched attitudes on both sides. The Loyalist community still dominated. The British government tried to introduce more equality with employment legislation and laws against incitement to hatred, but they had little effect.

Northern Ireland entered a military stalemate and political stagnation in the wake of Sunningdale. The IRA and the British government, now under Labour's Harold Wilson, came independently to the conclusion that they could not defeat each other militarily and so settled in for a long-haul conflict. IRA ceasefires came and went, punctuated by what it called 'spectaculars' – bombings that spread to English cities such as Birmingham and Guildford. In 1976, officials in Northern Ireland tried to appeal for peace with a publicity campaign featuring the slogan 'Seven years is enough'. Nationalists responded with the slogan '700 years is too much'. Meanwhile the world was losing interest in Northern Ireland, and it took a major bombing or murder to warrant any serious coverage.

An exception was to be the treatment of prisoners. In 1972, Whitelaw granted IRA prisoners Special Category Status after an inmate had gone on hunger strike in a bid to be classed as a political prisoner, believing that was preferential to letting the man die and suffering the inevitable backlash. The category gave IRA prisoners special privileges including being kept with other IRA men in separate compounds. Later, however, the British government embarked on a policy of 'criminalisation' which meant that IRA inmates would be treated as common criminals. The failed policy of internment ended at Christmas 1975 and it was decided that Special Category Status would end in March 1976, to coincide with the opening of the new specially designed HM Prison Maze, set out in H block shapes that had been built next to the internment camp of Long Kesh. The first IRA man taken to the Maze refused to wear the prison uniform, saying it would have to be nailed to him, and clothed himself in a blanket instead. More prisoners followed his lead, and smeared excrement on their cell walls. By 1978, there were 250 prisoners on the 'dirty protest' and they proved a PR disaster for Britain across the world. In 1979, the IRA assassinated ten prison officers in an attempt to make the British government relent, but to no avail. Margaret Thatcher was elected the Conservative and Unionist British prime minister in 1979 and her natural antipathy to the republican cause was reinforced by three major bombings in 1979, the year that she came to power. One of her closest political allies, the MP Airey Neave, was killed by a bomb planted by the republican splinter group the Irish National Liberation Army under his car which had been parked in Parliament's underground carpark. A few months later IRA bombs killed eighteen British soldiers at Warrenpoint and the Queen's cousin, Earl Mountbatten, on the same day as he sailed off the coast of County Sligo. Thatcher's response to these attacks was to add another 1,000 men to the RUC. She saw enhanced security and defeating the IRA as a more urgent priority than negotiations and reforms.[10]

Meanwhile, the IRA stepped up its campaign to gain Special Category Status for its members in prison. In 1980, they began a series of hunger strikes with prisoners prepared to starve themselves to death unless their demands were met. Bobby Sands began his hunger strike on 1 March 1981. As his health deteriorated, republicans decided to put him up as a candidate for a by-election to the British parliament. He won a resounding victory, sending shock waves through the Loyalist community and the political establishment both in Britain and the island of Ireland. Sands' victory was a major embarrassment for Thatcher. How could she dismiss him as a terrorist when he had just won the backing of the voters and been elected as a member of the British parliament? She dodged the issue and still refused to budge, even after Sands died on 5 May. Ten more hunger-strikers were to die before the IRA called off the campaign. They won some concessions but did not achieve the Special Category Status. To many across the world, however, they had won a moral victory.

The treatment of the hunger-strikers inspired yet more recruits to join the IRA. Perhaps more importantly, Sinn Féin realised that republicans could win elections. They started to consider the power of the ballot box. Sinn Féin publicity officer Danny Morrison addressed a 1981 party meeting with the famous phrase 'Will anyone here object if, with a ballot box in one hand and an armalite in the other, we take power in Ireland?' They started to win elections and would eventually overtake the SDLP as the voice of Catholic nationalists. In 1983, Gerry Adams defeated the SDLP's Gerry Fitt as MP for West Belfast. It represented a generational shift that signalled Sinn Féin's arrival as a major electoral force.

While the hunger strikes and various bombings and riots were grabbing the headlines in the early 1980s, work was going on behind the scenes without the knowledge of either the IRA or the Unionists. Mrs Thatcher had been warmly welcomed by Unionists when she came to power and her refusal to give into the IRA and the hunger-strikers added further reassurance that she was on their wavelength. Within a few years they were accusing her of betraying them. The Irish government had been dismayed by the failure of the Sunningdale power-sharing agreement and the ensuing stalemate between nationalists and Unionists. Successive Taoiseachs made discreet back-door approaches to No 10. For all her hard-line public stance, Thatcher was prepared to listen and held discussions with both Charles Haughey and then Garret Fitzgerald. Unionists were furious when they discovered talks had taken place without their knowledge.[11]

The IRA redoubled its military campaign following the treatment of the hunger-strikers. They planted more bombs in England, killing army band members and shoppers at the world-famous Harrods. Loyalists were carrying out killings of their own and in March 1984, Gerry Adams was shot in a UDA attack – he was injured but survived. Then in October 1984, the IRA planted a bomb in the Grand Hotel in Brighton where Thatcher's Conservative Party were staging their annual conference. Five people were killed, including deputy chief whip Sir Anthony Berry, and thirty-one were injured, including Cabinet minister Norman Tebbit and his wife Margaret. Thatcher herself only narrowly escaped with her life. The IRA claimed responsibility the next day and said that it would try again. Its statement read: 'Mrs. Thatcher will now realise that Britain cannot occupy our country and torture our prisoners and shoot our people in their own streets and get away with it. Today we were unlucky, but remember we only have to be lucky once. You will have to be lucky always. Give Ireland peace and there will be no more war.'[12] Thatcher began the next session of the conference at 9.30 a.m. the following morning, as scheduled. She said the bombing was 'an attempt to cripple Her Majesty's democratically elected government', adding, 'That is the scale of the outrage in which we have all shared, and the fact that we are gathered here now – shocked but composed and determined – is a sign not only that this attack has failed, but that all attempts to destroy democracy by terrorism will fail.'[13]

A month later she met Irish Taoiseach Garret Fitzgerald to discuss proposals for co-operation in the North. She famously dismissed them all with the words 'Out, out, out…'. Fitzgerald was dismayed but to everyone's subsequent surprise, negotiations went on behind the scenes. Then on 15 November 1985 Thatcher and Fitzgerald signed the Anglo-Irish Agreement. She believed it would help to secure Northern Ireland as part of the UK after Fitzgerald agreed to a clause that there could be no change in the North's constitution without the consent of the majority of the people. On the other hand, it also gave the Republic a consultative role in the affairs of the North, and that was too much for Unionists to stomach. The protests started before the ink on the agreement had dried.

To the nationalists, and the Irish and British governments, the Anglo-Irish Agreement was a significant but inoffensive development. It set up an Anglo-Irish Intergovernmental Council with offices in Belfast. One of its functions would be to enable Catholics to voice grievances to Irish officials, which would then be passed on to British officials to consider. The Irish government could also put forward proposals, but it was up to the British to decide whether or not to act on them. One of the main aims was to entice Unionists to edge back towards power sharing. The agreement meant that if a power was devolved to Northern Ireland, the Irish government would lose all input on that subject. The more powers that were devolved, the less influence for Dublin. On the other hand, if the Unionists wouldn't agree to share power then Dublin's influence would continue.

The Unionists rejected it completely, seeing it as some sort of trap to lure them towards more power for the south. They were also outraged that it had been introduced over their heads and without their knowledge. They set about strangling it at birth. Unionist MPs resigned to force by-elections to give the electorate a chance to voice their disapproval at the ballot box. Marches and rallies were called together with strikes. The British government stood firm and the RUC stepped in to prevent intimidation by Loyalist paramilitaries during marches and strikes. Northern Ireland Secretary Tom King and the RUC accused some Unionist MPs of rubbing shoulders with Loyalist terrorists.

Loyalist fury increased and the UDA and UVF started petrol bombing the homes of hundreds of police officers and launched attacks on the homes of Catholics. These were all measures that had enabled Loyalists to destroy political initiatives in the past – but not this time. Thatcher visited Belfast to reiterate her commitment to the Anglo-Irish Agreement. Her refusal to give in to the Unionists and scrap the Agreement led to an extraordinary outburst from Ian Paisley during one of his hellfire sermons: 'We pray this night that thou wouldst deal with the Prime Minister of our country. O God, in wrath take vengeance upon this wicked, treacherous, lying woman. Take vengeance upon her O Lord and grant that we may see a demonstration of thy power.'[14]

While the Unionists threw their energy into campaigning against the Agreement, Sinn Féin was turning its attention to elections, both in the North and the Republic. In the past, they had stood in elections in the Republic on the basis that they would not take up their seat because they did not recognise the legitimacy of the Dáil. By the mid-1980s, younger members like Gerry Adams were arguing that it made no sense to boycott an assembly that the Irish people recognised and accepted. It was a change of heart that was to see Sinn Féin develop into a political force that neither the British nor the Irish government could ignore. At the same time, the IRA got arms from Libya and used them to pull off devastating bomb attacks in both England and Ireland. The rising number of deaths and injuries involving innocent people made it impossible for the British government to speak with Sinn Féin or enter into negotiations with them – at least not in public.

Matters came to a head on 8 November 1987 when an IRA bomb exploded at a poppy day memorial ceremony in Enniskillen to commemorate those who fought in the two world wars. Eleven people were killed and many more were injured. Thatcher was furious and banned British radio and TV stations from broadcasting statements from Sinn Féin spokesmen. Their voices had to be dubbed by actors instead. It seemed a pointless gesture to many, but the main purpose was to isolate Sinn Féin from the political process.[15] The British military also stepped up its fight against the IRA. Eight IRA members were shot dead by troops as they prepared a bomb attack in Armagh. Three more were shot dead in Gibraltar. The deaths were controversial, and Britain was accused of operating a shoot-to-kill policy that overlooked such legal niceties as fair trials.

Every Bloody Sunday anniversary, families, friends and fellow citizens would gather for annual commemorations in Derry, and, for many, the annual march became an important gesture of public remembrance. Juliann Campbell wrote: 'The stigma of being associated with Bloody Sunday and thereby with "terrorism" persisted for many years. Lord Widgery's 1972 report did nothing to alleviate the suffering when it apportioned blame to the victims themselves. The immediate false narrative circulated by the British state thus became the "official" version of events, endorsed by the Lord Chief Justice of the day. Widgery was to prove a disaster for the British state and its relationship with Northern Ireland.' NICRA was instrumental in setting up an organisation to refocus attention. The Bloody Sunday Initiative was formally established in August 1989. The timing was spot-on as human rights issues came to the political and media forefront with the release of the Guildford Four and, in 1991, the Birmingham Six. Both miscarriages of justice fuelled efforts to win justice for the Bloody Sunday families. In December 1991, the Channel 4 documentary series *Secret History* broadcast a programme challenging the Widgery findings. The cause was boosted by more damning *Channel 4 News* reports, whistle-blowing former paras and explosive new documents released from the Public Records Office in London.[16]

The twentieth anniversary commemorations were not confined to Derry. A huge march was held in London, calling for British withdrawal from Ireland. Rock star Peter Gabriel voiced support for the demonstration, alongside MPs Peter Hain, Jeremy Corbyn and Tony Benn, filmmaker Ken Loach, journalist John Pilger, poet Adrian Mitchell and the belatedly freed Gerry Hunter and Billy Power of the Birmingham Six. A meeting was called in early February 1992 in the Pilot's Row Centre, built upon the killing ground of Bloody Sunday. Thirty-three people, mainly relatives but including four Englishmen, became the first members of the Bloody Sunday Justice Campaign (BSJC). The family-led campaign would stick to clear, simple demands: the repudiation of Widgery and the institution of a new inquiry, a formal acknowledgement of the innocence of all the victims, and the prosecution of those responsible for the deaths and injuries. The campaign welcomed 'anyone who supports our objectives irrespective of religion or political persuasion'.

On 15 April 1992, the newly established BSJC was officially launched in Pilot's Row Community Centre in the Bogside. In front of a huge crowd and TV cameras, Johnny Walker of the Birmingham Six said that the people of Derry deserved justice – and that he knew from personal experience what it was like to be denied justice for sixteen and a half years. In the weeks and months afterwards, families and activists travelled to Westminster at the invitation of Corbyn, to lobby parliamentarians, and to Leinster House in Dublin to lobby TDs. In Derry, relatives and campaigners embarked on a citywide campaign. 'After decades of comparative silence, previously disheartened relatives had the opportunity and the impetus to speak up, to share their grief and argue their case,' wrote Campbell. 'Collectively, they were to prove an unstoppable force.' Bishop of Derry, Dr Edward Daly – the priest whose image waving a bloodstained hankie would become synonymous with Bloody Sunday – pledged his support to the campaign. So too did SDLP Leader John Hume, who would later become the only person to receive the world's three most prestigious peace awards – the 1998 Nobel Peace Prize, the Gandhi Peace Prize and the Martin Luther King Award.

On Saturday 20 June 1992, the campaign launched a new postcard initiative urging British prime minister John Major to reopen the case. Family members set up a stall on Waterloo Place in Derry where they sat, often huddled under umbrellas, handing out the postcards. Each of the pre-addressed cards listed the three demands, and the public response was massive. The campaign was gaining attention in the USA, and in August 1992 relatives of the dead received commemorative parchments issued by the City Council of Chicago. A major source of funding was the Catholic, Irish-American organisation, the Ancient Order of Hibernians (AOH). However, support was hardly universal. Mary Robinson, President of Ireland at the time, refused to meet family members or lay a wreath at the Bloody Sunday memorial during a visit to Derry in September 1992. In October 1992, families sought the support of Ireland's Catholic Cardinal, Cathal Daly, and were shocked when he declined to meet them, as did Irish Taoiseach Charles Haughey later that year.

British Irish Rights Watch director Jane Winter agreed to research and draft a report to the United Nations. In Derry, the work continued unabated, with campaigners funding their efforts with dinner dances, concerts, raffles and campaign collection boxes throughout the city. The campaign organised public meetings and provided speakers for events in Derry, Belfast and Dublin. A succession of lawyers, authors, professors and human rights activists played fundamental roles. They included Patricia Coyle, a trainee solicitor for Madden & Finucane, who began an exhaustive, manual search of the Public Records Office in London.[17]

Throughout the 1980s and into the 1990s, the British and Irish governments kept in contact in search of a peace accord. New Northern Ireland Secretary Peter Brooke made two landmark speeches that helped to change people's thinking. In 1989, he declared that the IRA could not be defeated by military means. In 1990 he declared that Britain 'had no selfish, strategic or economic interest in Northern Ireland'. Unionists were unhappy about both declarations but in 1991 agreed to join exploratory talks. Those talks duly broke down but in what was later recognised as something of a breakthrough, the Unionists had shown that they were at least prepared to consider some settlement that involved the Republic.

On 20 January 1993, Major responded to a letter from Hume saying that those killed on Bloody Sunday 'should be regarded as innocent'. The families gave a guarded welcome to the long-overdue admission – but it was not enough. Despite her having refused three times to meet with the campaign, in June 1993 the BSJC again asked President Mary Robinson to receive a delegation. Once again, the President declined the families' invitation – pointing to the 'constitutional parameters' of her office. In the summer of 1994, protests and chaotic scenes greeted Prince Charles, Colonel-in-Chief of the Parachute Regiment, when he visited the city. Madden & Finucane also submitted its application to the European Court of Human Rights.

Throughout this period, Patricia Coyle continued to search out relevant material in the Northern Ireland Public Records Office (PRONI), and in archives and photographic libraries. Eventually, through Coleraine

Library, Coyle found a black trunk that contained twenty-one volumes of transcripts, one for each of the days of the Widgery Tribunal, which had lain undisturbed for twenty years. It further boosted demands for a new inquiry. Hume led a delegation to Downing Street to deliver a thirty-six-page British Irish Rights Watch report which defined the events of 30 January 1972 as 'summary and arbitrary execution of unarmed civilians'.

Operation Banner started to be scaled down in 1994 after the IRA declared a ceasefire as part of the embryonic peace process. This gradual withdrawal of troops continued intermittently until the operation officially ended on 31 July 2007. The Army and the paramilitaries had long recognised that no one could win such a war outright and that the only possible way out of the stalemate was to reach a political solution.[18] Negotiations between all the interested parties – republicans and Loyalists, and the British and Irish governments – proceeded slowly throughout the 1990s. John Major pragmatically supported steady progress despite himself being the target of a mortar bomb attack on Downing Street. Official figures show that British troops killed 305 people during Operation Banner throughout the duration of the Troubles. Of these, 156 were civilians, 127 were republican paramilitaries and thirteen were Loyalist paramilitaries. A total of 692 British soldiers were killed in the conflict, mainly by republican paramilitaries, and a further 689 died from natural causes, including suicide.

In Derry, the campaign continued unabated. Letters were still dispatched daily, relatives travelled to other cities and countries and, by 1995, the campaign had gathered momentum at home and abroad. Taoiseach John Bruton designated one of his own civil servants to act as liaison between the Irish government and the families. The tide was turning. On 16 February 1995, three years after she first refused to meet them, the Bloody Sunday relatives were finally granted an audience with President Mary Robinson, asking her again for her support and invited her to lay a wreath at the Bloody Sunday memorial the next time she was in Derry. This time she agreed tentatively.

Meanwhile, having discovered the original Coroner's Report in Belfast, Patricia Coyle knew the next step was to gain access to the Public Records Office in Kew Gardens, London, where the Home Office had lodged the Widgery Inquiry papers. A catalogue list showing categories of materials lodged by the original inquiry, thirteen of which were sealed for periods of either thirty or seventy-five years. She and her colleague Peter Madden applied to have those files released. With little finances to travel to and from London, they agreed to let fellow human rights campaigner Jane Winter to begin investigating the open material at Kew. In August 1995, Winter unearthed the infamous Heath-Widgery memo. Headed 'secret', it was a record of a meeting between then premier Edward Heath, Lord Chief Justice Widgery and Lord Chancellor Lord Hailsham in Downing Street the day after Bloody Sunday. In it, Heath advised Widgery to remember that 'we are in Northern Ireland fighting not only a military war but a propaganda war', while the Lord Chancellor suggested that the Treasury Solicitor would need to 'brief counsel for the army'. Its significance took some time to filter through, but eventually a press conference was called for 10 November 1995 at the Pat Finucane Centre. Winter flew from London for the press conference to discuss her find and copies of the memo were distributed to the media. That week's *Derry Journal* ran a front-page banner headline 'Widgery memo damns British' and claimed that the discovery of the confidential minutes would 'send shockwaves through the British establishment'. Relatives hailed the 'dynamite' find as the first major breakthrough in terms of incriminating the British government.[19]

During their campaign, families in Derry came across a bag of 1972 eyewitness statements which had been lying under the stairs in civil rights activist Brigid Bond's house for many years. Her husband had found the papers after her death, along with the original Bloody Sunday civil rights banner still stained with Bernard McGuigan's blood. In April 1996, the European Court turned down the families' case, but they campaigned on, sensing that the tide of public opinion had turned. In June they wrote a letter to Prince Charles asking him to condemn his soldiers' actions in Derry on Bloody Sunday, receiving a curt reply from his private secretary suggesting it was 'necessary to move on'.

Meanwhile, Patricia Coyle got the breakthrough she had hoped for. The Home Office finally granted her permission to see their classified files and she went to Kew to study them. The dusty, previously unseen documents revealed evidence that the statements of some soldiers had been tailored for Widgery and that lawyers for the families had received just a fraction of the information disclosed during the tribunal. She then discovered a draft version of the Widgery Report with a note scrawled on one of the pages: 'The LCJ (Lord Chief Justice) will pile up the forensic evidence against the deceased.' It was agreed that the new materials needed to be assessed by an independent legal expert, and the Bloody Sunday Trust subsequently commissioned Professor Dermot Walsh, Chair of Law at Limerick University, to do so.

By the twenty-fifth anniversary, public support for the campaign was at its highest point. On a crisp, cold Sunday afternoon, more than 40,000 people took to the streets and marched along the original 1972 route. The same week, relatives delivered a 40,000-strong petition to 10 Downing Street. They also took their campaign to the US Senate.

Channel 4 News broadcast the first of an explosive series of reports – an interview with an anonymous paratrooper who admitted that unarmed civilians had been targeted on Bloody Sunday. The same week saw more than a dozen Conservative and Labour MPs lodge early day motions at Westminster calling for a new independent, international inquiry.

On 20 February 1997, a busload of campaigners, lawyers and family members set off for Dublin for a series of meetings with various dignitaries, including the Taoiseach, John Bruton, his deputy, and Foreign Affairs minister. The Irish government, swayed by the mountain of new evidence, agreed to draw up a dossier of all the new evidence for submission to the British government. Another delegation embarked on a week-long lobbying trip to the US where they took part in New York and Boston St Patrick's Day parades, attended a St Patrick's Day event in the White House and spoke to Congressional leaders at Capitol Hill. Seventy-two Congressmen signed a letter supporting a new inquiry.[20]

The following month, the Dublin-based *Sunday Business Post* quoted a former para – known as Soldier 027 – alleging that his company had been told by their Lieutenant the evening before Bloody Sunday to 'get some kills'. He also alleged that some of his colleagues had been in possession of their own additional ammunition, including illegal dum-dum bullets, and that many soldiers' accounts had been doctored by lawyers to tally with the version of events favoured by the Army. Two days later, *Channel 4 News* broadcast an interview with another anonymous paratrooper who delivered an uncannily similar account to that of Soldier 027, admitting that 'hateful and disgraceful acts' had been committed in Derry.

In May 1997, Labour leader Tony Blair succeeded John Major as British prime minister. Almost immediately, pressure was put on him to resolve the Bloody Sunday issue. Just days after Blair entered No. 10, John Hume tabled a Commons motion urging the new prime minister to investigate the fresh evidence. As promised, the Irish government presented its 178-page dossier which included many previously unconsidered witness statements, an assessment of fresh information about the shootings, and a damning indictment of the Widgery report. When Bertie Ahern succeeded John Bruton as Taoiseach in June 1997, the new administration was equally supportive of the campaign.

In late summer 1997, leading global human rights groups threw their weight behind the campaign. Human rights watchdog Amnesty International called on the British government to repudiate the Widgery findings. The nationwide petition gathered pace throughout the summer of 1997, too, with relatives travelling to Belfast, Dublin and many other cities. Towards the end of November, John Hume took relatives and

Derry city councillors to Westminster. In December 1997, a Day of Action took place across Britain in support of the campaign, with protests held in several major cities. As the twenty-sixth anniversary loomed, support for the campaign had reached unprecedented levels. Bloody Sunday was being reported and debated all over the world.

Press Association political editor Jon Smith, who shadowed Blair on almost every trip of his premiership, said: 'In 1972 Blair was a long-haired wannabe rock star and music promoter, hanging out around west London clubs and music venues with business partner Alan Collenette in a battered old blue van. But it would be a mistake to assume that the terrible events of that year passed him by or that an apparently gilded life had left him unaware of bitter sectarian tensions or the actions of the British Army. He was acutely aware of The Troubles and later recalled watching the nightly horrors on television. His interest was also personal.'[21] Blair's mother, Hazel Corscadden, was born in the flat above her grandmother's hardware shop on Main Street, Ballyshannon, Donegal. The family were fiercely Protestant – Blair's grandfather had been a Grand Master of an Orange Order lodge – and his grandmother's last words to him were: 'Whatever you do, son, never marry a Catholic.' Which of course, he did.[22] Blair would holiday in Ireland most years visiting friends and family – until 1969. The visits stopped. Hazel had decided it was too dangerous, and in the few letters Blair received from friends later he was aghast at the slide into bigotry they displayed.[23] Perhaps it explained what was sometimes characterised as his 'messianic' approach to the peace process. Fast-forward more than twenty-five years and Blair needed pushing into announcing a new public inquiry into the events of Bloody Sunday – partly because it was yet another demand and partly because he genuinely believed such inquiries rarely proved useful. However, under pressure from the Irish government and the tide of nationalist opinion, he conceded. He was graceful enough to admit later: 'The report when published proved me wrong. It had been worth it.'[24]

On 29 January 1998, the families, survivors and campaigners gathered to hear Tony Blair announce the establishment of a new public inquiry into the events of Bloody Sunday.[25] Blair criticised the rushed process in which Widgery failed to take evidence from those wounded and did not personally read eyewitness accounts: 'The timescale within which Lord Widgery produced his report means he was not able to consider all the evidence available. Since his report was published much new material has come to light about the events of that day. It is the interests of everyone that the truth is established and told.'[26] He went on: 'We believe that the weight of material now available is such that the events require re-examination. We believe that the only course that will lead to public confidence in the results of any further investigation is to set up a full-scale judicial inquiry into Bloody Sunday.'[27] The inquiry would be headed by the eminent British law lord Lord Saville of Newdigate and two judges from Commonwealth countries, and it would have the legal power to subpoena witnesses and compel the disclosure of documents. The prospect of a fresh investigation formed part of the peace process negotiations and was viewed by many as a concession to Sinn Féin.[28]

The IRA declared another ceasefire as part of the ongoing negotiations towards ending violence and finding a political settlement that would be acceptable to both the nationalist and Loyalist communities, and the Irish and the British governments. The Good Friday Agreement (GFA), or Belfast Agreement, was signed on 10 April 1998 after three days of intensive talks during which Tony Blair effectively locked up the warring parties overnight and would not let them out until they had reached an agreement.[29] That agreement paved the way for a power-sharing assembly in Northern Ireland. It declared that Northern Ireland was part of the United Kingdom and would remain so until a majority of the people both of Northern Ireland and of the Republic of Ireland wished otherwise. Should that happen, then the British and Irish governments are under 'a binding obligation' to implement that choice. The agreement committed the participants to 'exclusively democratic and peaceful means of resolving differences on political issues'. This involved both the decommissioning of weapons held by paramilitary groups, and the normalisation of security arrangements in Northern Ireland. Both the British and Irish governments committed to the early release of prisoners serving sentences in connection with the activities of paramilitary groups, provided that those groups continued to maintain 'a complete and unequivocal ceasefire'. Cases were reviewed individually. There was no amnesty for crimes which had not been prosecuted.

A referendum on the Good Friday Agreement saw 71 per cent of people in the North voting in favour. Elections to a new Northern Ireland Assembly took place in June and a new power-sharing executive was due to be appointed the following year.

In a historic address to the Irish Parliament, Blair said that it was 'Time for the gun and the threat of the gun to be taken out of politics once and for all; for decommissioning to start. I am not asking anyone to surrender. I am asking everyone to declare the victory of peace. In Belfast or Dublin, people say the same thing: make the agreement work. It is never far from my mind. My sense of urgency and mission comes from the children in Northern Ireland. I reflect on those who have been victims of violence, whose lives are scarred and twisted through the random wickedness of a terrorist act, on those who grow up in fear, those whose parents and loved ones have died. And I reflect on those, who though untouched directly by violence, are nonetheless victims – victims of mistrust and misunderstanding who through lack of a political settlement miss the chance of new friendships, new horizons, because of the isolation from others that the sectarian way of life brings. I reflect on the sheer waste of children taught to hate when I believe passionately children should be taught to think. Don't believe anyone who says the British people don't care about the peace process. People in my country care deeply about it, are willing it to work. And in our two countries, it is not just the politicians who have a role to play. No one should ignore the injustices of the past, or the lessons of history. But too often between us, one person's history has been another person's myth. We need not be prisoners of our history. My generation in Britain sees Ireland differently today and probably the same generation here feels differently about Britain. We can understand the emotions generated by Northern Ireland's troubles, but we cannot really believe, as we approach the twenty-first century, there is not a better way forward to the future than murder, terrorism and sectarian hatred.'[30] Tragically, there were some who still disagreed with that.

Dissident republicans were intent on derailing the peace process, particularly hardliners who in October the previous year had broken away to form what they called the Real IRA with the intention of carrying on the armed struggle. They did so in a way which appalled millions. The group drove a bomb-laden saloon car into the busy town centre of Omagh, County Tyrone, on 15 August 1998. The 500-lb bomb exploded mid-afternoon when the town was crowded with families shopping. The bomb killed twenty-nine people, including a woman pregnant with twins, and injured some 220 others, making it the deadliest single incident of the Troubles. Telephoned warnings had been sent almost forty minutes beforehand but were inaccurate, and police had inadvertently moved people toward the bomb. The victims came from both sides of the community, Protestant and Catholic, Unionist and nationalist. The explosion burst a water main and sent a rush of water along the side of the street. An eyewitness described how the running water picked up human body parts and carried them along. She said: 'There were people, or actually pieces of people, bodies being washed in … they were basically piling up at the corner where the gully was … bits and pieces of legs, arms, whatever, were floating down the street.' A bus driver ferried some of the injured to hospital. He later described the journey: 'It was like a scene from hell. I wasn't able to drive fast because people were screaming in pain. As we went over the ramps into the hospital, I could hear the roars of pain.' Another eyewitness said: 'There were limbs hanging off, bodies being carried on doors, everything was chaotic. Then just as the bus was about to leave, the door opened and someone handed in a severed arm. I think that was just too much for the driver. I think he cried all the way to the hospital.'[31]

There was a wave of grief throughout the whole of Ireland and a sense of fury at the bombers who were continuing their campaign against the wishes of the people who had overwhelmingly endorsed the peace process in the referendum a few months earlier. The Omagh parish priest, Father Thomas Canning, said: 'I really don't know how the town of Omagh is ever going to come to terms with this awful catastrophe.' For a while, everyone held their breath fearing that the Good Friday Agreement and the move towards peace might fail, with a return to sectarian violence. Instead, the bomb seemed to galvanise everyone to work even harder. Sinn Féin president Gerry Adams urged the dissidents to give peace a chance and condemned the bombing, saying: 'I am totally horrified by this action. I condemn it without any equivocation whatsoever.' Martin McGuinness, who was Sinn Féin's chief negotiator in the peace process, said: 'This appalling act was carried out by those opposed to the peace process.' The Omagh bombing meant that the IRA came under added pressure to decommission its weapons, but the negotiations remained on track. The public outrage seemed to get through to the dissidents who issued an apology and then announced a ceasefire, although they did return to violence again later.

A few weeks after the bombing, US President Bill Clinton and Tony Blair arrived in Omagh to meet the 700 people who were injured and the families of those who had died. Clinton had devoted a great deal of his presidency to the peace process and Blair was similarly committed to finding a lasting, political solution. Within a month of Omagh it was clear that the bombers had failed in their attempts to derail the peace negotiations when Unionist leader David Trimble and Sinn Féin president Gerry Adams met for direct talks the first time. It wasn't necessarily a cordial meeting – they pointedly did not shake hands – but at least they were talking, and peace campaigners breathed a sigh of relief.[32]

The aftermath of the Omagh bombing sparked a series of controversies. There were allegations that the security forces in Ireland, Britain and the US had intelligence that could have prevented the bombing but failed to hand it over to the police. Police Ombudsman Nuala O'Loan held an inquiry into the RUC's handling of the Omagh bombing. Her report criticised them for failing to act on crucial intelligence and said they had ignored previous warnings about a bomb. The report said: 'The victims, their families, the people of Omagh and officers of the RUC were let down by defective leadership, poor judgement and a lack of urgency.' The Chief Constable of the RUC, Ronnie Flanagan, was furious with the findings and called the report 'grossly unfair'. He described it as 'an erroneous conclusion reached in advance and then a desperate attempt to find anything that might happen to fit in with that'.

Blair and Taoiseach Bertie Ahern agreed to cooperate to bring the bombers to justice but there have been no successful convictions. Twelve men were arrested on 22 September 1998 by the Gardai and the RUC but they were later released without charge. A conviction against another alleged bomber was quashed on appeal. On 15 March 2000, the families of the twenty-nine Omagh victims began a civil case against five men named in a BBC *Panorama* programme as being responsible for the bombing. On 8 June 2009, they were awarded £1.6m damages against four of the men. The fifth man was cleared of involvement.

Meanwhile, Lord Saville was ploughing on with his inquiry and the Bloody Sunday families continued their long, hard campaign to win posthumous justice for their loved ones.

8

The Saville Inquiry

'a catastrophe for the people'

The Bloody Sunday Inquiry took twelve years and cost almost £200 million, making it the longest and most expensive public inquiry in British legal history.[1] Its remit was to determine 'the events on Sunday 30 January 1972 which led to loss of life in connection with the procession in Londonderry on that day, taking account of any new information relevant to events on that day'. Those terms were almost identical to those set for Widgery, but the outcome was to be very, very different.

The inquiry was established under the Tribunals of Inquiry (Evidence) Act 1921 and chaired by Lord Saville. Born in 1936, Mark Oliver Saville, Baron Saville of Newdigate, was on paper at least just as much an Establishment figure as Widgery, but the nature of the Establishment had changed under Tony Blair's New Labour administration. Educated at a grammar school, he saw post-war National Service with the Royal Sussex Regiment in the mid-1950s, rising to second lieutenant. After that he graduated with a first-class honours Oxford degree in law. He was called to the Bar in 1962, becoming Queen's Counsel in 1975 and a High Court judge ten years later.[2] Married with two sons, his hobbies included sailing, flying and computers, and enjoying the company at London's Garrick Club.[3] His two eminent Commonwealth colleagues on the inquiry panel were less well-known in Britain, then as now. Born in Christchurch in 1928, Sir Edward Jonathan Somers QC was a New Zealand jurist and member of the Privy Counsel. William Lloyd Hoyt QC, born in 1930, was a Canadian lawyer and judge.

A driving force behind the inquiry was its Counsel, Christopher Clarke. Regarded by senior QCs as a man of a formidable legal skill, his intellect earned him the nickname 'Two Brains'. It was his task to deliver the inquiry's opening statement which lasted forty-two days and 1.25 million words – by far the longest in UK legal history. He made clear the inquiry was seeking to discover what really happened on Bloody Sunday. In his opening speech he said: 'What happened – whatever the truth of the matter – was a tragedy, the pain for which many have endured down the passage of years. The tribunal's task is to discover as far as humanly possible in the circumstances, the truth. It is the truth as people see it. Not the truth as people would like it to be, but the truth, pure and simple, painful or unacceptable to whoever that truth may be.'[4]

Except for some senior officers who gave evidence under their own names, military and security force witnesses were granted anonymity to protect them and their families. They were given ciphers – alphabetical for those who had fired rounds and lettered for those who had not. Civilians who had formerly been members of the Official or Provisional IRA or otherwise had connections with the republican movement were also given ciphers – numbers preceded by the organisation's acronym (for example, OIRA 1).

The Saville Inquiry proved a more comprehensive study than Widgery, interviewing a wide range of witnesses, including local residents, soldiers, journalists and politicians. Lord Saville declined to comment on the Widgery report and stressed that his probe was a judicial inquiry into Bloody Sunday, not Widgery. 'We are not sitting as a court of appeal from the Widgery Inquiry,' he said. 'It would be foolish for us to ignore the fact that there are allegations that some of those concerned in the events of Bloody Sunday were guilty of very serious offences, including murder.'[5] The inquiry proper opened with words from the chair: 'My name is Mark Saville. I am an English Law Lord.' Ulster TV correspondent Mark McFadden reported: 'That opening statement was delivered in the Guildhall in Derry. The location was symbolic. It was the destination chosen by anti-internment protesters on January 30th 1972... Few events in the dark history of Northern Ireland's Troubles have created such division, controversy, political dispute and intrigue. When Lord Saville entered the Guildhall there was a sense of anticipation. A sense that we were venturing into strange, new lands.' McFadden later broadcast: 'Saville knew from the start that his Inquiry was playing for high stakes. The reputation of the military and political establishment would be challenged by his investigation. But the spectre of Widgery could be felt throughout Saville's investigation. This new inquiry would not be quick and fast like Widgery. Saville would be painstaking and careful, examining not just the Bloody Sunday shootings but the events that led to them and also the wider political and military background of the early 1970s.'[6]

The inquiry opened properly in 2000 when formal public hearings began at the Guildhall. It held public hearings on 116 days over the first year, clocking up more than 600 hours of evidence, the vast majority of which was from eyewitnesses. Meanwhile, Somers resigned from the inquiry in 2000, and died of cancer two years later in his hometown of Christchurch. He was replaced by John Toohey QC, a former Australian High Court judge.

In August 2000, the inquiry ordered the soldiers who had opened fire to return to Derry to give their evidence. However, in December the Court of Appeal overruled that and accepted that the former soldiers would be in danger from dissident republicans should they return to Northern Ireland. The government demanded that the military witnesses and senior politicians should give their evidence in London. Such interventions, together with a general widening of the inquiry, meant that it dragged on years over-schedule.

The inquiry heard that there may be a 'wall of silence' in Derry over what exactly members of the Provisional IRA were doing on the day. The allegations persisted when a witness in February 2001 refused to name a man he said had fired at soldiers. After months of speculation, Sinn Féin's Martin McGuinness announced that he would give evidence to the inquiry. He stated that he was second-in-command of the Derry City brigade of the Provisional IRA and was present at the march. It was alleged at the inquiry that McGuinness was responsible for supplying detonators for nail bombs on Bloody Sunday. Paddy Ward claimed he was the leader of PIRA youth wing Fianna Eireann and also claimed that McGuinness and another anonymous PIRA member gave him bomb parts on the fateful morning. He said his organisation intended to attack city centre premises in Derry that day. In response McGuinness rejected the claims as 'fantasy', while Gerry O'Hara, a Sinn Féin councillor, stated that he and not Ward was the Fianna leader at the time.

By the time of the inquiry, McGuinness had risen from IRA commander in the Bogside to Deputy First Minister in Stormont. He had always refused to speak openly about his IRA past, so his appearance as a witness at the Bloody Sunday Inquiry in 2003 was a major media event. He said there were around forty–fifty Provisionals in Derry at the time. He told the inquiry the PIRA saw itself as in a state of war with British forces. Asked by Christopher Clarke if this meant shooting them, McGuinness replied: 'Absolutely, yes.' But on Bloody Sunday he claimed that PIRA in Derry obeyed orders not to attack soldiers at what was to be a peaceful demonstration against internment. 'The orders to the volunteers were very clear and the orders were that under no circumstances whatsoever were they to engage with the British army during the course of the civil rights protest,' he said.[7]

Bishop Daly repeated his affirmation that the protesters had not been armed, that armed men were likely present, but did nothing that would prompt the Army to open fire, and that soldiers had fired without warning on people who were fleeing or rushing to help the wounded. He said that the inquiry had left him 'full of hope' that justice would finally be served. Daly added: 'Certainly there was no threat posed to the army at the time they opened fire, none. I don't think there was any justification for it.'[8]

In her evidence to the inquiry, the republican Bernadette McAliskey (née Devlin) accused the government of murdering fourteen unarmed civilians in Derry on Bloody Sunday, and claimed the killings triggered almost three decades of conflict. She said that she had started her political career as a pacifist but changed her mind that day to support violence against the state. She denied, however, ever playing an active part. 'Three thousand and more coffins followed and years of imprisonment and torture and pain and sorrow, and it is highly arguable that without Bloody Sunday, where we are today we would have been in 1972,' she said. 'I cannot forgive the British government for that. The British army declared war on the people seeking justice in this country on that day.' She told Saville she did not believe a state-run inquiry could bring to book those she believed to be to blame. The only proper forum, she said, was the international court of justice in the Hague – 'somewhere else where the accused is not running the party'. She went on: 'It is, on the basis of personal experience, my honest belief that, at the highest level, British government, military and significant sections of the media acquiesced, conspired, organised and/or participated in and covered up terror and murder for political gain on 30 January 1972, and repeatedly thereafter.' She said she had no doubt the Army did all the shooting, but she had no idea whether the IRA moved all its weapons out of the Bogside before the march. Nor at the time did she know Martin McGuinness. She said: 'I keep feeling that I am being drawn further and further into matters of no consequence that I believe at the end of the day will become part of a great big cloud that will confuse the final issue: that the British government of the day ordered the army to shoot the citizens. That to me is all that matters.'[9]

Colonel Derek Wilford, however, claimed his soldiers had been fired at from several positions and had been attacked with petrol bombs and acid. He insisted the paratroopers had acted professionally and told the tribunal he saw or heard nothing which led him to believe paratroopers were out of control at any stage on Bloody Sunday. 'Nor did I see any shameful and disgraceful acts,' he said.[10]

Mike Jackson, by then the Army's most senior officer, found his appearance before the Saville Inquiry shrouded in controversy. The inquiry had uncovered a handwritten document composed by the then Captain Jackson within hours of the Bloody Sunday shootings. In this document, left inside an unlocked cabinet in a Derry army base, Jackson claimed the paratroopers shot at gunmen and bombers. He told Lord Saville: 'If it is to be suggested that there was attempt by anyone to sanitise ... a true version of events, for whatever reason, I would emphatically reject such a suggestion.'[11]

Many civilian witnesses were worried about a demand by the soldiers' lawyers for intelligence reports on them. Saville assured them that such information would not be brought up in cross-examination.[12] Many observers alleged that the Ministry of Defence acted in a way to impede the inquiry.[13] Over 1,000 army photographs and original army helicopter video footage were never made available. Additionally, guns used on the day by the soldiers that could have been evidence in the inquiry were lost by the MoD.[14] The ministry claimed that all the guns had been destroyed, but some were subsequently recovered in foreign locations such as Sierra Leone and Beirut.[15]

In 2002 the inquiry relocated to Westminster's Central Hall to hear evidence from former British Army soldiers who had claimed their lives would be endangered if they travelled to Derry.[16] Journalist Peter Oborne was not alone in labelling the inquiry a 'shambles'. He suggested that while 'most people ... accept that in Northern Ireland the only way forward is by casting a veil of obscurity over the past', the Saville Inquiry marked the 'one exception to this rule: the British army' whose 'conduct ... is being put under a microscope'.[17]

The judges finished hearing evidence on 23 November 2004 after more than 900 testimonies but reconvened once again on 16 December to listen to testimony from another person, known as Witness X, who had been unavailable earlier.[18]

UTV's Mark McFadden said: 'For journalists, the Inquiry has been a remarkable and exhausting journey. We have seen testimony from ex-Prime Minister Edward Heath and from former head of the Army General Sir Mike Jackson. We have listened to evidence from former IRA members including Martin McGuinness who spoke publicly for the first time about his role within the Provisional IRA. We have seen families reduced to tears as they saw and heard for the first time the Paratroopers who killed their loved ones. The witness stand at Saville became a "Who's Who?" of politics and the church, soldiering and terrorism. At the heart of it all, day after day, month after month, year after year, sat the Bloody Sunday families. When Saville concluded his investigation only one parent of the thirteen shot on Bloody Sunday remained alive. The remainder died waiting on their relatives to be cleared of wrong-doing. The families adopted the motto: "Set the Truth free". But Saville's lead counsel Sir Christopher Clarke made plain that the Truth can be difficult ... Saville's final report may not mark the end of the Bloody Sunday crusade, but it's an important step towards leaving Bloody Sunday to history. Thirty-eight years ago those anti-internment marchers never made it to the Guildhall. But their story goes out from there...'[19]

Several more years of sifting through the mountain of evidence, verbal and written, followed. In 2006 John Reid, while Home Secretary, queried soaring legal fees, prompting speculation that the inquiry had become a slow, lumbering, legal gravy train. In July that year a minister let slip that the expected cost could top £400 million, sparking suspicions it was aimed at blocking calls for another inquiry, this time into the 7/7 London terror bombings. Blair's official spokesman later agreed that costs had run out of control, saying that the inquiry had taken a 'long time and cost an awful lot of money'. Tory spokesman David Lidington said the costs were 'scandalous'. He cited Tory figures suggesting the inquiry has cost everyone in the country £6.64, while the forecast total could have financed a year's salary for more than 15,000 nurses, nearly 5,000 doctors and 11,000 policemen, or thirteen extra Apache helicopters for troops in Iraq and Afghanistan. In the event, the final cost – although hugely more than originally envisaged – was just under half the leaked figure.

The expected publication debate was pencilled in for the end of 2007, or possibly early 2008, by over-optimistic ministers and Whitehall bureaucrats. On 8 February 2008, Northern Ireland Secretary Shaun Woodward revealed that the inquiry was still costing £500,000 a month even without hearings, and that the total cost by the previous December was £181.2 million – more than half of which was spent on legal bills, and the report itself was set to run to more than 5,000 pages. The likely publication date was put back to the second half of 2008. But in November, Saville himself estimated at least another year of work. That too proved wildly optimistic. Saville put the deadline back another year to March 2010, a delay which he admitted was 'extremely disappointing'.

Woodward icily said he had been 'profoundly shocked' by the new delay, adding: 'I am concerned at the impact on the families of those who lost loved ones and those who were injured'.[20]

The Saville report was indeed handed to government lawyers on 24 March 2010, twelve years after the inquiry was established. The government lawyers then checked it for evidence which might pose a threat to 'national security'. The report was given to new Secretary of State Owen Paterson, who had replaced Woodward, who then had to decide an appropriate publication date. John Kelly, whose brother Michael was killed on Bloody Sunday, said the families feared the report 'will fall victim to selective leakage and other partisan usage long before the full report sees the light of day' and urged Paterson to publish as quickly as possible. On 26 May 2010 it was announced that the report would be published on 15 June. The media emphasised the financial cost and length of the inquiry, and the ways in which that could overshadow its legal and moral value.[21]

Legal affairs correspondent Joshua Rozenberg struck a note of cautious complaint: 'The Bloody Sunday report will no doubt be welcomed by the families of those killed when British troops opened fire in Derry more than thirty-eight years ago. But it will not be welcomed by the legal establishment, which regards Lord Saville's inquiry into the events as an embarrassing failure of the judicial process and the waste of a promising career. There is no doubt that the first judicial inquiry into Bloody Sunday was perfunctory. Completed two-and-a half months after the day on which thirteen civil rights demonstrators were killed, with another person dying of injuries later, it ran to just thirty-nine pages. While none of those killed or wounded was "proved to have been shot while handling a firearm or bomb", the former Lord Chief Justice had "a strong suspicion that some others had been firing weapons or handling bombs in the course of the afternoon". Clearly, unspecified allegations such as these should not be allowed to stand unless they can be justified. If there is proof individual soldiers behaved recklessly, they should be identified and the others exonerated. If there is evidence that demonstrators had been handling firearms or explosives, they should be named and the others cleared.

'But the antidote to a report that was too short is not one that is too long. By all accounts, Lord Saville's report will be too large to publish in the traditional way and certainly too lengthy to read and absorb in the seven-and-a-half hours ahead of formal publication that has been offered to those most closely involved. Nobody asked Saville to go into such detail. On the contrary, parliament told him that the subject of his inquiry was a matter of "urgent public importance". That was more than twelve years ago. And Saville's report will be published some five years later than he had predicted. Saville's gross under-estimate of the time it would take to complete, for which he has never offered an adequate explanation, hardly inspires confidence. I understand that at least one former soldier may face a police investigation and possible charges arising from the inquiry. He should not have had to wait so long to find out where he stands, just as other troops and civil rights campaigners should have been cleared much more quickly. Never again will we see a judicial inquiry that has lasted so long or cost so much. Nor can we expect any truly independent judicial inquiries in future. Five years ago, parliament passed legislation that gives a government minister power to change a judicial inquiry's terms of reference. If it acts outside those terms, the minister may sack the judge or cut off his funding. Other killings in Northern Ireland provided the impetus for the 2005 legislation. But it is hard to escape the conclusion that ministers thought the Bloody Sunday inquiry was running out of control. Any judge asked to conduct an inquiry in future – such as the one William Hague has promised into torture allegations – should study the reaction to Saville's report this month before deciding whether to give up the day job.'[22]

Shortly before publication, it was announced that the following October soldiers from the Parachute Regiment would return to Helmand Province, Afghanistan, for the third time in four years. Commanders feared the report could cause a 'morale-damaging backlash' against the British Army if it was not viewed in the context of the violence and chaos that engulfed Northern Ireland in 1972. While there should be no attempt to justify the killing of civilians by British paratroopers, senior defence officials emphasised that the events of Bloody Sunday were 'a tragedy which belonged to another era' and should not reflect badly on the present day's armed forces.[23]

The *Independent*'s David McKittrick wrote: 'Northern Ireland has, of course, been transformed since 1972. Today Mr McGuinness is second-in-command of Northern Ireland's Government. But Bloody Sunday is still part-history, part-current affairs. Lord Saville has a much better chance of producing a report that might command the sort of widespread acceptance that Lord Widgery's never did. Yet it is unlikely that his conclusions will satisfy everyone: those who are unshakably convinced that British ministers ordered a deliberate massacre of innocent civilians will not be satisfied. There will certainly be much debate on a venture which has generated such a gigantic amount of documentation. In paper form the material is said to fill a lorry. No one yet knows, however, whether this colossal exercise will unearth what most can accept as the truth, bring closure to the bereaved, and at last lay to rest the ghosts of Bloody Sunday.'[24]

On the morning of 15 June 2010, thousands of people walked the path that the civil rights marchers had taken on Bloody Sunday, holding photos of those who had been shot.[25] The families of the victims received advance copies inside the Guildhall.[26] John Kelly, whose brother was among the dead, said: 'When 'Soldier F', the person who murdered Michael, came into London to give his evidence I remember that morning before I went to the hearing getting on my knees in the hotel and praying to Michael and my mother and father to help me get through that day.' Kelly said it was ironic that the Saville report would be officially announced by a Conservative prime minister in the Commons, given that it was a previous Tory government that ordered the paras into Derry. 'State murder happened in this city and the British government has to answer for that,' he said. 'The present government has to accept that this is the truth. The prime minister should say that.' Damien Donaghey, wounded in the firing and branded a nail-bomber by the Army, said: 'I can feel it building up inside me. But it will be a weight off my mind once it's over and a relief ... well, maybe ... hopefully.'[27] By then, around half of the injured survivors had died and never got to see the end of the inquiry.

The Saville report proved to be a demolition job of Widgery, finding that soldiers lied about their actions and falsely claimed to have been attacked.[28] It agreed that all of those shot were unarmed, that none were posing a serious threat to life or injury, that no bombs were thrown and that soldiers 'knowingly put forward false accounts' to justify their firing.[29] Soldiers had repeatedly denied on oath shooting the named victims and also denied shooting anyone by mistake. Saville was having none of that. The contrast between the Saville report and Lord Widgery's whitewash could hardly have been more stark. Widgery largely exonerated British soldiers and condemned the victims; Saville condemned the soldiers and exonerated their victims. Widgery reported that there was 'not a shred of evidence' to support claims that 1 Para was sent in to give Derry residents a 'rough handling'. Saville found that Army Commander Major General Robert Ford 'referred in particular to the "Derry Young Hooligans" as a factor in the continued destruction of the city and expressed the view that the army was "virtually incapable" of dealing with them. He also expressed the view that he was coming to the conclusion that the minimum force required to deal with the

"Derry Young Hooligans" was, after clear warnings, to shoot selected ringleaders.'[30] Widgery accepted that 1 Para's Colonel Wilford did not exceed his orders. Saville said: 'Colonel Wilford either deliberately disobeyed Brigadier MacLellan's order or failed for no good reason to appreciate the clear limits on what he had been authorised to do. He was disturbed by the delay in responding to his request to mount an arrest operation and had concluded that, by reason of the delay, the only way to effect a significant number of arrests was to deploy Support Company in vehicles into the Bogside.'[31] Widgery ruled that there was no breach of Army discipline. Saville found that 'soldiers reacted by losing their self-control and firing themselves, forgetting or ignoring their instructions and training and failing to satisfy themselves that they had identified targets posing a threat of causing death or serious injury ... our overall conclusion is that there was a serious and widespread loss of fire discipline among the soldiers of Support Company.'[32]

On the key question of who fired first, Widgery said he was 'entirely satisfied' that soldiers were the first targets. Saville concluded: 'Despite the contrary evidence given by soldiers, we have concluded that none of them fired in response to attacks or threatened attacks by nail or petrol bombers. No one threw or threatened to throw a nail or petrol bomb at the soldiers on Bloody Sunday.' Widgery praised the quality of military testimony which he believed to be truthful apart from 'one or two exceptions'. Saville said: 'In the course of the report we have considered in detail the accounts of the soldiers whose firing caused the casualties, in the light of much other evidence. We have concluded, for the reasons we give, that apart from Private T many of these soldiers have knowingly put forward false accounts in order to seek to justify their firing.'[33]

Later in the report, Saville said: 'We appreciate that soldiers on internal security duties, facing a situation in which they or their colleagues may at any moment come under lethal attack, have little time to decide whether they have identified a person posing a threat of causing death or serious injury; and may have to make that decision in a state of tension or fear. It is a well-known phenomenon that, particularly when under stress or when events are moving fast, people often erroneously come to believe that they are or might be hearing or seeing what they were expecting to hear or see. We have borne this in mind when assessing the state of mind of the soldiers responsible for the casualties. It is also possible that in the sort of circumstances outlined in the previous paragraph, a soldier might fire in fear or panic, without giving proper thought to whether his target was posing a threat of causing death or serious injury.' On the issue of false accounts, the report added: 'We have also borne in mind that the fact that a soldier afterwards lied about what had happened does not necessarily entail that he fired without believing that he had identified a person posing a threat of causing death or serious injury, since it is possible that he was at the time convinced that he was justified in firing, but later invented details in an attempt to bolster his account and make it more credible to others. We have borne this possibility in mind when seeking to decide whether or not each of the soldiers of Support Company who fired and whose shots killed or injured civilians believed, when he did so, that he was justified in firing.'[34]

The report concluded that an Official IRA sniper fired on British soldiers, although on the balance of evidence his shot was fired after the Army shots that wounded Damien Donaghey and John Johnston. The inquiry rejected the sniper's account that this shot had been made in reprisal, stating the view that he and another Official IRA member had already been in position, and the shot had probably been fired simply because the opportunity had presented itself. Ultimately the Saville Inquiry was inconclusive on Martin McGuinness's role, due to a lack of certainty over his movements, concluding that while he was 'engaged in paramilitary activity' during Bloody Sunday, and had probably been armed with a Thompson sub-machine gun, there was insufficient evidence to make any finding other than they were 'sure that he did not engage in any activity that provided any of the soldiers with any justification for opening fire'.[35]

Saville conceded: 'When shooting breaks out in an urban area, as it then did, it is often difficult or impossible to establish who is firing, from where the firing has come, in what direction it is going, and the type of weapon being used. The same applies to explosions and we have little doubt that the sound of the firing of baton rounds could in some circumstances have been mistaken for the explosion of bombs. In Londonderry these factors were magnified by what was known as "the Derry sound", which was the echoing effect created by the City Walls and adjacent buildings (including the high Rossville Flats) and which could multiply the sound of gunfire and explosions and create false impressions of the direction from which these sounds were coming. In circumstances such as we have described, there is a risk that soldiers, mistakenly believing themselves or their colleagues to be under lethal attack, lose their self-control, forget or ignore their training and fire without being satisfied that they have identified a person posing a threat of causing death or serious injury.'[36]

The report stated: 'The firing by soldiers of 1 PARA on Bloody Sunday caused the deaths of thirteen people and injury to a similar number, none of whom was posing a threat of causing death or serious injury.' It went on: 'The immediate responsibility for the deaths and injuries on Bloody Sunday lies with those members of Support Company whose unjustifiable firing was the cause of those deaths and injuries.' Saville stated that British paratroopers 'lost control', fatally shooting fleeing civilians and those who tried to aid the civilians who had been shot by the British soldiers.[37] Saville stated that the civilians had not been warned by the British soldiers that they intended to shoot. The report states, contrary to the previously established belief, that none of the soldiers fired in response to attacks by petrol bombers or stone-throwers, and that the civilians were not posing any threat. Saville said British soldiers should not have been ordered to enter the Bogside area as 'Colonel Wilford either deliberately disobeyed Brigadier MacLellan's order or failed for no good reason to appreciate the clear limits on what he had been authorised to do'. The report stated five British soldiers aimed shots at civilians they knew did not pose a threat and two other British soldiers shot at civilians 'in the belief that they might have identified gunmen, but without being certain that this was the case'.[38]

Of those in charge of army operations, Saville's verdict was mixed. Major General Ford, the commander of land forces who set the British strategy to oversee the civil march in Derry, was broadly cleared, but his selection of 1 Para, and in particular that of Colonel Wilford to be in control of arresting rioters, was found to be disconcerting, specifically as '1 PARA was a force with a reputation for using excessive physical violence, which thus ran the risk of exacerbating the tensions between the Army and nationalists'. Wilford was found to have 'deliberately disobeyed' his superior Brigadier Patrick MacLellan's orders by sending Support Company into the Bogside and without informing MacLellan. Wilford's front-line subordinate, Major Ted Loden, was cleared of misconduct; Saville said that Loden 'neither realised nor should have realised that his soldiers were or might be firing at people who were not posing or about to pose a threat'. The inquiry found that Loden could not be held responsible for claims, malicious or otherwise, by some of the individual soldiers that they had received fire from snipers.[39]

Captain Mike Jackson, the second in command of 1 Para on the day, was cleared of 'sinister' actions following his compiling of a list of what soldiers told Major Loden on why they had fired. This list became known as the 'Loden List of Engagements' which played a role in the Army's initial explanations. Brigadier Pat MacLellan, the operational commander, was cleared of any wrongdoing as he was under the impression that Wilford would follow orders by arresting rioters and could not be blamed for Wilford's actions. Intelligence officer Colonel Maurice Tugwell and army press officer Colin Wallace were also cleared of wrongdoing. Saville believed the information they released through the media was not down to any deliberate attempt to deceive the public but rather due to much of the inaccurate information they received at the time.[40]

Regarding individual soldiers, Saville concluded that Private R, who probably shot Jackie Duddy as he was running away, possibly 'fired in a state of fear or panic, giving no proper thought to whether his target was posing a threat of causing death or serious injury'. Margaret Deery was probably shot by Lance Corporal V, again possibly 'in a state of fear or panic, without giving proper thought to whether his target was posing a threat of causing death or serious injury'.[41] Michael Bridge was probably shot by Lieutenant N, once again possibly 'in a state of fear or panic, without giving proper thought to whether his target was posing a threat of causing death or serious injury'. Such verdicts were levelled at Private Q who shot Michael Bradley, and Sergeant O, Private R and Private S who fired the shots that indirectly injured Patrick McDaid and Pius McCarron.[42] But such 'excuses' did not apply to other soldiers whose behaviour was scrutinised in dept by Saville.

Lance Corporal F, who killed Michael Kelly as he cowered behind a rubble barricade, 'did not fire in panic or fear, without giving proper thought to whether he had identified a person posing a threat of causing death or serious injury. We are sure that instead he fired either in the belief that no-one at the rubble barricade was posing a threat of causing death or serious injury, or not caring whether or not anyone at the rubble barricade was posing such a threat'.[43] Later the report said: 'We have no doubt that Lance Corporal F shot Patrick Doherty and Bernard McGuigan, and it is highly probable that he also shot Patrick Campbell and Daniel McGowan. In 1972 Lance Corporal F initially said nothing about firing along the pedestrianised area on the southern side of Block 2 of the Rossville Flats, but later admitted that he had done so. No other soldier claimed or admitted to firing into this area. Lance Corporal F's claim that he had fired at a man who had (or, in one account, was firing) a pistol was to his knowledge false. Lance Corporal F did not fire in a state of fear or panic. We are sure that he fired either in the belief that no-one in the area into which he fired was posing a threat of causing death or serious injury, or not caring whether or not anyone there was posing such a threat.'[44]

Claims by Corporal P, Lance Corporal J and Corporal E that they fired at armed men in Rossville Street, killing William Nash, John Young and Michael McDaid, were rejected by Saville. The report said: 'We are sure that these soldiers fired either in the belief that no-one in the areas towards which they respectively fired was posing a threat of causing death or serious injury, or not caring whether or not anyone there was posing such a threat.' The same was true of Private U who fatally wounded Hugh Gilmour as he was running away from the soldiers. Either Private L or Private M shot and mortally wounded Kevin McElhinney as he was also crawling away from the soldiers, probably on the orders of either Colour Sergeant 002 or Corporal 039 or both. The unidentified soldier who shot and injured Alexander Nash while he was tending his dead or dying son William at the rubble barricade 'could not have believed that he had or might have identified someone posing a threat of causing death or serious injury'.[45]

Along with Lance Corporal F, Saville identified Corporal E, Private G and Private H as the soldiers who went into Glenfada Park North, between them killing William McKinney and Jim Wray, injuring Joe Mahon, Joe Friel, Michael Quinn and Patrick O'Donnell, and possibly injuring Daniel Gillespie. All claimed that they had identified and shot at people in possession of or seeking to use bombs or firearms. The report said: 'In our view none of these soldiers fired in the belief that he had or might have identified a person in possession of or using or about to use bombs or firearms. All four soldiers denied shooting anyone on the ground, but Jim Wray was shot for a second time in the back, probably as he lay mortally wounded.' Private G shot Gerard McKinney in Abbey Park; his shot passed through this casualty and mortally wounded Gerald Donaghey. Private G may not have been aware that his shot had had this effect but falsely denied that he had fired in Abbey Park.[46]

Saville found that Support Company fired in all over 100 rifle rounds on Bloody Sunday after they had gone into the Bogside but 'with the probable exception of shots fired by Sergeant O at what he described as a gunman on a balcony of Block 3 of the Rossville Flats, we found no instances where it appeared to us that soldiers either were or might have been justified in firing'. In comparison, Saville found that outside of Support Company, no other members of 1 Para fired a single shot, including those who had also gone into the Bogside on foot.[47]

In a key section of the report's final chapter, Saville said: 'We have concluded that the explanation for such firing by Support Company soldiers after they had gone into the Bogside was in most cases probably the mistaken belief among them that republican paramilitaries were responding in force to their arrival in the Bogside. This belief was initiated by the first shots fired by Lieutenant N and reinforced by the further shots that followed soon after. In this belief soldiers reacted by losing their self-control and firing themselves, forgetting or ignoring their instructions and training and failing to satisfy themselves that they had identified targets posing a threat of causing death or serious injury. In the case of those soldiers who fired in either the knowledge or belief that no-one in the areas into which they fired was posing a threat of causing death or serious injury, or not caring whether or not anyone there was posing such a threat, it is at least possible that they did so in the indefensible belief that all the civilians they fired at were probably either members of the Provisional or Official IRA or were supporters of one or other of these paramilitary organisations; and so deserved to be shot notwithstanding that they were not armed or posing any threat of causing death or serious injury.'

In a damning final line, the report said: 'What happened on Bloody Sunday strengthened the Provisional IRA, increased nationalist resentment and hostility towards the Army and exacerbated the violent conflict of the years that followed. Bloody Sunday was a tragedy for the bereaved and the wounded, and a catastrophe for the people.'[48]

In the House of Commons, Conservative prime minister David Cameron acknowledged, among other things, that the paratroopers had fired the first shot, had fired on fleeing unarmed civilians, and shot and killed one man who was already wounded.[49] He described what British soldiers had done as 'both unjustified and unjustifiable, it was wrong'.[50] He also said that this was not a premeditated action, though 'there was no point in trying to soften or equivocate' as 'what happened should never, ever have happened'. Cameron then apologised on behalf of the British government.[51] A survey later found that 61 per cent of Britons and 70 per cent of Northern Irish agreed with Cameron's apology.[52]

Relatives of the civilians who were fatally shot by the British soldiers gave a 'thumbs up' to the crowd which gathered outside the Guildhall to hear the conclusions of the report and to listen to Cameron's apology. The statement on behalf of the families declared: 'The victims have been vindicated. The Parachute Regiment has been disgraced. The truth has been brought home at last. Widgery's great lie has been laid bare.' Crowds of people applauded upon hearing that apology broadcast live on a giant screen which had been erected in the city. They did so again when it became clear that police would open a murder investigation into the killings.

Historian Paul Bew wrote: 'It is astonishing to think that when the tribunal, chaired by Lord Saville, began its work in 1998, David Cameron was not even in Parliament. Now, thirty-eight years after the event itself, Bloody Sunday has come back to haunt another British prime minister.'[53] After reading Saville, even observers who were natural supporters of the British Army now regarded Widgery as discredited. The conservative historian and commentator Max Hastings, for example, described the Widgery report as 'a shameless cover-up'.[54]

Protestant church leaders were warmly applauded in Catholic Bogside in an historic gesture they hoped would help bridge the city's traditional divide. Church of Ireland Bishop of Derry Ken Good said people now needed to seize on the new opportunity to heal differences after the findings of the Saville Inquiry. Along with the moderator of the Presbyterian Church, the Reverend Norman Hamilton, and Methodist Church president the Reverend Paul Kingston, Bishop Good met with victims' families at a monument to the dead. There, the church leaders handed the relatives a replica of Maurice Harron's *Hand Across the Divide* sculpture which stands at the west end of the city's Craigavon Bridge. Bishop Good said a cloud had been lifted from Derry during the momentous scenes at the city's Guildhall, giving an historic opportunity for bitter rivalries to be settled. 'I want us to have a more open, more transparent, a more natural and a more easy relationship with one another in this town that we all love so well,' Bishop Good said. And in a reference to the Phil Coulter song about the city's troubles he added: "We don't want there to be a divide.'[55]

But the Saville report, and its implications for future prosecutions, did not receive universal acclaim. Many were dismayed that blame was ring-fenced around one officer, Derek Wilford, and a number of rank-and-file soldiers and did not place any blame on the military and political elite. The finding on Gerald Donaghey – that he was 'probably' carrying nail bombs when he was shot, but that this did not justify his shooting – was also met with some shock. Saville's qualification of his innocence left his family without the full relief felt by others.[56]

The *Daily Mail* said that Cameron's apology was following an example set by Labour of 'sealing off nagging historic disputes by saying sorry'.[57] Labour MP Harriet Harman said that while the report spoke for itself, many disparate groups would regrettably identify enough in it to justify a predictable 'flogging of traditional hobby horses'.[58] One lawyer representing soldiers involved in the enquiry claimed that Saville 'cherry picked' the evidence in his inquiry and felt under pressure to give a verdict that was not borne out by the available evidence.[59]

This view was later echoed by a former paratrooper who wrote that the Saville report was one-sided and did not reflect events of the day as he experienced them.[60]

General Sir Mike Jackson said Saville's findings had left him with a 'sense of shock'. He rejected accusations he had been responsible for concocting a false account of what happened on the day, which claimed the victims were bombers and gunmen. 'I don't lie. I gave evidence on oath to Lord Saville. I am afraid rather more has been made of the mechanical compilation, the first attempt to put together a sequence of firing on that dreadful afternoon has resulted in this allegation,' he said. 'The purpose of what I did – which was actually copying out somebody else's list, I was a scribe not an author – was not some sort of cover-up at all. I am sorry if anybody senses a conspiracy. There was not.'[61]

Political responses also followed a wearingly familiar sectarian line. Ulster Unionist Party leader Sir Reg Empey criticised the inquiry itself, questioning the benefit of reliving the 'darkest years' of Northern Ireland's history after forty years, and also contrasting the £200 million probe into thirteen deaths with the lack of any comparable inquiries into the deaths of people at the hands of paramilitary groups during the same period. That was echoed by Protestant correspondents who claimed that the report created an unjust hierarchy in which the victims of Bloody Sunday were unfairly elevated above the more numerous victims of IRA violence.[62]

Battle-hardened Colonel Richard Kemp said his immediate instinct on hearing the findings of the Saville Inquiry was that guilty soldiers should be jailed for a long time. 'I think that the actions we have heard described are much more like the actions of Nazi stormtroopers than British paratroopers,' he said. Kemp, who commanded all British troops in Afghanistan, initially thought the full wrath of the law should come down on the killers. But he argued that, on further refection, the death toll was really the fault of the British state rather than the individuals concerned. 'We have also seen under the Good Friday Agreement a large number of terrorist murderers let off and let out of prison early and in some cases not prosecuted,' the former terrorism advisor to the Prime Minister said. 'All these things need to be taken into account when the Director of Public Prosecutions weighs up whether or not it is in the public interest to imprison these people.'[63]

Northern Ireland's Public Prosecution Service (PPS) said it was investigating, along with Crown prosecutors, whether witnesses committed perjury at the inquiry. 'The PPS has now received a copy of the Saville Report which refers to certain witnesses providing evidence to the inquiry which was knowingly untrue,' a spokesman said. 'It is noted that some evidence was given to the inquiry sitting in London. The PPS will consider in consultation with the Crown Prosecution Service where jurisdiction lies in regard to any possible offences that arise.' Earlier, Michael Mansfield QC, who represented the families of some of the victims, urged prosecutors to bring charges against soldiers accused of lying to the inquiry as Saville had concluded that some members of the Parachute Regiment 'knowingly put forward false accounts' to justify opening fire on unarmed protesters. Mansfield said that while witnesses to the inquiry were given immunity from prosecution if they incriminated themselves in evidence, that did not cover false testimony. He went on: 'Given the strength and clarity of the conclusions ... the Director of Public Prosecutions should consider whether it is so serious – because the rule of law has been flagrantly breached on this occasion by a number of soldiers on a number of UK citizens – that consideration should be given to a prosecution.'[64]

When, many years later, the question of prosecutions finally came to a head, Lord Saville insisted that his inquiry had not been 'a question of prosecutions'. Instead, he told the BBC, the purpose was simply 'to try to find out what happened'.[65]

9

Bloody Culture

'broken bottles under children's feet'

Bloody Sunday sparked an outpouring of artistic and cultural effort. Some of it may have been opportunistic, exploitative and moronically simplistic, but much of it was motivated by a genuine, deep-felt mixture of compassion and rage. And, helped by its catchy, two-word title, it ensured that the event remained in the public consciousness for generations. First out were two of the newly disbanded Beatles pop group.

Paul McCartney, of Irish descent on his mother's side and later knighted, recorded 'Give Ireland Back to the Irish' just two days after the event. Written with his wife Linda and recorded at Abbey Road Studios, it was the debut single of their new post-Beatles group Wings. It was the band's first song to include Protestant Ulster lead guitarist Henry McCullough.

The lyrics, tame from today's perspective but apparently dynamite at the time, include the lines: 'And he dreams of God and country/ And he's feeling really bad/ And he's sitting in a prison/ Say, should he lie down, do nothing'.

McCartney had spent Christmas and New Year in New York visiting his wife's family and rebuilding his relationship with former bandmate and co-writer John Lennon after bitter feuding since the break-up of the Beatles. McCartney was appalled at the unfolding events he watched on TV the following day and immediately began writing the song. He was also inspired by being around Lennon and the politically radical mood of Greenwich Village where Lennon and Yoko Ono were living. McCartney later recalled: 'I wasn't really into protest songs – John had done that – but this time I felt that I had to write something, to use my art to protest.'[1] Before leaving New York for London, McCartney arranged a session with Wings to rush-record the single. Having never released an overtly political song before, McCartney was condemned by the British media for his seemingly pro-IRA stance. Music critics regarded the lyrics as overly simplistic and an attempt by him to gain credibility for his new band on the back of a pressing political issue.[2] The single was banned in the UK by the BBC, the Independent Television Authority and Radio Luxembourg, and was shunned by most US radio outlets. It peaked at number 16 on the UK singles chart and 21 on the US Billboard Hot 100 but topped the national chart in Ireland. John Peel, one of the few British DJs to support McCartney, said: 'The act of banning it is a much stronger political act than the contents of the record itself. It's just one man's opinion.'[3]

McCartney later said: 'From our point of view, it was the first time people questioned what we were doing in Ireland. It was so shocking. I wrote 'Give Ireland Back to the Irish', we recorded it and I was promptly 'phoned by the Chairman of EMI, Sir Joseph Lockwood, explaining that they wouldn't release it. He thought it was too inflammatory. I told him that I felt strongly about it and they had to release it. He said, "Well it'll be banned", and of course it was. I knew 'Give Ireland Back to the Irish' wasn't an easy route, but it just seemed to me to be the time to say something.' The pop magazine *Melody Maker* summed up his response to the ban: 'Up them! I think the BBC should be highly praised, preventing the youth from hearing my opinions.'[4] While rehearsing at his home, McCartney told an ABC reporter that he did not plan to focus on politics in his work, but that 'on this one occasion I think the British government overstepped the mark and showed themselves to be more of a sort of oppressive regime than I ever believed them to be'. Wings performed the song throughout their February 1972 campus tour and when asked by a reporter whether the shows were fundraisers for the IRA, McCartney said: 'We're simply playing for the people.' McCullough's brother Samuel was beaten up in an Irish pub in Kilburn, North London, following a row about the song.[5]

There was a widely held suspicion amongst fans and critics that the song was McCartney's attempt to impress John Lennon who, unlike himself, had been vocal in his support for Irish republicanism. Music critic Chris Ingham said of the Wings single: 'The record managed to irritate everyone, not least for its naive, simplistic attitude to a complex situation … but also for its musical mediocrity. The BBC banned the record, granting it a notoriety disproportionate to its importance.'[6]

New Musical Express critic Bob Woffinden described the song as in the mould of 'Lennon's least successful diatribes'. He added that McCartney's song 'gave the appearance of being an exploitation single every bit as much as "tribute" singles that are rushed out in the wake of the death of a star name'. He added that Lennon would soon 'do far worse'.[7] That comment may have been harsh, but it was prophetic.

John Lennon's 1972 album *Some Time in New York City* featured 'Sunday Bloody Sunday' in direct response to the event and 'The Luck of the Irish' which dealt with the overall conflict. The lyrics of the former were a lot harsher than McCartney's and included the lines: 'Well, it's always Bloody Sunday in the concentration camps/ Keep falls road free forever from the bloody English hands/ Repatriate to Britain, all of you who call it home'.

Lennon, also of Irish descent, had the previous August joined a 'troops out' protest in London shortly before moving to New York.[8] As the lyrics showed, he responded to the Derry shootings with rage. Lennon explained: 'Here I am in New York and I hear about the thirteen people shot dead in Ireland and I react immediately. And being what I am I react in four-to-the-bar with a guitar break in the middle. I don't say "My God, what's happening? We should do something." I go "It's Sunday Bloody Sunday and they shot the people down." It's all over now. It's gone. My songs are not there to be digested and pulled apart like the Mona Lisa. If people on the street think about it, that's all there is to it.'[9]

Beatles biographer John Blaney felt that Lennon's need to express his disgust at the incident caused him to write a song that is 'a piece of pro-Republican propaganda that ignored the historical facts in favour of emotional blackmail'. Blaney felt that the lyrics supporting the Irish republican movement were hypocritical given the movement's own history of violence and Lennon's prior expressed commitment to pacifism.[10] Music critic Paul du Noyer similarly described it as too simplistic to address the complexity of the issues, although he acknowledged that they were 'heartfelt'.[11] Journalist Robin Denselow wrote that 'the suggestions at the end of *Sunday Bloody Sunday* that the problem be solved by shipping back to Britain the Protestants who had lived in Ulster for more than 300 years were scandalous, naive and even racist. Lines like "You anglo pigs and scotties sent to colonise the North", "Repatriate to Britain all of you who call it home" or (worst of all) "Internment is no answer, it's those mothers' turn to burn" simply weren't worthy of Lennon, especially with his concern with racial problems, and his earlier avowed pacifism'.[12]

Lennon donated the royalties from the song to the civil rights movement in Northern Ireland and spoke at a protest in New York in support of the victims and families of Bloody Sunday. The song was covered by the Irish nationalist band The Wolfe Tones on their 2004 album *The Troubles*. They toned down the lyrics, removing 'English pigs' and 'concentration camps' and replacing the last verse with a verse that called on the British government to apologise for its long-term treatment of the Irish.

The British heavy metal band Black Sabbath swiftly got in on the act with *Sabbath Bloody Sabbath* on their 1973 eponymous fifth album. The track was written by Geezer Butler, of Irish descent, who later wrote: 'the Sunday Bloody Sunday thing had just happened in Ireland, when the British troops opened fire on the Irish demonstrators... So I came up with the title "Sabbath Bloody Sabbath", and sort of put it in how the band was feeling at the time, getting away from management, mixed with the state Ireland was in'. The core music was branded as 'the riff that saved Black Sabbath' because Tony Iommi, who wrote most of the band's music, had been suffering from writer's block. The band's management rented the supposedly haunted Clearwell Castle to inspire him.[13]

Folk/rock singer-songwriter Roy Harper's song 'All Ireland', written in the days following Bloody Sunday despite his being confined by illness, raged at the military action but then looked at solutions. He wrote later that his message was 'there must always be some hope that the children of "Bloody Sunday", on both sides, can grow into some wisdom'.[14]

More than a decade after the event, the Irish rock band U2 came up with 'Sunday Bloody Sunday' – not to be confused with Lennon's song – as the opening track from their album *War* which was released as the album's third single in March 1983 in Germany and the Netherlands. It remains one of U2's most overtly political songs, its lyrics describing the horror felt by an observer of killings. The song helped U2 reach a wider listening audience and was generally well received by critics.[15] It has remained a staple of the band's live concerts, and became one of its signature tunes, but it drew controversy from its earliest performances, with lead singer Bono having to constantly stress its anti-sectarian message.

The song had grown from a guitar riff and lyric written by The Edge during a period of depression and Bono had reworked the lyrics after an encounter with Provisional IRA supporters in New York City. U2 manager Paul McGuinness, purely as a gimmick, made arrangements for the band to appear in the city's St Patrick Day's Parade but found that there was a possibility that IRA hunger-striker Bobby Sands, who had starved to death behind bars the previous year, would be the parade's honorary absent marshal. McGuinness and the band, feeling that IRA tactics were prolonging the violence, decided to withdraw. McGuinness met with one of the parade's organizers in a New York bar to arrange the cancellation and ended up in a heated debate about the IRA. McGuinness recalled: 'He kept telling me to keep my voice down. The place was full of New York policemen – Irish cops – and he thought I was going to get us killed.'[16] The band recorded the song at Windmill Lane Studios in Dublin. It consciously took the standpoint of someone horrified by the cycle of violence in the province. Early versions opened with the line 'Don't talk to me about the rights of the IRA, UDA.' U2 bassist Adam Clayton confirmed that better judgment led to the removal of such a politically charged line, and that the song's 'viewpoint became very humane and non-sectarian ... which, is the only responsible position'.[17]

Drummer Larry Mullen said in 1983: 'We're into the politics of people, we're not into politics. Like you talk about Northern Ireland, "Sunday Bloody Sunday", people sort of think, "Oh, that time when thirteen Catholics were shot by British soldiers"; that's not what the song is about. That's an incident, the most famous incident in Northern Ireland and it's the strongest way of saying, "How long? How long do we have to put up with this?" I don't care who's who – Catholics, Protestants, whatever. You know people are dying every single day through bitterness and hate, and we're saying why? What's the point? And you can move that into places like El Salvador and other similar situations – people dying. Let's forget the politics, let's stop shooting each other and sit around the table and talk about it... There are a lot of bands taking sides saying politics is crap, etc. Well, so what! The real battle is people dying, that's the real battle.'[18] U2 were aware when they recorded 'Sunday Bloody Sunday' that its lyrics could be misinterpreted and could even put them in danger.

The band were particularly nervous about playing the song in Belfast, and at the Maysfield Leisure Centre, Bono stated 'It's not a rebel song'. He attempted to further clarify this point by reciting the entire second verse and adding: 'If you don't like it, you let us know.'[19] The Edge recalled that 'the place went nuts, it drew a really positive reaction', also saying that 'We thought a lot about the song before we played it in Belfast and Bono told the audience that if they didn't like it then we'd never play it again. Out of the 3,000 people in the hall about three walked out. I think that says a lot about the audience's trust in us.'[20]

In November 1987, during a long-renowned concert at McNichols Sports Arena in Denver, Colorado, Bono interrupted the song to condemn the Remembrance Day bombing in Enniskillen: 'And let me tell you somethin'. I've had enough of Irish Americans who haven't been back to their country in twenty or thirty years come up to me and talk about the resistance, the revolution back home ... and the glory of the revolution ... and the glory of dying for the revolution. Fuck the revolution! They don't talk about the glory of killing for the revolution. What's the glory in taking a man from his bed and gunning him down in front of his wife and his children? Where's the glory in that? Where's the glory in bombing a Remembrance Day parade of old age pensioners, their medals taken out and polished up for the day. Where's the glory in that? To leave them dying or crippled for life or dead under the rubble of a revolution that the majority of the people in my country don't want. No more!'[21]

The song has been covered or adapted by numerous singers and groups, including Ignite, Paramore, The Roots and Jay-Z. In 2010, *Rolling Stone* ranked 'Sunday Bloody Sunday' 272nd on its list of its 500 greatest songs of all time, while the Rock and Roll Hall of Fame named it as one of the 500 songs that shaped rock and roll. 'Sunday Bloody Sunday' was commemorated in Christy Moore's *Minds Locked Shut* on the album *Graffiti Tongue* and named the dead civilians; the Celtic metal band Cruachan included the song 'Bloody Sunday' in their 2004 album *Folk Lore*; and in 2010 the band T with the Maggies released the song 'Domhnach na Fola' (Bloody Sunday) on their debut album.

Irish poets took the tragic event as inspiration – Thomas Kinsella's 1972 poem 'Butcher's Dozen' was a furiously satirical response to the Widgery tribunal and Seamus Heaney's 1981 work 'Casualty' castigated Britain.

Playwrights also saw Bloody Sunday as prime material for the stage. Brian Friel's 1973 *The Freedom of the City* took the viewpoint of three civilians.[22] Friel had completed the first version of his play ten months before Bloody Sunday and set it in 1970 in the aftermath of a civil rights meeting. It follows protesters who mistakenly find themselves in the mayor's parlour in the Guildhall and the authorities mistakenly assume it is an 'occupation'. The play illustrated their final hours in the Guildhall, their failed escape and the tribunal into their deaths. Friel took part in the NICRA march and saw some of the ensuing mayhem. He then adapted the play to ensure the audience recognised resonances with Bloody Sunday. Still set in 1970 Derry, the play interweaves the deaths of the three unarmed citizens at the hands of the security forces, the reaction of the population, and a judge's verdict that the shootings were justified and that the victims were armed. *The Freedom of the City* was first performed at the Abbey Theatre, Dublin, on 20 February 1973 with the anti-hero leads taken by Niall O'Brien, Dermot Crowley and Colm Meaney.[23]

In 2005 journalist Richard Norton-Taylor distilled four years of evidence-taking into the two-hour play *Bloody Sunday: Scenes from the Saville Inquiry*. It opened in London's Tricycle Theatre to glowing reviews. The *Times* critic pronounced it 'devastating'; the *Independent* called it 'a necessary triumph'; and the *Daily Telegraph*'s critic wrote: 'I can't praise this enthralling production too highly ... exceptionally gripping courtroom drama.'[24] The play portrayed the 'greater human experience of the Inquiry'. He continued: 'The layout of the Guildhall and the equipment they had, the money they had, and the suits and the boots and the accents, the way they were seated and the way they spoke, the permission that had to be gained in order to say or not to say, and the conflict between the counsel and the witnesses and the judges... The Imperium had arrived in one of the provincial cities and it just spoke theatre to me. I also felt that one of the impacts of the Saville Inquiry was a narrowing of the language into a very narrow legal discourse, and I kept feeling there would be opportunities for expanding that. The legal process is vital and essential, but I think there are other processes, in particular those that use the imagination, that can assist in a wider salving of the hurts that an event like Bloody Sunday has left with individuals and the community.'[25] The production was later adapted as a BBC radio drama. A key line was: 'Thirteen shot dead. Fifteen wounded and injured. There's arithmetic for you. One-three. One-five. Two-eight. Could be a phone number. Something you'd dial and it would ring out all over the world. Ring and ring and ring and keep on ringing until somebody, somebody answered.'

Two 2002 television films clashed unfortunately in the timings of their broadcasts, weakening to some extent their impact. First out – by a few days – was Granada TV's *Bloody Sunday*, written and directed by Paul Greengrass. It portrayed the events of the day through the eyes of Ivan Cooper, played by James Nesbitt. The actor, like the real-life SDLP MP and march organiser, is an Ulster Protestant. A departure from his previous largely comedic roles, the film was a turning point in his career – he won a British Independent Film Award and was nominated for a Bafta for best actor. The film was inspired by Don Mullan's influential book *Eyewitness* and was shot mainly in Ballymun, North Dublin, but some location scenes were shot in

Derry, in Guildhall Square and in the Creggan on the actual route of the march. The soundtrack contains only one piece of music, a live version of U2's 'Sunday Bloody Sunday', which plays over the closing credits. In recognition of the role his book played in getting the Saville Inquiry set up, his book's inspiration for the movie, and the fact that he was a schoolboy witness to the tragedy, Don Mullan was asked by director Greengrass to appear as a Bogside priest. Gerry Donaghy was played by Declan Duddy, nephew of Jackie Duddy, one of those killed. A number of the military characters were played by ex-members of the British Army, including Simon Mann – later jailed for his part in a failed coup in Equatorial Guinea – who played Colonel Wilford. General Ford was played by Tim Pigott-Smith, Brigadier Maclellan by Nicholas Farrell, Chief Superintendent Lagan by Gerard McSorley, and Eamonn McCann by Gerard Crossan, while Bernadette Devlin was played by Mary Moulds.

Shot documentary style with hand-held cameras, the film is gritty and realistically confusing with the viewing audience left to work out who is who and what is happening. The first third intercuts the preparations of the march organisers and the paras, the middle section covers the march and massacre in roughly real time, and the final third propels the view into the grief-stricken aftermath as families swamp the local hospital in search of their loved ones. In the film, General Ford is portrayed as ruthless and determined to teach the 'hooligans' a lesson they will not forget, Brigadier McLellan as decent but ineffectual, Colonel Wilford as a cold-hearted professional, and Superintendent Lagan as desperate to avoid a bloodbath. The soldiers are shown as, by turn, scared, gung-ho and pumped up by adrenalin. The script has one – 'Private Lomas' – shocked by the murder of civilians but forced to lie by both peer pressure and the chain of command in his witness statement. The film's events gel largely with the narrative supplied by Saville almost a decade later, with a few exceptions. They include soldiers planting nail bombs on Gerry Donaghy as he lies dead in a car, and two scenes in which local people wrestle guns off IRA men. A scene in which, after the massacre, young men queue to collect rifles from a PIRA arsenal may be fanciful in its depiction but is broadly accurate in portraying the boost it gave to the paramilitaries.

It premiered at the Sundance Film Festival on 16 January, a few days before its screening on ITV on 20 January, and then in selected London cinemas from 25 January. The film was critically acclaimed, winning the Audience Award at Sundance and the Golden Bear at the Berlin International Film Festival plus the Hitchcock d'Or best film prize at the Dinard Festival of British Cinema.[26] The Rotten Tomatoes website gave it a review aggregate of 92 per cent and its consensus reads: 'Bloody Sunday powerfully recreates the events of that day with startling immediacy.'[27]

Film critic Roger Egbert wrote that the subject is 'still an open wound in the long, contested history of the British in Northern Ireland'. He went on: 'Cooper is played by Nesbitt as a thoroughly admirable man, optimistic, tireless, who walks fearlessly through dangerous streets and has a good word for everyone. He knows the day's march has been banned by the British government but expects no trouble because it will be peaceful and non-violent. As Cooper hands out leaflets in the streets, Greengrass intercuts preparations by the British army, which from the top down is determined to make a strong stand against "hooliganism". More than two dozen British soldiers have been killed by the Provisional IRA in recent months, and this is a chance to crack down ... Greengrass re-creates events with stunning reality. Communications are confused, orders are distorted as they pass down the chain of command, and soon rubber bullets and gas grenades are replaced by the snap of real bullets.'[28]

Bloody Sunday appeared eight days before writer Jimmy McGovern's TV film on the same subject, *Sunday*, and McGovern criticised Greengrass's film for concentrating on the leadership of the march, and not the perspective of those who joined it.[29] *Sunday*, produced by Sunday Productions for Channel 4, screened on 25 January 2002 and directed by Charles McDougall, indeed dramatised the events through the eyes of the families of the dead and injured, specifically those of Leo Young, older brother of John Young. Also, unlike the Greengrass film, it covered events prior to Bloody Sunday, and subsequent events up to and including the Widgery Tribunal. Transmission was followed by a live studio debate about the issues involved.

The crew filmed the majority of its scenes in Derry itself; streets and open spaces where the actual events happened were used, including William Street, the Creggan, Craigavon Bridge and Harvey Street, where Father Daly was filmed waving a bloodstained handkerchief escorting men carrying Jackie Duddy. Cairan McMenamin and Barry Mullan played Leo and John Young, Paul Campbell played Jackie Duddy, Christopher Eccleston played General Ford, Sean Chapman played Brigadier McLellan, Brian Devlin played Father Daly, Stephen McCole played Para F, and Corin Redgrave played premier Ted Heath. The film was the debut of Clare Crockett, who gave up acting to become a nun and died aged thirty-three during missionary work in Ecuador in 2016.[30]

Liverpool-born McGovern, then best known for his psychological crime series *Cracker*, had been a teacher in deprived areas and well knew the mean streets his pupils lived in. McGovern was a regular visitor to Northern Ireland when researching his script which, like his earlier drama-documentary *Hillsborough* on the Liverpool FC disaster, focused on heroic families trying to both get justice and clear their loved ones' names.[31] Director McDougall was renowned then for his groundbreaking TV series *Queer as Folk,* and later for *Desperate Housewives* and *Sex and the City*.

The film, like Greengrass's, is gritty and realistic, although the most emotionally charged of the two. But it fashionably plays around with continuity and employs slick cinematic tricks such as using Derry girl Dana's Eurovision Song Contest hit *All Kinds of Everything* on the soundtrack. The Establishment figures are cartoonishly cynical and morally corrupt. A drunken para, for example, grins at TV coverage of grieving relatives and bawls: 'Can't you take a fucking joke.' Widgery is reptilian and General Ford completely callous. The action scenes are masterful, however, and the funeral scene provides a masterclass of the compassionate observation of grief.

In a later article, McGovern wrote: 'A rule I stick to: you don't write drama-docs to further your career. You write them because the victims or their families have asked you to write them. Yet another rule I stick to: those in power hate drama-docs, because the camera goes to places where they do not want it to go.' After he made a drama-documentary on a Liverpool dock strike, Gaslight Productions 'asked me to write the story of Bloody Sunday. I had been asked before but always refused, arguing that it was a story that should be told by the Irish themselves. But this time I travelled over to Derry and met a few of the bereaved families. It was then I realised that Bloody Sunday was our story, too. A story of how, in 1970-71, we faced the prospect of rampant Irish republicanism. We went in hard and that brought about the thing we most feared: rampant Irish republicanism. It was, I realised, a classic tragedy of colonial power (currently being replayed in Iraq). I felt that, as a son of the colonial power, I had every right to tell that story and so I began work.

'I interviewed in their homes all the families of the dead, all bar three of the wounded, eyewitnesses and former IRA men. In Britain and Belfast, I interviewed British soldiers who were there on the day. More than sixty people in total; Katy Jones went on to interview 100 more. Frankly, it was the kind of effort that puts the Guardian and the rest of the British press to shame. When I was two years into that three-year process, Paul Greengrass arrived in Derry. He, too, was going to tell the story of Bloody Sunday. In fact, he had already completed the first draft of a script based on Don Mullan's excellent book, Eyewitness Bloody Sunday. Now, I'm not attacking Paul Greengrass, a fine film-maker, when I say that he did not feel the need to interview the people whose story he was telling; he had adopted a different approach. Little wonder, therefore, that his film, Bloody Sunday, and ours, Sunday, were very different: his, loosely based on a book, focused on a politician trying to keep two warring factions apart; ours, based on personal testimony, focused on the people on whom a drama-doc should always focus: the victims and their families.

'I have never knocked Greengrass's version in public. I'm not going to knock it now. Two Englishmen fighting over an Irish bone is an appalling spectacle. But a recent Guardian interview with Paul appeared to knock ours, so we have to defend it. Sunday was the most meticulously researched drama that British television has ever seen. We (Gaslight Productions, Box TV, Channel 4, Katy Jones and myself) stand by every word of it.'[32]

Stephen Gargan, the film's co-producer and director of *Gaslight Productions* in Derry, said the story was one that had to be told: 'We wanted to communicate the local truth about Bloody Sunday to a wider audience... I think the film made, and continues to make, a contribution to telling that story and communicating that story to a wider audience. In particular, I think we tried as best we could within the confines of television to humanise the people who were killed that day, and to give the wider public a better understanding of the impact on families and on communities when a loved one is taken from them. Myself and Jimmy McGovern initially started with the families and then moved out to the surviving wounded and then witnesses and IRA members, and we had a parallel research team running in England talking to former British soldiers and other personnel, so the script was very much grounded in fact. But beyond that we were trying to get to an emotional truth and a factual truth, and I think that's the power of a drama documentary, in that it can communicate that emotional truth.' Of the funeral scenes, he added: 'It was a very cold night, and we had all the coffins laid out and people started to carry them towards St Mary's church. The individual families actually formed up behind their own particular coffin, and in some parts helped to carry them, and if you look at the scenes now you do see actual family members in them. I think they felt themselves that they were making a contribution to their own family's story.'[33]

Mark Cunliffe, giving the film four stars, wrote: 'McGovern's script is very impressive and effective; minor details like the sole coming away from a shoe will take on greater, tragic significance, whilst details like a wounded father having to watch his son's funeral on TV from his hospital bed, whilst being subjected to an RUC officer's questions, have the air of poignant, bewildering authenticity.'[34] The IMDb website concluded: 'Told primarily from the perspective of the Derry community, juxtaposed with the British Army/state's preparations and reaction to the day, *Sunday* communicates the forensic and emotional truth of what happened.'[35]

10

The Decision to Prosecute

'We are the victims here.'

The Police Service of Northern Ireland (PSNI) began a murder investigation in 2010 headed by its Legacy Investigations Branch which focused on eighteen former paratroopers. One of those soldiers died in 2018, and a decision on whether or not to prosecute the other seventeen for criminal offences dragged on into 2019. All sides held strong views apart from, it seemed, the main author of the damning report which had sparked the probe.

Lord Saville, when asked if he accepted that without it the prospect of former soldiers being prosecuted may not have happened, he said: 'I simply don't have the answer. The campaign by the families was for a new inquiry. Some thought that those soldiers who were found responsible should be prosecuted but overall the campaign for Bloody Sunday originally was for an inquiry to find out what happened and why, rather than a question of prosecutions.' Former soldiers were granted anonymity and assured that their evidence to the Saville Inquiry wouldn't be used in any subsequent criminal proceedings. 'If we had not given those assurances, backed by the director of public prosecutions, people could quite legitimately have refused to answer questions on the grounds that answering might incriminate them,' he said. 'So, we were there to find out what happened rather than investigating criminal offences. We sought assurance and gave it to those people, which is protected in law.' When asked if he, like many, took the view that the Saville report would draw a line under Bloody Sunday, he replied: 'I didn't know what was likely to happen. We hoped the inquiry would help the situation in Ireland and I think and hope it did to a degree. The question as to whether it draws a line under events or whether there should be prosecutions is not one for me, it's one for politicians and prosecuting authorities. If people want more and feel that justice can only be served by prosecutions against those that they believe to be responsible, then that is a matter again on which I can't really comment. I think we did a pretty thorough job and I was satisfied we had done a fair job at finding out what happened that day as was realistically possible. Our job was to do as thorough and fair a report as we could as to what happened on that day.'[1]

Hard-line Unionists and Loyalist paramilitaries championed the paras for their own purposes as the investigation dragged on. In 2012 a serving British Army soldier from Belfast was charged with inciting hatred against a surviving relative of the deceased with social media to promote sectarian slogans about the killings while featuring banners of the Parachute Regiment logo. In January 2013, shortly before the annual Bloody Sunday remembrance march, two Parachute Regiment flags appeared in Loyalist areas of Derry. They were condemned by the Ministry of Defence and removed to be replaced by Union Flags.[2] In the run-up to the Loyalist marching season in 2013 the flag of the Parachute Regiment appeared alongside other Loyalist banners in other parts of Northern Ireland. In 2014 Loyalists in Cookstown erected similar flags close to the route of a St Patrick's Day parade. In November 2015, a sixty-six-year-old former para was arrested for questioning over the deaths of William Nash, Michael McDaid and John Young. He was released on bail shortly after.[3] And so it went on, illustrating ongoing tensions long after the Good Friday peace agreement.

Forty-seven years after Bloody Sunday, in March 2019, the PNSI finally brought murder charges against one former British soldier for the murders of James Wray and William McKinney, and for the attempted murders of Patrick O'Donnell, Joseph Friel, Joe Mahon and Michael Quinn. It emerged that Soldier F – the lance corporal condemned for his actions by Saville – had joined the Parachute Regiment in 1966 and left the Army in 1988. The former soldier admitted firing thirteen rounds on Bloody Sunday in Derry in 1972. The Saville Inquiry stated that there was 'no doubt' Soldier F had shot Patrick Doherty and Bernard McGuigan, both unarmed. Soldier F admitted at the inquiry he had shot Michael Kelly, saying he had only fired at people with bombs or weapons, a claim rejected by the inquiry. Anonymity orders – covering the seventeen soldiers and two suspected Official IRA men who were investigated – remained in place.[4] The ex-paratrooper was identified as 'Dave' by eyewitness accounts and faced a seventh supporting charge of the attempted murder of a person or persons unknown on the day he fired thirteen bullets. The PNSI said there was insufficient evidence to prosecute sixteen other soldiers and two Official IRA men, all of whom had been investigated since the publication of the Saville report.[5] PSNI Director Stephen Herron said: 'It has been a long road for the families ... and today will be another extremely difficult day for many of them. We wanted to meet them personally to explain the decisions taken and to help them understand the reasons.'[6]

The reasons behind the decision to bring charges against Lance Corporal F for murder and attempted murder on Bloody Sunday – and not against other members of the Parachute Regiment – were set out. One of the central issues was that evidence presented to the Saville Inquiry could not be relied upon for a criminal trial. Additionally, the standard of proof for conviction in a court – beyond reasonable doubt – is different to the inferences that the inquiry could make.

The PSNI said: 'A court would not permit the prosecution to rely upon the majority of the previous accounts provided by the soldiers as evidence against them in a criminal trial. This is because of the circumstances in which they were obtained [often by military authorities without a caution being administered]. This has meant that, when applying the test for prosecution in these cases, a large volume of material that played a central role at the inquiry was not available to us in order to support potential prosecutions.'

In its section on the shootings by soldiers in Glenfada Park North and Abbey Park, the PNSI said: 'In relation to Soldier F it has been concluded that there is a reasonable prospect of conviction and Soldier F is to be prosecuted for the murders of James Wray and William McKinney [as well as] the attempted murders of Joseph Friel, Michael Quinn, Joe Mahon and Patrick O'Donnell.' Altogether four soldiers were reported in connection with those casualties: soldiers F, H, G and E. Soldiers G and Soldier E had since died. The statement added: 'In relation to Soldier H the position was that there was no evidence capable of proving that he fired upon entering Glenfada Park North (in other words, when these casualties were sustained) other than his own inadmissible accounts. In these circumstances there was no reasonable prospect of conviction and a decision was taken not to prosecute Soldier H.'

The prosecutors, referring to army shootings in the car park area at the front of the Rossville Flats where Jackie Duddy died, admitted: 'A fundamental difficulty in relation to this sector was in attributing responsibility for the various casualties to particular soldiers. The Bloody Sunday inquiry, with the benefit of much material that would not be admissible in criminal proceedings, was able only to say that a particular soldier probably shot a particular casualty.' It added: 'The prosecution was not able to identify sufficient admissible evidence to prove with any degree of certainty the actions of the soldiers in this sector. In some cases the only evidence of what individual soldiers did was contained within their own accounts – which are inadmissible against them. In other cases there was evidence from their co-accused – but it was concluded that this evidence would be inadmissible against the soldiers or that, even if it was admissible, it did not provide evidence of criminal conduct."[7]

The Bloody Sunday families, some of whom had expected up to four paratroopers to be charged, had gathered in the Guildhall to hear the decision and immediately vowed to legally challenge the decision which they described as a 'slap in the face' for their justice campaign. At a press conference in the Guildhall the families said the full cost of Bloody Sunday 'cannot be measured just in terms of those who suffered that day but must also be measured in terms of those who suffered because of that terrible day'.[8]

Linda Nash, whose nineteen-year-old brother William was shot dead, said she felt 'let down by a law and a justice system that's supposed to protect people. I'm feeling devastated. The most difficult thing I had to do today was to call my children and tell them that there are no prosecutions for their granda and uncle. My heart is broken. I am devastated. This is our worst day since Bloody Sunday. But we will dust ourselves down and the fight will go on. I left home certain that I would get justice for Willie. I am shocked, absolutely gutted, that I did not. I am delighted for the Wray and McKinney families, but the decision is a huge slap in the face for the rest of us. But we have no intention of giving up.'[9]

John Kelly, whose seventeen-year-old brother Michael was killed, said: 'It is unbelievable that only Soldier F will be prosecuted. It is scandalous. In my view every one of them should be prosecuted for murder and attempted murder. We had heard rumours that there would be four – and we were disappointed at the thought of that – but I am totally devastated in the fact that Soldier F has got away with Michael's murder. We have walked a long journey since our fathers and brothers were brutally slaughtered on the streets of Derry on Bloody Sunday. Over that passage of time all of the parents of the deceased have died. We are here to take their place. Bloody Sunday was not just a wanton act carried out by a trained army against defenceless civil rights activists. It also created a deep legacy of hurt and injustice and deepened and prolonged a bloody conflict unimaginable even in those dark winter days of 1972.'

Michael McKinney, whose brother William was the victim of one of the two murders Soldier F was charged with, said he shared the disappointment of the other Bloody Sunday relatives, while they shared his family's relief. James Wray's brother Liam said he was 'very saddened for the other families' of those killed on Bloody Sunday, adding:

'Their hearts must be broken. It has been a sad day but the Wray family are relieved. There are a lot of sad and heartbroken people today.'

Sinn Féin deputy leader Michelle O'Neill said that her party shared the families' disappointment and 'incredulity' that only one soldier would be charged but that prosecution was still 'a significant achievement'. SDLP leader Colum Eastwood said the decision to prosecute only one paratrooper did not vindicate the actions of the others. The families' justice campaign had been met with 'prevarication, equivocation and obstruction at every level', he added.[10]

There was a mixed reaction among Unionist politicians. DUP MP Gregory Campbell said the IRA's murder of two RUC officers in the days leading up to Bloody Sunday was being airbrushed from history. 'The facts also remain that 90 per cent of deaths in Northern Ireland were at the hands of illegal terrorist groups who existed solely to murder and cause destruction,' he said. 'There is still a disproportionate focus however on the small proportion of the 10 per cent of deaths attributed to those who were attempting to serve the community in difficult and often very dangerous situations.'

TUV leader Jim Allister said there was too much focus on security force killings and that IRA victims were being forgotten. He was one of many who referred to the July 1972 PIRA bombings of Bloody Friday in Belfast which in eighty minutes killed five civilians, two British soldiers, a RUC reservist, and a UDA member, while 130 were injured. He said: 'Why is Bloody Sunday more important than Bloody Friday? While insatiable demands for wholesale prosecutions may have perished on the rock that prosecutions are only possible where there is sufficient evidence, the hierarchy that has elevated Bloody Sunday families above all others is hard to take. In 1972, we also had Bloody Friday, but IRA murders don't count it seems when it comes to this distorted dealing with the past. The pursuit of soldiers while terrorists continue to go scot-free is now very much part of the rewrite of history so promoted by IRA/Sinn Féin, who themselves still withhold information on multiple murders.'

Ulster Unionist MLA Doug Beattie said: 'The PSNI looked at the evidence, passed it to the PPS and they decided – based on the evidence – to prosecute one former soldier. This is the law, it must be respected by all and it is now for the courts to decide. Nobody is above the law and nobody should be held to a greater or lesser standard than anyone else. My thoughts remain with the families of all the innocent victims of the Troubles.' Lowry Mathers, whose wife Joanne was shot dead by the IRA in Derry while collecting census forms in 1981, said: 'It's all very well getting justice for Bloody Sunday. But what about me? What about my son? There is absolutely no justice for us and that leaves a bad taste in my mouth.' Kenny Donaldson of Innocent Victims United said: 'Our organisation holds a consistent policy on criminal violence whether perpetrated by terrorists or individual members of the security forces. The PPS has found that tests have been met for Soldier F to face prosecution for two deaths and a number of other attempted killings; the law must now run its course.' But he added that the 'overwhelming majority' of security force members had 'performed their role with honour, integrity and immense restraint'.[11]

There was no ambivalence from John Kelly and his family whose lives have been dominated by Bloody Sunday. When TV dramatist Jimmy McGovern filmed *Sunday*, his award-winning account of the massacre, Kelly's son Niall acted the part of his uncle Michael, including the graphic depiction of his death that afternoon. They shared the burning desire among all relatives and survivors to erase what they regard as slurs or libels on the dead. 'When our parents received £250 in ex-gratia payments for Michael's death in 1974, the *Sun* newspaper decided to have some fun at our expense,' Kelly said. 'It was around Christmas time and the paper printed a cartoon of Santa Claus delivering a sack to Derry with £250 painted on it.'

Kelly's friend Damien Donaghey survived being shot on Bloody Sunday. He was fifteen when he was wounded in the femur after two paratroopers identified during the hearings as Soldiers A and B opened fire on a crowd. When Saville was published, he was waiting for surgery for a new knee and was due to be treated in the same hospital, Altnagelvin, that he was taken on the day of the massacre. During the inquiry Donaghey said: 'When I was in hospital after being shot the police came in and took my trousers away which were in shreds because the medical staff had to cut them up. The police took the trousers away for forensic tests and they found there were no traces of explosives or evidence of any nail bombs being thrown. Up to this day I have never been charged with anything yet I was branded a nail bomber by the paratroopers on the day and that has still stuck to me to this day. That's why everyone has to be cleared, the dead and those who survived, totally innocent.' After Donaghey's cousin Gerald was shot dead, paratroopers alleged they had found nail bombs in his pocket. 'This soldier originally said he saw that Gerald had nail bombs on him even though other soldiers admitted that no nail bombs were found in his pocket. The soldier who made that allegation never turned up to give evidence at the inquiry. He had disappeared, some said to Thailand. I feel lucky at least that I survived to see these lies exposed, to see the report.' Given the cost and length of the inquiry, many outside Derry have questioned if it was worth it, but Donaghey said: 'People don't understand when they go on about the fees that we, the victims and survivors, never got one 1p out of the £191m. What is money if you get the truth? How much is a life? Is somebody saying that all those people lying in a cemetery are not worth £191m?'[12]

The prosecution sparked a heated debate, still ongoing, well beyond the borders of Derry and Northern Ireland about attempts to bring justice for the families of republican victims, but not those who fell victim to paramilitaries freed under the terms of the Good Friday Agreement. Unusually, the opposing sides in the debate did not always slip neatly into niches of the Left or Right, republican or Unionist, soldier and civilian. A senior army officer who served several tours in Northern Ireland and elsewhere was reluctant to be directly quoted but said: 'The general view of the rest of the Army was that the Paras had grossly over-reacted on Bloody Sunday. We were appalled. Of course, it acted as a recruiting sergeant for PIRA. There is no way I would have opened fire if I was there. There was both a failure of command and discipline.'[13]

Douglas Murray, who had sat for months in the Saville Inquiry courtroom, wrote in the centre-Right *Spectator* magazine that while it was right 'that the sight of terrorists benefiting from an immunity denied to our soldiers is grotesque, there are competing qualms. Not only because British soldiers should be held to a higher standard than terrorists. But because, having watched all of the Bloody Sunday shooters testify, I can say with certainty that they include not only unapologetic killers, but unrelenting liars.' He went on: 'As one soldier after another appeared before Lord Saville, it became clear that the soldiers of 1 Para were intent on spurning this last effort to get to the truth of what happened that day. Almost without exception they stonewalled, sticking to the testimony they had given in 1972, repeating claims that had been repeatedly disproven and, when in difficulty, pleading forgetfulness. Not a plausible forgetfulness, but a highly selective, implausible type. Their evidence was evasive, frustrating and self-damning. The Saville inquiry had promised immunity from further legal action to all witnesses who told the truth about their actions on the day. In that quiet inquiry room, the soldiers of 1 Para might have come clean and admitted what they had done before sinking back into anonymity and retirement. Instead they stuck to their lies. For example, on the day itself, four soldiers — E, F, G and H — moved as a brick into one of the more concealed areas of the Bogside. By their own evidence they were responsible for at least half of the deaths that day. By the time of the Saville inquiry, soldiers E and G were dead, but F and H were not, were called and clearly reluctantly appeared. H was the soldier who had fired the most shots that day, including nineteen he said he fired at a single window that did not shatter. But it was soldier F — who fired thirteen rounds on the day — whose performance in 1972 and 2003 was most disturbing. It always seemed to me that if anyone was deserving of prosecution, then it was him.

'F started lying from the moment the shooting stopped. Like every other soldier who had fired, F was immediately asked to give the Royal Military Police (RMP) his justification for, and direction of, each shot. So in the early hours of January 31 1972 F pointed on a map to a number of positions where he claimed to have fired at gunmen and nail-bombers. At no stage did he admit to firing at the rubble barricade where Michael Kelly had fallen, shot side-on in the abdomen. Yet while F was speaking to the RMP, at the nearby hospital a 7.62mm calibre bullet was being dug out of the spine of Michael Kelly's body.

'In the weeks that followed the rifles of the soldiers who had fired were sent to a Belfast laboratory for testing. Realizing that unmentioned shots would be traced to his gun, F chose to radically alter his story. So at Lord Widgery's inquiry, several weeks after the day, F decided to recall firing at a 'bomber' at the rubble barricade. There was no bomber at the barricade. But the bullet that had lodged in Kelly's body was indeed shown to have come from F's rifle. And so at that earliest stage of the search for the truth, F's first lie — and first murder — was exposed. And nothing happened. F stayed in the army and periodically received promotion. Under questioning in 2003, the short and stocky F — then in late middle age — was reduced to monosyllabic answers, generally of either "yes" or "no". He claimed to remember almost nothing of the day, despite it being his first visit to Londonderry and — by his own admission — the most shots he had fired on any deployment up to that date. Under devastating questioning, F was shown to have killed at least four people that day. One of them was Patrick Doherty, shot through a buttock as he was crawling away. One more killing which soldier F had "forgotten" about when first questioned by the RMP.

'Then, while Doherty lay crying in agony, a forty-one-year-old man called Barney McGuigan stepped out from behind a block of flats to try to get help for the dying man. McGuigan was waving a white handkerchief. According to the testimony of numerous witnesses, including an officer from another regiment stationed on the city walls, soldier F — positioned on the other side of the road — got down on one knee and shot McGuigan through the head. No one who saw the mortuary photos of the exit wound in McGuigan's face will forget what just that one bullet of soldier F's did.

'In 1972 Dave — F — committed perjury in front of Lord Chief Justice Widgery. He perjured himself again before Lord Saville in 2003. Perhaps on that disastrous day in 1972 he thought he was teaching the citizens of Londonderry some kind of lesson. Or perhaps — under what he presumed to be suitable cover — he just seized an opportunity to kill with impunity on British streets. It is true that few people are comfortable with retired soldiers being prosecuted. But if soldier F did indeed presume he could get away with murder that day, who is comfortable with that presumption proving right?'[14]

The week the prosecution was announced, American author Lionel Shriver was interviewed by the *Belfast Telegraph* about her appearance at the *Imagine* festival. Her most famous novel, *We Need to Talk About Kevin*, which documented a mother's attempts to understand why her son carried out a mass killing at a school, was later turned into a film. Her earlier novel, *Ordinary Decent Criminals*, was set against the backdrop of the conflict in Northern Ireland. During her research she had instinctively sided with the Unionists, saying: 'When I arrived I did not think the lack of civil rights and the injustices going on were of such egregious character that they merited violence and therefore I found myself completely at odds with the IRA. Liberal Americans from an ocean away may have regarded the IRA as some kind of left-wing liberation movement but I found it to be a right-wing nationalist retrograde movement which was authoritarian and thuggish. Historically I have talked a little less about loyalist violence which no sane person endorsed either. At least one could say it was reactive, no matter how distasteful. I threw them (terrorists) all into the same lot but the IRA were better organised and were often misrepresented as heroes while violent loyalists didn't have much of a constituency.'

Asked why she had strongly opposed the prosecution of police officers or soldiers for historic crimes, including the killings on Bloody Sunday, she replied: 'I think that you cannot have it both ways. You cannot let terrorists go and still hold soldiers to account. I realise there is an argument that soldiers should be held to higher values, but I think the more persuasive argument was that the Good Friday Agreement was supposed to draw a line under all that. It was not a perfect justice but even an imperfect justice has to be an imperfect justice for everyone. In the context of Northern Ireland anyone who is in the police or Army enjoys none of the clemency that the Good Friday Agreement gives to terrorists. It seems to work out that as long as your morals are in the gutter you get out of jail free. Terrorists are rewarded but the forces of law and order are pursued.'[15]

Peter Hitchens, a former Trotskyist who swung far to the maverick, independent Right, was even more forthright: 'The decision to prosecute one of the Bloody Sunday soldiers is straightforward victor's justice. And if you still haven't grasped who won in the war between Britain and the Provisional IRA, perhaps the truth will now at last sink in. All war is crime. But only the losers ever face trial for it. Whether 'Soldier F' is guilty or not is a matter for the courts and should stay that way. I have nothing to say about it. But the long, dragging process which has led to his being charged is political, far more a matter of power than of justice. It is because we were the vanquished and the Provisional IRA, backed with all the might of the USA, were the winners in 1998 that this is happening at all. If we had won, scores of IRA and 'Loyalist' murderers (freed as a sop to the Protestant killer gangs) would still be doing time. And our police and courts would still be hunting down the culprits of hundreds of terrorist crimes which will now never be punished. And there would not be the slightest chance that a long-retired ex-paratrooper would be preparing for his trial, for actions allegedly taken while under army discipline.

'If you are sharp-eyed, you will have noticed that the body which announced the prosecution is called the Public Prosecution Service, not the Crown Prosecution Service. That should be a helpful hint. Britain's continued rule in Northern Ireland is provisional, in more senses than one. So the Crown, the symbol of British authority which adorns every courthouse and prison (and every embassy abroad), and is to be found on the cap-badge of every police officer and all service personnel, has already been abolished in Northern Ireland. Our flag has been hauled more than halfway there. In Northern Ireland now, the Union Jack can only be flown on public buildings in limited circumstances. Everybody there knows that one day soon, the referendum promised in the 1998 surrender to the IRA will be held, and the whole thing will be handed over to Dublin rule.'[16]

Army veterans in Parliament also had their say, often with the benefit of direct personal experience. Conservative MP Colonel Bob Stewart, who was UN officer commanding in the Bosnia conflict, said: 'I served for more than three years in Northern Ireland, on seven operational tours. I first went there in 1970. Sadly, I lost six men who were directly under my command, and many more in my unit. Almost fifty of the men under my command were wounded — thirty-five in one incident. I have been involved in several fatality shootings. We were sent to save lives, to look after people. We were given a yellow card, which was approved by Parliament, and that yellow card told us what we could and could not do under fire. We trained very hard on it. We memorised it. We rehearsed it. Colleagues are nodding their heads. We practised on exercise incidents so that we would learn.

'Army training screams out against opening fire in peacekeeping. That decision is an incredibly difficult one to make and it is very difficult in an urban environment because soldiers are thinking, "If I open fire, who else am I going to hurt?" How many times did I see instances of our soldiers not firing when under fire because of the possibility that children or women would be caught in the crossfire? That tactic was used by our opposition. There is huge inhibition to opening fire, and the decision to do so has to be made in milliseconds by our young men. When that decision and those actions are judged, it is in some courtroom, warm and nice with time and lawyers. A judgment is being made about a decision taken by someone who is panicking like hell.

'We must remember that most of our young men were eighteen or nineteen years old. They were kids. My soldiers looked so young that they could have been in year 9 or 10 at school. Firearms were used as a last resort. On the yellow card it says, in capitals: FIREARMS MUST ONLY BE USED AS A LAST RESORT. That was drilled into us. A challenge had to be given before someone could open fire, unless doing so, it says on the yellow card, would increase the risk of injury or death to others or oneself. That challenge was clear: "Army. Stop or I fire." Again the yellow card is specific: opening fire was allowed only if lives were endangered by someone firing a weapon at a soldier or someone they were protecting, or if someone was planting or throwing an explosive device – the card specifically mentions petrol bombs. One third of my platoon were injured by petrol bombs in 1970 on the streets of Londonderry, at the Rossville Street/William Street junction – one third burned, and we had not opened fire at all. And nor did we. If someone is driving at a soldier, that soldier is allowed to open fire. Finally, if a terrorist has killed someone or is in the act of killing someone, a soldier can open fire if they cannot make an arrest in any other way.

'We could only open fire with aimed shots, not with machine gun fire; we did not do it automatic. We had to use "the minimum force" – that, again, is on the yellow card – and we had to be careful that we did not hit innocent people. That little phrase stopped so many British soldiers from firing, particularly in Belfast on the Falls Road. Most men on the ground were petrified that, by accident, they would kill an innocent person. That was a factor in the decision to open fire, in those milliseconds.

'I know what happens in the case of a fatality, as I was involved in such an investigation. The Royal Ulster Constabulary and the Special Investigation Branch of the Royal Military Police hauled us over the coals. Even though we had just acted to save our life or someone else's life, we were treated as though we had done something wrong. Soldiers are separated, questioned individually and kept in isolation. They are not given assistance and they have a very uncomfortable interview. The weapons they used are seized and checked; all the ammunition is counted, and they have to account for every single round. That is what happened to our men, and some women, when they were involved in fatality shootings.

'Detailed reports were produced. The problem is that those reports are usable by the Director of Public Prosecutions; they are dug up, and some people go to court. In 1978, I had a very uncomfortable interview with two soldiers who were working with me. They were not infantry. I told them they had to go to court and would be charged with manslaughter. They went ballistic. They said, "Sir, you bloody officer. You are actually going to ditch us. You are going to abandon us; you are going to let us go to a court." I felt rotten, because I agreed with them, but the Royal Ulster Constabulary told me that I had to instruct those soldiers to go to court and I had to support them, because if they went to court on a charge of manslaughter and that court proved there was no case to answer, the case would be dismissed and they would never hear about it again. Well, will they?

'We always acted within the law. If we did not, as we have heard already, we should be prosecuted, but this card was given to us by our predecessors in this place as a protection, as well as instructions as to how we should act. Terrorists just disappear. There is no record of what they have done; they just kill. We must not judge them in the same way as soldiers. It is so easy to go after men in uniform who went out at our bidding and acted within the law, with everything written down. It is so much more difficult to get evidence on a terrorist. To veterans, it seems like our Government – or Governments, because this includes the Labour Government as well – are giving those guys get-out-of-jail cards. So many of our veterans feel really bitter about that.

'Our men and women who served in uniform require us to act. We need a statute of limitations for Northern Ireland veterans. It is absolutely right that we have a statute of limitations for people serving outside the UK, but what is the difference? Someone putting on a uniform was more likely to be shot in Northern Ireland than someone doing it in Iraq or Afghanistan. I can tell you that in Northern Ireland, our casualty rate was pretty big. The casualties we had in Northern Ireland outstrip the casualties we have had in Iraq and Afghanistan. Not just that: there were people who were really badly injured. I had three who lost their legs.'[17]

Earlier, Stewart had said: 'In 1978, I told two soldiers who were with me that because they had been to court and been proved innocent and had acted within the law, they would never, ever be asked to do such a thing again. How the hell can our Government allow such people possibly to be investigated again?'[18]

One-time Tory Leader Iain Duncan Smith, another veteran, recalled 'it being drilled into our heads that a 7.62 round would travel through two levels of brick and kill something on the other side. That often gave our soldiers cause for hesitation, even when thinking about returning fire.'[19]

In December Joe Mahon, who as a teenager pretended to be dead after being shot by Soldier F, was awarded £250,000 in damages as compensation for serious injuries. That brought the total to more than £3m paid out to Bloody Sunday families in a series of settlements and awards made against the Ministry of Defence. With liability accepted in all cases, proceedings brought by Mahon centred on the level of payout. He was shot in the hip and abdomen as he tried to flee gunfire at Glenfada Park. The Saville Inquiry found the same bullet probably struck both Mahon and McKinney. Along with the physical pain he still suffered in his hip and back, Mahon was said to be plagued by guilt that he survived while others died. At the time of the shootings he had arranged to leave school to start a joinery apprenticeship, but due to his serious injuries and subsequent poor health, he only secured steady employment in 2009 when he obtained a job as a supervisor. Now aged sixty-three, Mahon sued for aggravated damages and loss of earnings. Outside court, Mahon's solicitor said: 'My client has already achieved his primary aim of securing the exoneration of his own character and establishing the innocence of all of those who were murdered and wounded, yet he still carries with him the physical and mental scars of the events of that day. He has continued to hold the state accountable for its actions on Bloody Sunday and will continue to do so until those responsible have been successfully prosecuted.'[20]

In August, the Larne-based Clyde Valley Flute Band provocatively paraded with Parachute Regiment and Soldier F emblems sewn on their shirts. But a subsequent Apprentice Boys parade in Derry passed off without violence. Graeme Stenhouse, the governor of the Apprentice Boys, echoed a view from civic leaders that it was important to restore good relations and promote mutual respect in the city. 'We have to remember this is a predominately nationalist city but having said that, we have every right to parade in this city,' he said. 'We have been around for over 300 years, so it is only correct that we get that right – to celebrate our culture and our identity but as always conduct ourselves in the proper manner.'[21]

For the rest of 2019 proceedings against Soldier F were bogged down into the inevitable legal morass, with contested arguments about the venue for the trial, its legitimacy and procedures governing the calling of witnesses. In August, committal papers were given to Soldier F and the following month twenty-eight Bloody Sunday family members marched from the city's Diamond to Bishop Street and crammed into the public gallery in Londonderry Magistrates' Court for the formal committal proceedings. Missing was Soldier F himself. One of his lawyers told the court that a mass of evidence needed to be properly scrutinised, and the defence wanted to consider what witnesses would need to appear at a later stage. A prosecution lawyer agreed that it was a complex matter involving a significant number of documents. The case was duly adjourned, and the defendant walked out with both his bail and anonymity intact. BBC correspondent Julian O'Neill commented: 'The families came to court knowing this would be the start of lengthy process – and this could be the first delay of many.' He was not wrong.[22] Outside after the hearing, Ciaran Shiels, solicitor for the McKinney family and the four wounded victims, said the relatives knew they faced a long journey through the courts, adding: 'The families are in it for the long haul, as they always have been.'[23]

In September 2019 the families of the massacre victims marched to court as veterans warned against turning the prosecution of a former paratrooper into 'a media circus'. The barrister representing Soldier F told the court he would be challenging any attempt to send him to Crown Court for trial. The defence sought to cross-examine witnesses at a committal hearing in a procedure that will seek to have the case thrown out at the earliest possible stage. He faced a seventh supporting charge of the attempted murder of a person or persons unknown on the day. Relatives of victims of Bloody Sunday gathered in the Diamond area of Londonderry city before walking together towards the courthouse. Outside court, Mickey McKinney, the brother of William McKinney, said: 'This is a very significant event for us on the journey towards achieving the third and final demand of the Bloody Sunday justice campaign – the prosecution of a soldier for murder and attempted murder on Bloody Sunday.' Liam Wray, the brother of James Wray, described the first court hearing as an 'historic day'. He added: 'I am very nervous this morning. We are glad and relieved that this day has arrived, it's been forty-seven-and-a-half years.'

Soldier F did not appear in court but another paratrooper, who had been accused of attempted murder but subsequently told no charges would be brought against him, warned against the case becoming a *cause celebre*. Sergeant O said: 'This prosecution is in danger of becoming a media circus. They are trying to sway the courts but it won't work. The courts must do their job properly.' Sergeant 0 added: 'I sympathise 100 per cent with Soldier F. He should not be going through this especially at his stage in life. What good is it going to do prosecuting a seventy-year-old? It is going to take years and years to go through the courts before they can bring it to trial. It is time to call it quits.' The case against Soldier F was heard before a district judge in Londonderry Magistrates' Court. At the brief hearing Mark Mulholland QC, representing the former paratrooper, confirmed he would be challenging the attempt to send him to Crown Court trial by calling witnesses at a mixed committal hearing.

The case was adjourned to December to allow defence and prosecution to prepare for the committal proceedings. District Judge Barney McElholm granted an interim anonymity order to continue the protection of the accused's identity. He said he accepted it would 'take some time' before the committal could proceed. 'It's important that this is all done with a degree of fairness to all concerned in these matters,' he said.[24]

The December hearing was adjourned, and again in January 2020 awaiting a final decision on the venue for future hearings following pressure from Soldier F's legal team for a trial in Belfast on the grounds that a local one could be prejudicial. There were also security concerns about staging it there and practical issues about the size and acoustics of the court facilities in the city. Liam Wray said after that postponement: 'The atrocity happened in Derry. It was witnessed by many, many people. The majority of witnesses in this case are going to be Derry people. For them to have to trip up to Belfast, which is not an easy journey, would be ridiculous. The issue here is we are talking about open justice. Justice for all and the experience we have had over the forty-eight years that we have been campaigning in regards to our relatives who were the victims of Bloody Sunday has been that the initial inquiry (Widgery) happened in Coleraine, we have seen the way that left people feeling about justice, then we had the soldiers' evidence in the Bloody Sunday inquiry in London. It's about time people got real, it's about time to say justice should be seen to be done and it should be heard to be done too in this courthouse.'

McKinney's brother Mickey echoed such concerns, saying: 'It's very important, this is where the crime was committed, not half a mile from where we are standing here. We are the victims here. The people who are standing here this morning are the victims. This is where the case should be heard, not Belfast because of one man (Soldier F).'[25]

In March Judge McElholm adjourned the case yet again, saying: 'A lot of work has been going on in the background in regards to assessing the feasibility of different venues with regards to space and the need to accommodate as many people who wish to obviously participate as possible. Those things are not simple.' He pledged that the submissions of the families and of the defence would be taken into account.[26]

As the Soldier F proceedings slowly dragged on, the issue of historic military prosecutions provided a difficult sideshow for Boris Johnson and an administration preoccupied by delivering Brexit and economic promises and by handling a tsunami of crises, including flooding, the first signs of coronavirus and the collapse of relations between No. 10 and the civil service. A legal claim lodged in the High Court accused ministers of discriminating against British Army veterans, saying that soldiers were fifty-four times more likely to be prosecuted than terrorists over deaths during the Troubles. The judicial review of the prosecution of Dennis Hutchings, a seventy-eight-year-old great-grandfather suffering terminal cancer, over a 1974 fatal shooting in Northern Ireland was deeply embarrassing for premier Johnson as he had repeatedly promised to end prosecutions of troops over historic allegations where no new evidence had come to light. Hutchings' lawyers argued that veterans are being taken to court 'disproportionately' compared to alleged terrorists.[27] Hutchings, a former Life Guard, pleaded not guilty in a Diplock court with no jury present to charges relating to the death of John Patrick Cunningham, a twenty-seven-year-old with learning difficulties, who was fatally shot in the back as he ran away from an army patrol near Benburb in County Tyrone on 15 June 1974.[28] That, and the parallel Soldier F proceedings, put a spotlight on Boris Johnson's pledges and performance up to any beyond his December 2019 general election landslide.

In July 2019 it was announced that a new Office for Veterans' Affairs was being created to 'provide lifelong support to military personnel'. Army veteran Johnny Mercer, an outspoken critic of the historical investigations process, was made the minister responsible for delivery. He said that the prime minister had 'tasked me to end the repeated and vexatious pursuit of veterans' over offences allegedly committed in the line of duty. And ahead of the election the Conservatives marked Armistice Day with pledges to improve the lives of UK service personnel and their families, including a new law to protect veterans from such 'vexatious' pursuit. Legislation would ensure that the Law of Armed Conflict has primacy and that peacetime laws are not applied to service personnel on military operations. Under the proposals, he said the Tories would amend the Human Rights Act so it does not apply to issues – including deaths during the Troubles in Northern Ireland – that took place before it came into force in 2000. Johnson said: 'As we remember the ultimate sacrifice made by our brave men and women for their country just over a century ago, it is right that we renew our commitment to the soldiers, sailors, marines, airmen and veterans of today.' Defence Secretary Ben Wallace told BBC Radio 4's Today programme any changes would not affect current criminal prosecutions brought against service personnel, but in future, those who wanted to pursue complaints against the forces would have to go to the European Court of Human Rights rather than UK courts. 'At the moment, because of the Human Rights Act, people can go via our courts and use our systems to constantly reopen this and we don't think that is right or fair,' he said.

Both Sinn Féin and Unionists in Northern Ireland condemned the pledge. The UUP's Doug Beattie - a retired Army captain – said it would allow for 'terrorists... to get away scot-free', while Sinn Féin's Linda Dillon said it was 'unacceptable' to give soldiers, past and present, 'immunity'. Irish Deputy Prime Minister Simon Coveney also said the proposal was 'very concerning', tweeting: 'The law must apply to all, without exception, to achieve reconciliation.' Conservative plans to exempt British troops from human rights laws during combat were first announced in 2016 by Johnson's predecessor, Theresa May, but they had yet to be put into law.

BBC defence correspondent Jonathan Beale wrote: 'This isn't the first time the Conservatives have promised to end what they've called "vexatious legal claims and prosecutions against British soldiers accused of wrongdoing on the battlefield' – such as allegations of abuse or unlawful killing. The past four Tory defence secretaries have all pledged to introduce legislation to protect serving personnel and veterans, but have so far failed to deliver. The thorniest issue has been what to do with killings and deaths that took place during the Troubles in Northern Ireland. The Tories now believe they might have a solution by amending the Human Rights Act so it does not apply to incidents before 2000. But recent history has shown any change will be easier said than done.[29]

After what appeared to be a political breakthrough, Boris Johnson said Stormont's new power-sharing deal strikes a 'balance' between supporting veterans and giving victims of the Troubles the chance to seek justice, with plans for a new body to investigate Troubles murders revived. The revived 2014 Stormont House agreement included the creation of the Historical Investigations Unit (HIU) to take on the criminal justice element of looking into the past. A separate truth recovery mechanism would offer bereaved relatives the chance to learn more about the circumstances of their loved ones' deaths without the prospect of conviction.

The HIU's predecessor, the Historical Enquiries Team, was criticised by the police watchdog, which concluded it treated cases where the state was involved with 'less rigour' than those not involving military personnel. The Public Prosecution Service in Northern Ireland has said that of the so-called Troubles 'legacy' cases it has taken decisions on since 2011, seventeen relate to republicans, eight to Loyalists, five are connected to the Army and three involve police officers.

The prime minister told a press conference in Belfast: 'I think that the parties here who have revived Stormont have done a very good job of finding a balance between giving people who are in search of the truth the confidence that they need, but also giving people who served our country in the armed services the confidence and certainty that they need. Nobody thinks that people should get away with crimes. What we're saying is that people should be protected from unfair vexatious prosecutions when there's no new evidence to be found, and those positions, I think, are wholly compatible.' His spokesman also said the government had 'always been clear we would implement the Stormont House agreement in a way that provides certainty for veterans and justice for victims'.[30]

In March 2020 Boris Johnson's government announced new legislation to protect military personnel and veterans from prosecution for alleged historical offences in conflicts overseas. Veterans Minister Johnny Mercer said it would tackle 'vexatious claims'. Defence Secretary Ben Wallace confirmed the bill would 'deal with overseas operations' only. The legislation proposed a five-year limit on criminal prosecutions from the date of an incident – unless there is compelling new evidence – and a six-year limit for any civil case involving personal injury or death. It would also compel any future government to consider a derogation – effectively opting out – from the European Convention on Human Rights in any conflict overseas. But human rights groups have expressed anger, saying the legislation would place the military above the law and undermine existing international conventions. The plans for Northern Ireland would see only cases where there is 'new compelling evidence and a realistic prospect of a prosecution' move to a full-blown investigation. And once a case has been considered there will be a legal bar on any future investigation, which the Northern Ireland Office said would 'end the cycle of reinvestigations'.[31] Only a small number of Troubles killings will receive 'full-blown' investigations under the new approach, disappointing hundreds of families. It would see the vast majority of almost 2,000 unsolved cases closed and prevented in legislation from ever being reopened. The Northern Ireland Office said: 'Once cases have been considered there will be a legal bar on any future investigation occurring. This will end the cycle of reinvestigations for the families of victims and (army) veterans alike.'[32]

At a preliminary hearing of Derry's magistrates' court, it was suggested to district judge, Barney McElholm that the case be moved to Belfast because Derry's Bishop Street courthouse was not large enough to facilitate such a hearing. However, the move was opposed by the families, who were determined that Soldier F should stand trial in the city where their loved ones were killed. Lance Corporal F and the still-grieving families were expecting a breakthrough in the legal morass in March 2020 – and then the coronavirus pandemic hit.

Michael McKinney said the latest delay was, 'while entirely understandable, nevertheless frustrating'. He went on: 'The Bloody Sunday families have fought a long campaign for justice for my brother, Willie and all the dead and victims and that campaign will continue. There have been many obstacles along the path of this campaign and the coronavirus is another although it is by far the biggest obstacle given this is a world pandemic. But we will overcome this as we have every other obstacle. No one should doubt for a single second our determination to keep going. What drives us – and all the Bloody Sunday families – is a burning passion for justice.'[33]

And so it dragged on. And on. And on. In May 2020, following a case review, the trial was postponed to the middle of July when it was planned to be held remotely. William McKinney's brother Mickey said provision was being made to allow families to 'attend or observe future hearings remotely' if the coronavirus pandemic means they cannot attend court in person. 'We consider this a positive development as the participation of the families and wounded is central to this,' he said.[34] It was then put back to September because of the pandemic. Solicitor Ciaran Shiels, who represents several of the victims' families, applied to District Judge Ted Magill to have an anonymity order granted to Soldier F lifted. He said in other murder cases in Northern Ireland involving members of the security forces, military and police witnesses were named during the court proceedings. The judge agreed to review the application, which meant the trial would have to be in a new court term. Evidence via sightlink would be heard from witnesses from the UK and from Europe during which documents and maps would have to be shown to some of the witnesses, which raised practical difficulties as the system constantly experienced operational difficulties.[35]

Meanwhile, civil damages to relatives of the dead and others wounded topped £3 million in government compensation. In one case, the High Court heard that the wounded Patsy O'Donnell was allegedly humiliated by a soldier threatening to put another bullet in him. Lawyers for his family claimed one of the paratroopers grabbed him by the hair and told colleagues: 'Chaps, there will be blood flowing tonight.' Aged forty when he was shot in the shoulder by the soldier, O'Donnell died in 2006, but relatives of the father-of-six sued the Ministry of Defence for the injuries and damages inflicted on him. Karen Quinlivan QC said he had been shot while taking cover at Glenfada Park North, was arrested and escorted to Columbcille Court, the court heard, where he was photographed and struggled to assume a search position due to his injuries. 'He described a soldier pulling his head back by the hair and saying to him 'You are a Fenian b****** and I hate Fenian b*******',"' Quinlivan alleged. 'He also said "You have a bullet in you and when we get you down to the barracks you'll have another one in you. You mark my words."' The counsel added: 'Despite his injuries, soldiers instead of seeking medical attention for Mr O'Donnell subjected him to violence and further humiliation.' Following his release from hospital, he was unable to return to his job with an asphalt company for eight months. It was claimed that he was frequently stopped by soldiers and police, and had his home raised, after Bloody Sunday. His work as a roofing contractor was also allegedly frustrated by being detained during trips across the border into Co Donegal. 'Patsy O'Donnell regarded his identification with Bloody Sunday as a lifelong burden,' Quinlivan contended. 'It led to his being harassed by the Army and police.' In a statement to the Saville Inquiry before he died at the age of seventy-four, Mr O'Donnell said: 'I do, however, still feel bitter about what happened to me and the fact that I am probably classed by some people as a gunman and am under suspicion for doing something wrong. I am not and have never been involved in that sort of thing. I hope that this Inquiry will get to the truth.'[36]

At the end of September 2020, following a review of the cases of fifteen Army veterans, the Public Prosecution Service stuck to its original decision to bring charges against no more than one soldier in relation to Bloody Sunday. No new evidence was submitted for the review and solicitors for the families sent detailed submissions to the PPS setting out why they believed the previous year's decisions were wrong and why another ten soldiers should be facing prosecution for murder and attempted murder. The review was carried out by senior PPS assistant director Marianne O'Kane, who had not been previously involved in the cases, who looked at the deaths of ten victims and ten others wounded. She said: 'I have concluded that the available evidence is insufficient to provide a reasonable prospect of conviction of any of the fifteen soldiers who were the subjects of the reviews. Accordingly, the decisions not to prosecute these fifteen individuals all stand. I know that today's outcome will cause further upset to those who have pursued a long and determined journey for justice over almost five decades. I can only offer reassurance to all of the families and victims of Bloody Sunday, and the wider community, that my decisions were conducted wholly independently and impartially, and in accordance with the Code for Prosecutors.'

The response was predictably swift. Irish Taoiseach Micheál Martin expressed his 'deep disappointment' with the PPS decision and said it will 'bring back pain and loss' for the Bloody Sunday victims and families. Kate Nash, whose brother William was among those killed, said: 'I'm deeply disappointed that after a further review the correct decision's still not been reached.' Her solicitor, Darragh Mackin, said they would be seeking a judicial review of the decision: 'The issue of joint enterprise and conspiracy remains entirely up in the air and a decision was allowed to be taken premised on the actions of individuals and soldiers falling between the gaps of the grey area as to who actually fired the fatal shot. As we all know in the issue of joint enterprise, where two or more individuals act collectively in a specific act, the charge can be brought.' John Kelly, whose brother Michael was killed, said: 'We are not finished. Even though we have another knockback, and we have had many over the years, we will continue on to achieve truth and justice. Michael was seventeen, Michael cannot speak for himself. I will do it for him.' SDLP leader Colum Eastwood said that the families 'are people who have walked this very long walk, full of dignity and full of pride and not deterred by anybody'. But DUP MP Gregory Campbell questioned the potential cost of a judicial review: 'Is that going to mean further trauma and delay for all of those involved? I think more and more people will be saying how much further is this going to go on, because there are families today across Northern Ireland who are still grieving.'[37]

By Christmas 2020, with Britain in mostly severe tiers of coronavirus restrictions, Soldier F was one of six Army veterans facing prosecution and the political row over historical cases erupted again. Two elderly ex-soldiers – known as A and C – faced a murder trial over the 1972 death of IRA commander Joe McCann, who at the time was suspected of being involved in the killing of a soldier. Another veteran was charged with the murder of a fifteen-year-old boy in Londonderry and another, David Holden, was charged with manslaughter over a shooting at an army checkpoint in 1988. The sixth, Dennis Hutchings was twice cleared of the 1974 attempted murder in the fatal shooting of unarmed twenty-seven-year-old John Pat Cunningham in County Tyrone but faced another trial under the 'legacy' proceedings. The former coal miner, who was in the Life Guards for twenty-six years, was first cleared in 1974 following a five-month investigation and again in 2013. But the case was examined once more by a 'legacy' team with the Police Service of Northern Ireland after the government apologised for Cunningham's death and Hutchings was arrested at home in 2015. A soldier in a nearby patrol who witnessed the incident through the magnifying sight on his rifle came forward who claimed that Hutchings aimed all three of his shots into the air as warnings to Cunningham. Hutchings had always maintained that he only fired warning 'air shots'.

Meanwhile, the Overseas Operations Bill making its way through Parliament would curb prosecutions against troops and veterans from Iraq and Afghanistan – but offers no such protection to those who served in the Troubles. In contrast, Tony Blair's government told almost 200 wanted IRA terrorists nearly twenty years before they would not be prosecuted. Tory MP Jack Lopresti said: 'We mustn't let this politically motivated witch-hunt continue, which hounds and ruins the lives of former servicemen who have served our country bravely in Northern Ireland and who should be enjoying a well-deserved retirement.' John Ross, a former paratrooper in Ulster, added: 'The prosecutions are disgusting. It was a very dangerous situation during the Troubles. It was worse than a war zone in many ways. I was in the Falklands and at least you knew who the enemy was. In Northern Ireland you went out on patrol and you were on edge. There were people hell-bent on killing you.'[38]

11

The Trial That Never Was

'a bad day for justice'

The Covid-19 pandemic continued to put the Soldier F trial on hold as the question of the historic prosecutions of security forces again became a political hot potato. A perfect storm of factors combined to deliver more grief to the Bloody Sunday families.

The family of Bernard McGuigan, known as Barney, lodged a legal challenge against a PPS decision not to charge the former soldier with his murder. They said the PPS had confirmed that an undertaking by the attorney general meant testimony given to the Saville Inquiry could not be used in criminal investigations, nor could oral evidence given by Soldier F to the earlier Widgery Tribunal. The family stated: 'The PPS still contend, in effect, that F was acting "under orders" to give evidence at Widgery. As far as we are concerned the evidential test is more than met in respect of the murder of our father in such callous well-known circumstances, witnessed by many including other soldiers.'[1]

Committal proceedings against Soldier F opened in March 2021 but there was more confusion and disappointment for the families. The prosecution made opening remarks but reporting restrictions imposed on the hearing prevented the media from publishing any of the details. Soldier F was granted anonymity by District Judge Ted Magill, to the disgust of the families. Soldier F and victim family members listened to the proceedings remotely.[2]

As the Soldier F proceedings unfolded at glacier pace, the fragility of Northern Ireland peace was yet again exposed. Violence returned to the streets of Derry and Belfast in April 2021 as mainly Loyalist youths went on the rampage, injuring more than eighty police officers with petrol bombs and masonry over several nights. The protests were over the Brexit border deal and the DPP's decision not to prosecute any of the 2,000 mourners who attended the funeral of former IRA intelligence chief Bobby Storey's funeral in breach of covid rules. BBC home affairs correspondent Julian O'Neill reported: 'There has been a concern that loyalist anger would eventually make its way onto the streets. You could say the writing was on the wall – literally – since January and growing tension over the Irish Sea border. But there is a melting pot of grievances, largely bottled up by lockdown. This ranges from policing to politics to societal problems. The rioting was low-level, relatively scattered and localised – there is no sense of a broader, joined-up orchestration. Several agendas are at play, including the South East Antrim UDA kicking back at the PSNI after a clampdown on its criminality.'[3]

On the thorny issue of historic military prosecutions, Tory MP Johnny Mercer was sacked by text as a defence minister ahead of the Overseas Operations Bill returning to the Commons. The new law was designed to protect veterans from unfounded prosecutions, but British soldiers who served in Northern Ireland were excluded from the legislation. The MP – a former Army captain – wrote that the government had 'abandoned people in a way I simply cannot reconcile' in allowing 'endless investigations' into historic killings to continue. He added: 'Veterans are being sectioned, drinking themselves to death and dying well before their time, simply because the UK government cannot find the moral strength or courage we asked of them in bringing peace to Northern Ireland in finding a political solution to stop these appalling injustices.'

The government aimed to restrict the number of Troubles killings which could be fully investigated under a new approach where 'new, compelling evidence' would be required. But the bill went further for other veterans, such as those who served in Iraq or Afghanistan, proposing a five-year limit on criminal prosecutions. In 2019, the Public Prosecution Service in Northern Ireland said of thirty-two 'legacy cases' it had ruled on since 2012, seventeen related to republicans, eight to Loyalists, and five were connected to the Army. Mercer said that 'no discernible efforts have been made' to introduce similar legislation to cover Northern Ireland veterans, despite previous pledges, adding: 'I can see no prospect of this changing.' He was 'deeply proud of my predecessors who served in Northern Ireland', adding they were 'not second-class veterans' and deserved 'the protection of the Overseas Operations Bill like everyone else'.[4]

Mercer's dismissal sparked more calls from Unionists that the UK government should 'honour its commitment' to offer legal protection from prosecution to former soldiers who served in Northern Ireland. DUP MP Sir Jeffrey Donaldson, a former Ulster Defence Regiment soldier, said Troubles-related investigations have 'disproportionately' focused on the Army and police. 'We have thousands of victims who are not having the opportunity to have their cases looked at and they are the victims whose loved ones were murdered by paramilitary terrorist organisations,' he said. 'This is unacceptable, we cannot go on like this,' he continued. 'There are thousands of innocent victims who are waiting for their cases to be looked at. I won't stand by a narrative that suggests that you've got victims on one side and police and soldiers on the other. There were far more soldiers and police officers who were killed during the Troubles than there were people who were killed by soldiers and police officers, we shouldn't lose sight of that.'

Sinn Féin assembly member (MLA) Gerry Kelly said victims should be at the 'core' of the discussion and dismissed claims that there had been attempts to rewrite history. 'The families would like him to rectify history because they were told lies and are still being told lies and are still being frustrated at getting to the truth,' Kelly said. 'It's a nonsense to think that the British Crown Prosecution Service would be pursuing either unfounded or vexatious prosecutions against its own former soldiers. What about those who have been waiting, some of them for fifty years, forty years, thirty years, for some sort of truth and justice? Surely that's at the core of it.' Claire Hanna, SDLP MP for South Belfast, described legacy issues as a 'thorn that has to be grasped now'. She continued: 'Everybody is equal before the law and everybody wants legacy issues addressed, for families who need closure and to allow society to heal and go forward, but it has to be done in a way that is about victims. Families who have been waiting, many for decades in many cases, who every time this issue is discussed the offer that comes down to them is reduced and it seems that interests of those who created victims in paramilitaries or state forces always seem to come ahead of those who have lost someone.'

John Kelly, whose brother Michael was shot dead on Bloody Sunday, said the debate about protecting former soldiers from prosecution was 'the same old' and an attempt to 'deny Irish people the right to justice'. He added: 'No soldier, no matter where they served, in any part of this world, should be immune from prosecution for wrongdoing.'[5]

As that debate raged, the family of the only woman shot on Bloody Sunday was awarded almost £270,000 in damages. Peggy Deery, a widowed mother of fourteen, was thirty-eight when she was shot in the leg and died from a heart attack in 1988. The High Court judgement included compensation for her injuries and for the subsequent years of mental distress. Mr Justice McAlinden described the behaviour of the soldiers who wounded and verbally abused Mrs Deery as 'imbued with a degree of malevolence and flagrancy which was truly exceptional'. He said Mrs Deery was a woman of good character who attended the civil rights march in support of a society based on fairness and equality. Mrs Deery's family had sued the Ministry of Defence (MoD) for the injuries they claim contributed to her death. Counsel for the family argued that the paratrooper who shot her probably knew she posed no threat. The court was told after being shot Mrs Deery was carried into a house on Chamberlain Street to be treated by members of the Knights of Malta. The court heard soldiers then entered the property and allegedly directed foul language at the widow. Mrs Deery, who lost her husband to cancer months before Bloody Sunday, spent four months in hospital, developed a chronic kidney disease and was effectively housebound for the rest of her life. Her daughter Helen Deery told the court how they carried out cooking and cleaning duties in a house with no central heating or washing machine. A barrister representing the MoD argued her heart problems were probably due to a heavy smoking habit of forty cigarettes a day. In judgement, Mr Justice McAlinden said: 'Any claim that she was anything other than an innocent demonstrator was a fabrication constructed and perpetuated by the perpetrator or perpetrators of a wrong in an attempt to avoid personal or collective responsibility for any wrongdoing.' Awarding £250,000 to Mrs Deery's estate, the judge added a further £17,028 in special damages for the cost of care provided to her. 'This will take into account the mental distress which she undoubtedly suffered by reason of the approach adopted by the defendant to those killed and injured during Bloody Sunday in the period between the end of January 1972 and the date of the deceased's death in January 1988', he added. He said because Mrs Deery died before the Saville Inquiry into the events of Bloody Sunday, the 'cloud of imputed culpability would, at least to some extent, have cast an intermittent shadow over her'.[6]

Meanwhile, the High Court also granted permission to the families of five Bloody Sunday fatalities to challenge a decision not to prosecute former soldiers.[7] But Soldier F's prosecution was again thrown into the air in May 2021 when the trial collapsed of two more paratroopers accused of the murder of an Official IRA man just a few months after Bloody Sunday and they were formally acquitted.

Joe McCann, twenty-four, was shot in in the Markets area of Belfast and was evading arrest when the soldiers opened fire, killing him. Soldiers A and C, both in their seventies, had pleaded not guilty, saying they were acting lawfully when they shot the fugitive. Both soldiers were interviewed by a police legacy unit, the Historical Enquiries Team (HET), in 2010 and it was this evidence that formed a substantial part of the prosecution's case. The judge ruled that evidence as inadmissible and the Public Prosecution Service (PPS) confirmed it would not appeal against that decision, meaning the case could not proceed. McCann's daughter Aíne said there had been 'a failure of the state at all levels' in relation to her father's death. 'The RUC [Royal Ulster Constabulary] failed, the criminal justice failed, not only in this case but in the case of many other families,' she said. Those families would, it would transpire, include those of the Bloody Sunday victims.

The court was told that evidence implicating the soldiers came from two sources – statements given to the Royal Military Police in 1972 and interview answers given to the HET in 2010. The PPS accepted that the 1972 statements would be inadmissible in isolation, due to deficiencies in how they were taken including that the soldiers were ordered to make them and they were not conducted under caution. However, prosecutors argued that the information in the 1972 statements became admissible because they were adopted and accepted by the defendants during their engagement with the HET in March 2010. However, the judge said it was not legitimate to put the 1972 evidence before the court 'dressed up and freshened up with a new 2010 cover'. He questioned why the HET's re-examination did not prompt a fresh investigation by the Police Service of Northern Ireland (PSNI), with the veterans interviewed under caution. The judge suggested that course of action might have made a prosecution more sustainable.[8]

Inevitably, the collapse of that trial upped political pressure to abandon all prosecutions, including that of Soldier F. Other cases included: seven former soldiers who operated plain clothes in the Military Reaction Force facing charges including murder relating to shootings and Soldier B charged with the murder in Derry of a teenager, both also in 1972; and up to forty more potential prosecutions from the same decade. The *Times* editorialised that during the Troubles more than 250,000 military personnel served in Northern Ireland at various times and killed around 300 from the overall death toll of 3,650. It stated: 'It was a mission to maintain peace, preserve order and protect civilians from violence. A democracy rightly demands that its armed forces scrupulously adhere to the rule of law in peacekeeping operations and in war zones...

The continued pursuit of elderly former service personnel on the basis of flimsy evidence for alleged acts committed in this desperately difficult military deployment is politicised and unjust. The acquittals must mark the end to it.'[9]

However, the same week as the McCann acquittals, the question of historic blame was widened when the police ombudsman ruled that officers who killed four people at the start of the Troubles were never held to account due to investigative failings. And the ombudsman, Marie Anderson, also stated the use of machine guns by officers to deal with rioting in Belfast in August 1969 was 'disproportionate and dangerous'.

Nine-year-old Patrick Rooney – the first child killed in the Troubles – was hit in his bedroom by one of the shots fired to disperse rioters at Divis flats. A separate incident in the same area also claimed the life of off-duty soldier Hugh McCabe, twenty, killed by a police marksman who stated he was returning gunfire, though no witnesses saw anyone armed. Samuel McLarnon, twenty-seven, was shot dead while he stood at a window in his house at Herbert Street in Ardoyne. Michael Lynch, twenty-eight, was killed in nearby Butler Street by an officer who claimed he had seen 'gun flashes'. Anderson's 128-page report concluded that 'even allowing for the tumultuous circumstances of the time', the Royal Ulster Constabulary (RUC) failed to effectively investigate any of the deaths. It noted there had been limited enquiries, inadequate forensic examinations and no evidence any officer had been interviewed for potential criminal or misconduct offences. Anderson said: 'Unfortunately, responsibility cannot be determined over fifty-one years later, given the passage of time and the fact many witnesses and former police officers who may well have been able to assist are now deceased or unwell.'[10]

Ahead of the Covid-delayed 2021 Queen's Speech, Taoiseach Micheál Martin warned the UK that any unilateral move around Troubles-related prosecutions of veterans would be a 'breach of trust'. He added: 'For us the victims are the priority and the victims will remain the priority.' The proposed UK legislation to limit prosecutions for offences committed before the signing of the 1998 Good Friday Agreement had been leaked on the eve of polling day for elections in England, Scotland and Wales and helped secure more wins in former English Labour heartlands.

Sinn Féin president Mary Lou McDonald said the move was an 'attack on the rule of law' and 'an attempt to put British soldiers above the law and prevent investigations into murder, torture, shoot to kill and collusion involving British forces in Ireland'. She added: 'Let's be clear, this is not about dealing with the legacy of our past; this is about continuing the decades-long cover-ups and frustrating families in their efforts to get truth and justice.' Colum Eastwood branded the plan 'the biggest betrayal of victims by the British government' and said it would 'put a huge obstacle in the way of true reconciliation'. He went on: 'It is the most shabby government I have ever come across, they are so cynical and so untrustworthy, I don't think anybody would trust them. Society needs to move on but on the basis of truth and justice. You cannot do it by hiding the past and this government is more concerned with backbench Tory MPs with military constituencies than actually looking after the victims of the past.'

BBC Northern Ireland correspondent Julian O'Neill broadcast: 'I don't think we should be surprised by this development. It was the direction of travel that the government has been on since it announced it wanted to shut down the majority of investigations, close them, for good. This was the mechanism by which the Conservative Party would honour its manifesto commitment to end prosecutions of veterans who served in Northern Ireland. What has become clear is that in order to do this, the government would have to apply some type of mechanism across the board. So, as well as restricting or banning further prosecutions of veterans, this new piece of legislation would mean former paramilitaries would not be prosecuted either."

When that sank in, Unionists matched the fury of republicans. Ulster Unionist Party (UUP) MLA Doug Beattie said this was an amnesty for all: 'Everybody will get away with this. This is a line under the sand.' Alliance Party leader Naomi Long tweeted it 'typifies the contempt with which Govt are treating victims'. Traditional Unionist Voice (TUV) leader Jim Allister said: 'Amnesty for terrorists in the tailwind of action to protect veterans is not acceptable, either by reason of the equivalence it embraces or the disproportionate advantage to terrorists.' Amnesty International said no one can be above the law or beyond accountability. 'This reported plan is an insult to victims on all sides and the latest gross betrayal of victims who remain determined to seek the truth, justice and accountability to which they are entitled,' said Grainne Teggart, the organisation's Northern Ireland campaign manager. 'We urge the government to abandon this offensive plan and revert to the UK's commitments to deliver mechanisms capable of vindicating the rights of victims.'[11]

Almost fifty years after the Ballymurphy massacre (*see Chapter 2*) the families of the ten fatal victims finally got some degree of justice. The inquest, which opened in November 2018, heard almost 100 days of evidence from more than 150 witnesses which included more than sixty former soldiers, more than thirty civilians and experts in ballistics, pathology and engineering. The coroner, Mrs Justice Keegan, was hampered by suspiciously missing documents, including 1972 statements from soldiers saying they had shot someone – the coroner knew their names but the public did not. She said that the deaths took place in a 'highly charged and difficult environment' but concluded: 'What is very clear, is that all of the deceased in the series of inquests were entirely innocent of wrongdoing on the day in question.' The effects of the killings on the families of the ten victims had been 'stark'.

On the killings of Father Hugh Mullan and nineteen-year-old Francis Quinn, she found both men were shot by the Army although neither was armed; she was convinced Fr Mullan was a 'peace-maker' and that 'the use of force was clearly disproportionate'. On the killings of mother-of-eight Joan Connolly, Daniel Teggart, Noel Phillips and Joseph Murphy, she said they were innocent, unarmed and were 'posing no risk'. On the death of thirty-one-year-old Edward Docharty, she said he was not linked with the IRA and was an innocent bystander caught in the line of fire when a British soldier, known as M3, fired in response to a petrol bomber. On the killings of Joseph Corr and John Laverty, she found that on the balance of probability, both men were shot by the Army, it was wrong to describe them as gunmen and that the Royal Military Police investigation at the time was inadequate.[12]

Sinn Féin's Michelle O'Neill said: 'My first thoughts today are with the families of those killed in the Ballymurphy massacre. All were innocent and today their families have been vindicated. Today is their day; it is a day for truth. What happened in Ballymurphy was state murder and for decades the British government have covered it up. Now the truth has been laid bare for all to see. But still this British government are attempting to slam the door to justice, closed in the face of these families and others killed by the state or as a result of collusion. As the findings from the inquest were being read, the British government was announcing its plans to legislate to cover up its role in the conflict and to put current and former British soldiers beyond justice and the law. British state forces cannot be above the law.'

Colum Eastwood said: 'I'm so inspired by the fearless dedication of these families to fight for truth and justice for their loved ones.' The Alliance's Naomi Long said: 'This is vindication – still, to this day, the families have had to deal with sneers and slurs from those linking the victims with the IRA. To have it finally put into public record – the truth they have stated all these years – they were entirely innocent – is justification for their brave stand and dedicated campaigning for so many years. The UK government now needs to step up and formally apologise for the actions of the Army on the day in question. We saw how much a similar apology in relation to Bloody Sunday meant to the families there, and I encourage the government to acknowledge the courage of the Ballymurphy families with a similar statement.'

Jeffrey Donaldson of the DUP said: 'We're very clear where people have been killed who are innocent, then of course, people in those instances have the right to have their case put forward. That has been done in this inquest. But, in terms of the way forward, we want to see a legacy process that enables innocent victims – particularly those who were victims of terrorism – to have the opportunity of access to justice. At the moment there isn't a process that delivers this for all victims and that is wrong.'

Shadow Northern Ireland Secretary Louise Haigh said the families' fifty-year wait was a 'profound failure of justice. For them, the standard to which we hold ourselves as a nation has fallen far short. Many more families affected by the conflict are, too, still fighting for answers. The case for a comprehensive legacy process, with families able to discover the truth about what happened to their loved ones and where possible, justice, is strong and compelling. Ministers promised victims such a process, they owe it to families to deliver on their commitments.'

And Irish Taoiseach Micheál Martin said that 'the inquest has been very, very clear in its conclusions that all were entirely wrongly killed, that all were entirely innocent. I toured that area myself as minister for foreign affairs and I acknowledged the extraordinary perseverance and commitment to the families involved who waited a long, long time – for fifty years – to get some sense of justice for their loved ones. The Irish government has supported the Ballymurphy families for many years and we will continue to stand in solidarity with them. The legacy of violence in Northern Ireland remains a deep wound.'

BBC News NI reporter Will Leitch, who covered the inquest during sixteen months of hearings, dubbed it his 'longest and most difficult assignment'. He wrote: 'It was a cry of horror. A sharp, sudden cry of pain, of grief, of deep, deep sorrow. A visceral cry which must have pierced the heart of every single person who heard it echo around courtroom 12 of the Laganside Courts complex in Belfast. The courtroom gasped as waves of emotion rippled out from the jury box, where the families were sitting to watch witnesses give evidence on day thirty-three of the Ballymurphy Inquest.

'The daughters of Joan Connolly comforted their sister. She had just heard, for the very first time, graphic details of how her mother was shot, and died, alone and in great pain, just feet from a house where another woman inside was frantically trying to save her. That woman, now in the witness box, paused, and looked anxiously at the coroner to see if she should continue her evidence. Margaret Elmore had, under oath, described what she remembered from August 1971, and knew that in doing what the court asked, had inadvertently awoken great sorrow. The court rose, to allow time for everyone to recompose themselves. That was just one painful moment in March 2019 during the Ballymurphy Inquest, but one which has stayed with me. This story was about ordinary people and the quest for the truth of what happened fifty years ago. I have watched and listened to many sad or upsetting court cases in my thirty years as a reporter. But nothing prepares you for the cries of a woman who had just heard how half her mother's face had been shot off.'[13]

Premier Boris Johnson bungled the subsequent UK government apology. Downing Street claimed that the PM had 'apologised unreservedly' and in a telephone call described the events as 'tragic'. But he left it to Northern Ireland Secretary Brandon Lewis to make a Commons statement; Lewis said that the government 'profoundly regrets and is truly sorry' for the events surrounding Ballymurphy. John Teggart, whose father Danny was among those who were killed, said of Johnson's comments: 'The apology was to third parties, it wasn't to the Ballymurphy families. It's not a public apology. What kind of insult is it to families that he couldn't have the conversation with ourselves?' Briege Voyle, whose mother Joan Connolly was killed, said the prime minister's message 'means nothing'.

Johnson finally did apologise personally in Parliament, beginning prime minister's questions by reading the names of the victims and going on to say that he was sorry for how the investigations were handled and for the pain endured by the families. He said: 'No apology can lessen their lasting pain. I hope they may take some comfort in the answers they have secured and in knowing this has renewed the government's determination to ensure in future that other families can find answers without distress and delay.' Johnson also told Parliament that the UK government was committed to introducing legislation in the current session to address the legacy of the Troubles, 'and to introduce a fair package for veterans as well, to protect them from unfair, vexatious litigation where no new evidence has been brought forward'. That was to include a ban on all prosecutions prior to 1998 under a statute of limitations. BBC Northern Ireland home affairs correspondent Julian O'Neill wrote: 'Amnesty is a word which dare not cross the lips of government as it sets out its latest change of approach around the legacy of the Troubles. There has yet to be a clear, public enunciation of what is proposed. But it is this: a statute of limitations which would ban all prosecutions related to the Troubles. Not just future cases, but potentially, those already in train. It would apply across the board – to army veterans and former paramilitaries – on everything which happened before the Good Friday Agreement in 1998.' He added: 'The legacy plan would involve some form of investigations for families of the bereaved. But they would be investigations for the purposes of information recovery, not prosecutions. The government believes this is the key.'[14]

Scores of others legacy inquests were scheduled to run over five years, many dealing with state actions from the 1970s and 1980s. Added to that, almost 1,000 unresolved Troubles cases still in the hands of the Police Service of Northern Ireland, two thirds of them relating to deaths caused by republican and Loyalist paramilitaries, plus 250 or so killings being independently reinvestigated. There were also calls for public inquiries into the Omagh, Enniskillen and La Mon bombings, and the murder of solicitor Patrick Finucane.[15] It all amounted to a legal and logistical quagmire.

When his committal proceeding renewed in June 2021, Soldier F was allowed to retain his anonymity because, the court heard, he would be a 'prime target for anyone seeking vengeance for the terrible events of Bloody Sunday'. District Judge Ted Magill said Soldier F had enjoyed anonymity at both the Widgery and Saville inquiries and in respect of these proceedings since September 2019. Two threat assessments had found that he was at 'low' risk from dissident republicans, both in Northern Ireland and in England, but the judge said this could rise if he was named. The judge accepted the evidence of Alan McQuillan, a former assistant chief constable of the Police Service Northern Ireland, who said that Soldier F 'would have to look over his shoulder for the rest of his life'. Judge Magill said that the threat was not only from dissident republicans, but 'from a lone actor, not a member of any organisation, but someone who might be prepared to carry out an attack'. He added that 'a real threat does exist' and Soldier F is right to 'feel genuine fear'. The judge ordered that the anonymity order should be maintained.

As the Bloody Sunday families waited for the Soldier F trial, legacy cases continued to hit the headlines. The long-delayed inquest into Derry woman Kathleen Thompson, shot dead in the garden of her Creggan home during an Army raid in November 1971, focused on a former soldier identified only as Soldier D.

The former Royal Green Jacket testified to firing shots in the direction of where Ms Thompson was shot, claiming to have seen a gunman, but could not recall who was with him on the operation. It was put to him that regimental colleagues had erected a 'wall of silence' to protect him because it was well known he had been involved in the shooting of Mrs Thompson.[16]

And then, on 2 July 2021, the bombshell the families had long feared dropped. The prosecutions of Soldier F and Soldier B, charged with the murder of Derry teenager Daniel Hegarty, were dramatically dropped.

Reviews of both cases were prompted by the collapse of the earlier Joe McCann murder trial in which the court had ruled statements by Soldiers A and C as inadmissible. When interviewed in 1972, they admitted shooting McCann but they were not cautioned and had no access to legal advice. In 2010, they were re-interviewed by the police Historical Enquiries Team (HET), but they were not under arrest nor was any mention made that they were under suspicion for murder. Their 1972 statements were read into the record also and this, claimed the PPS, made them admissible. But the judge decided otherwise. The PPS said that given 'related evidential features' it was concluded 'there was no longer a reasonable prospect of key evidence in proceedings against Soldier F and Soldier B being ruled admissible'.

The Director of Public Prosecutions, Stephen Herron, travelled to Derry to personally inform families in a hotel suite of the decisions. Afterwards, Herron said: 'I recognise these decisions bring further pain to victims and bereaved families who have relentlessly sought justice for almost fifty years and have faced many setbacks. In both cases I would like to emphasise that this outcome does not undermine previous findings that those killed and injured in these tragic incidents were entirely innocent. These decisions were taken only after a most careful consideration of all relevant legal matters by a team of experienced and senior prosecutors.'[17]

The parallels with the McCann case were at first rejected by prosecutors in the case of Soldier F. His original 1972 statements were made without caution, but it was felt that statements made in the same circumstances by other soldiers identifying him as firing shots could be admitted as 'hearsay evidence' come his trial. That view was significantly changed by the collapse of that trial. In an eleven-page statement, the PPS stated: 'The stance taken by the court in A and C demonstrated in clear terms that compelled statements are regarded as legally flawed and evidentially diminished. It was concluded there was no reasonable prospect of a court acceding to an application to admit as hearsay evidence the 1972 compelled statements.'

The reaction was, inevitably, one of anger, grief and pain. The Bloody Sunday families said the decision was a 'damning indictment of the British justice system' and they would be challenging it: 'The actions of Soldier F resulted in the two women being robbed of their husbands, twelve children being orphaned of their father, and dozens of young men and women deprived of a brother. These are the clear findings of the Bloody Sunday Inquiry and the responsibility that it attaches directly and unequivocally to the actions of Soldier F.'

Liam Wray, brother of Bloody Sunday victim James, said: 'The decision today does not make Jim any less murdered than he was in 1972.' John Kelly, brother of Michael, said: 'It's a day of devastation. The fact that justice has been denied to the people of Derry, to the families – highly disappointed. But one point is we're never going to give up. We'll find some way of seeing [Soldier] F in a court of law.'

Colum Eastwood described the decision as 'bitterly disappointing' for the families. The Social Democratic and Labour Party (SDLP) leader said it is 'also devastating for the message it sends to the world. The people of Derry have stood with them [the families] on every step of their long march toward justice, we're with them today and we'll be with them until the end.' Sinn Féin's Gerry Kelly said that the decision 'once again highlights the need for a comprehensive mechanism to deal with the legacy of the past'. Michelle O'Neill, Sinn Féin vice-president, said it was a 'bad day for justice'. She added: 'The message is clear: British state forces who gunned down peaceful protestors and a child in Derry acted with impunity and will be allowed by the state to get away with murder.' Shadow Secretary of State for Northern Ireland Louise Haigh said 'the ongoing failure to deliver a process to deal with the legacy of the past remains an open wound which is failing victims and their families'.[18]

The defence of the decision was equally predictable. Northern Ireland's veterans commissioner Danny Kinahan said his thoughts were with the families and said 'the pressure is now on everyone to find a way forward'. He went on: 'Veterans don't want an amnesty or equivalence; they want the rule of law in place but they feel everything that's happening is very lopsided. They came in to stop the Troubles, to protect society and stop a civil war and they did that and there are some awful side effects – this is one of them.' Conservative MP Johnny Mercer tweeted: 'Another veteran's life ruined. Investigated, dropped, investigated, dropped, charged, dropped. This government's shame highlighted in another tragic case – for all sides.' Paul Young from the Justice for Northern Ireland Veterans and Northern Ireland Veterans Movement said: 'It will be a huge relief for the families of Soldier B and F and a sense of relief and joy within our veteran community. It was obvious to veterans that the cases against them were unsound since the case against Soldier A and C collapsed.'

The Democratic Unionist Party's Gregory Campbell said victims' families were unlikely to find closure by way of the courts, adding: 'It is going to be almost impossible in my view, and in the view of many, as years go on and we get further and further and memories become even more distant, to get to an accurate recreation of what happened, and how it happened, and thereby then try and bring closure to families who desperately want it.' Ulster Unionist Party (UUP) leader Doug Beattie said that the long passage of time had led to the decision: 'We've to have trust in our justice system, this has got a long way to run, I do think it's difficult to get evidence that will stand up in a court of law that will get any form of convictions this far on.'

BBC Northern Ireland home affairs correspondent Julian O'Neill wrote: 'Prosecutions for events from fifty years ago are very problematic. Evidence can be scarce, protagonists deceased and, because of the peace process, jail time on conviction of a Troubles-related offence is capped at two years. Legacy issues are also politically toxic. Twenty-three years on from the Good Friday Agreement, how to deal with the past is still unresolved. These events coincide with government attempts to win agreement on a proposal to ban all Troubles-related prosecutions. The discontinuation of the prosecutions of Soldier B and Soldier F will be used to advance its argument.'[19]

Two weeks later the court hearing to withdraw the murder charges was adjourned after the court heard that 'certain matters' regarding Soldier F's anonymity have been referred to the Attorney General.[20]

By then, the real name of Soldier F had been plastered over a wall at Free Derry Corner for several weeks but Colum Eastwood caused outrage when he used parliamentary privilege to identify him. The DUP's Gregory Campbell described Eastwood's actions as 'reckless and downright dangerous'. Speaking outside parliament, Eastwood said that Soldier F's name had gone viral on social media, adding: 'The people of Derry know his name. There is no reason for him to be granted anonymity. No other perpetrator involved would be given anonymity, for some reason Soldier F is a protected species.'[21] He later received death threats. Given the court rulings guaranteeing anonymity, it is understandable that the media did not follow suit. But there was a reason behind Eastwood's alleged misuse of the privilege – which protects MPs from libel and other prosecutions both criminal and libel. It was the growing realisation that Boris Johnson was using the collapse of the Soldier F prosecution and others to deliver a statute of limitation on ALL historic Troubles cases.

All hell broke loose.

12

Amnesty

'... so it's alright to push us to the one side.'

On 16 July 2021, after several days of astounding leaks, Boris Johnson did something that no other UK prime minister had every achieved: he united all the main political parties in the Stormont government, republicans and Loyalists, former soldiers and terrorists, Catholic and Protestant church leaders, police and civil rights activists, lawyers and victim support groups, the old and the young, jailbirds and peaceniks. All united in disgust over his decision to legislate for a statute of limitations on Troubles crimes and an end to all prosecutions for such offences committed before the 1998 Good Friday Agreement, both criminal and civil. He stated that he wanted to 'draw a line' under the decades of murder and mayhem and instead create a Nelson Mandela-style process of 'reconciliation'. He told the Commons that the measures he was bringing forward were 'balanced and have a wide degree of support', including from former Labour prime ministers. He clearly believed, with some justification, that the British electorate as a whole were tired and increasingly uninterested in historic crimes and wanted the whole mess to be shunted aside.

As always, he left it to others to spell out the details. Brandon Lewis, his hapless Northern Ireland Secretary of State, said current and future generations would be 'condemned' to division, and reconciliation would be impended if the government did not act. The package included a new independent body that would focus on the recovery of information relating to Troubles-related deaths, a major 'oral history' initiative and the statue of limitations. 'It is, in reality, a painful recognition of the very reality of where we are,' he told the Commons. He added: 'We know that the prospect of the end of criminal prosecutions will be difficult for some to accept, and this is not a position that we take lightly. But we have arrived at the view that this would be the best way to facilitate an effective information retrieval and provision process, and the best way to help Northern Ireland move further along the road to reconciliation. Ongoing litigation processes often fail to deliver for families and victims, and their continued presence in a society which is trying to heal from the wounds of its past risks preventing it being able to move forward.' Others saw it as, in reality, a general amnesty for heinous crimes committed by terrorists on all sides introduced to protect a handful of ageing Army veterans. It went beyond a ban on Troubles-era prosecutions, of which there had been just nine in the past six years. Ending legacy inquests and civil actions is arguably of greater impact. At the time of the statement, there were thirty-six inquests relating to the Troubles due to be heard, many relating to killings by the Army and police, and more than 1,000 civil claims lodged against the Ministry of Defence and other state agencies.[1]

It was instantly condemned by all five of the main political parties in Northern Ireland and by the Irish government. DUP leader Sir Jeffrey Donaldson said the proposal was an 'effective amnesty' and was 'totally unacceptable'. He added: 'Victims will see these proposals as perpetrator-focused rather than victim-focused and an insult to both the memory of those innocent victims who lost their lives during our Troubles and their families.' Justice had been 'corrupted' in 1998 with the release of prisoners and then by Tony Blair's On-the-Run amnesty letters. 'Understandably many victims will feel that these proposals represent a further denial of the opportunity to secure justice for their loved ones,' he said. 'There can be no equivalence between the soldier and police officer who served their country and those cowardly terrorists who hid behind masks and terrorised under the cover of darkness. We find any such attempted equivalence as offensive.'

Deputy First Minister and Sinn Féin vice-president Michelle O'Neill said the government has 'yet again shown a blatant disregard' for victims. She questioned why the government was moving in such a direction when all the main Stormont parties and victims' groups were opposing the move. 'There is no room for an amnesty in terms of dealing with the past,' she said. The government's intention was to 'cover up' its role during the Troubles. 'I look towards the Irish government; they need to hold the British government to account,' she said. 'We are certainly not going to take this lying down.'[2]

UUP Leader Doug Beattie said that the announcement 'reinforces the injustice which has already been dealt to victims', adding 'It's the wrong path and will tread on the emotions of innocent victims and their families. Nobody has the right to deny them the hope that someday, finally, they might see justice being done. The Ulster Unionist Party has been consistent and unequivocal in its opposition to any proposals for an amnesty. We warned about this when some were championing a statute of limitations despite the inevitable conclusion that it would lead to an amnesty for terrorists.'

SDLP Leader Colum Eastwood raised the 1990 case of Patsy Gillespie and asked would the NI secretary come with him to meet his widow and explain 'why he wants to protect his killers from prosecution and investigation'. He said that the government's approach was a 'serious act of bad faith that will breach obligations undertaken in successive all-party agreements and the international treaty signed at Stormont House', adding: 'You cannot draw a line in the sand on injustice.'[3]

Alliance deputy leader Stephen Farry said the proposals were 'an assault on the rule of law and human rights' and an 'insult to victims from all backgrounds', adding: 'The UK government has unilaterally abandoned the Stormont House Agreement, something agreed by two governments and most local parties. This approach is framed solely around the perceived need to address what is a false narrative of vexatious investigations of Army veterans.'

The Irish government also expressed disgust and dismay. Minister for Foreign Affairs Simon Coveney said: 'We do not believe the UK proposals published today can be the basis for dealing with legacy cases or would be supported by the parties or people in Northern Ireland.' He added that 'there will be a strong onus on the UK government in the engagement process to explain how their proposals could fully comply with their ECHR and other legal and international human rights obligations, or properly meet the needs of victims and their families'.[4]

At Westminster, Labour leader Sir Keir Starmer said a blanket amnesty was 'plain wrong' and not supported by victims. Shadow Northern Ireland Secretary Louise Haigh said it was 'deeply regrettable' that the government's approach on legacy has put victims' trust in the government at 'rock-bottom'. She accused Mr Johnson's the government of having taken a 'sledgehammer' to promises it made to victims a year before.[5]

Rattled by the response, Johnson defended his government's plans as 'measured and balanced'. He old MPs: 'The sad fact remains that there are many members of the armed services who continue to face the threat of vexatious prosecutions well into their seventies and eighties. We are finally bringing forward a solution to this problem, to enable the people of Northern Ireland to draw a line under the Troubles and to enable the people of Northern Ireland to move forward.'[6]

But it was indeed the response of the victims of all sides, of terrorism and state-sanctioned murder, which was to prove the most resonant. Not just of the Bloody Sunday and Ballymurphy massacres, but those of the Birmingham pub bombings and Loyalist hit squads, tit-for-tat killings and 'punishment' executions which were an almost daily feature during the worst days of the Troubles.

John Kelly, whose brother Michael was killed on Bloody Sunday, said the reported proposals deny many victims' families justice. 'The message they are sending out is that if you wear a British army uniform you are protected,' he told BBC Radio Foyle. 'We are hoping it does not happen and we will fight it as best we can.'[7] Mickey McKinney, whose brother William was one of the victims, said that an amnesty only adds to the pain of Bloody Sunday. He said: 'I don't trust the British government. Would you trust them if they murdered your brother and told lies about him?' The Ballymurphy Massacre victims' families issued a statement: 'We see this as the British government's cynical attempt to bring in an amnesty and a plan to bury its war crimes. The Ballymurphy Massacre inquest findings in May this year is the perfect example of why there should not be a statue of limitations.' John Teggart, whose father Danny was one of the victims of the Ballymurphy shootings, said the proposals were a 'slap in the face' for victims. 'It dances on the graves of all our loved ones and all those who were affected in the conflict', he said.[8]

Bernadyne Casey's brother Robert, a Catholic man who was a former soldier, was one of three men shot dead by the Army during an incident in Newry, County Down, in October 1971. 'We never, ever, got the truth about why they were shot,' she said. On the government's proposals, she asked: 'Whose authority had they to do that? Who said they should take that decision?' Ms Casey said she learned about the plans by watching the news. 'It makes you very bitter,' she added.

Such sentiments were shared by those who lost loved ones to the paramilitaries. Relatives of victims of the Birmingham pub bombings described the plans as 'obscene'. Julie Hambleton, whose older sister Maxine was among twenty-one people killed in the 1974 blasts, wrote to No 10: 'Tell me prime minister, if one of your loved ones was blown up beyond recognition, where you were only able to identify your son or daughter by their fingernails because their face had been burned so severely from the blast and little of their remains were left intact, would you be so quick to agree to such obscene legislation being implemented?

You would do everything in your power to find the murderers and bring them to justice, which is exactly what we campaign for every day. At what point did your government lose all sight of its moral, ethical and judicial backbone? How is this considered to be a deterrent for any future terrorist organisations?'[9]

Mary Hamilton, injured in the 1972 Claudy bombings which claimed the life of her brother-in-law, said a blanket ban on prosecutions would both anger and disgust victims' families and the wider public. The government was effectively saying the lives of those killed before 1998 'were not worth anything', she said.[10]

Kathleen Gillespie's husband Patsy was killed in a particularly brutal IRA attack – in 1991 the father of three was kidnapped, chained to a van containing a 1,200-lb bomb, and ordered to drive to the Coshquin army base near the Irish border to save his family who were held at gunpoint. The bomb exploded, killing him and five soldiers. She said: 'I feel robbed. I have this thing in my head that when it's an important person that's been killed, their thing is investigated, and their thing is solved. We're just the ordinary common people so it's alright to push us to the one side.' Serena Hamilton, whose father Corporal David Graham was an Ulster Defence Regiment soldier killed by the IRA in Coalisland, County Tyrone, in 1977, said: 'How can you move forward when you haven't got justice in the first place for such heinous crimes that happened to the likes of my father?'

The WAVE Trauma Centre stated: 'Victims and survivors should not be treated this way,' adding that if ministers were 'serious about effectively dealing with legacy' they 'must talk to those most impacted by pain and trauma'.

Eugene Reavey, whose three brothers were killed by the Loyalist Glenanne gang in 1976, said: 'People have been traumatised all their lives and yesterday's news is just going to traumatise these people all over again.' He vowed to write to Nancy Pelosi, the Speaker of the US House of Representatives, to ask the United States not to sign a trade deal with the UK until 'this is sorted out'. The Reverend Alan Irwin's father Thomas and uncle Fred, both part-time Ulster Defence Regiment soldiers, were killed in separate incidents in the 1970s and 1980s. 'They've said they're listening to us, but they're not listening and we've lived with betrayal after betrayal, particularly since the Belfast Agreement of 1998,' the Church of Ireland canon said. 'This betrayal hits an all-time low. How any government, no matter where they are, but our sovereign government, to stoop to something that is both morally and ethically wrong goes against the grain. I just cannot see how anyone in a civilised democracy could ever support such a thing.'[11] Amnesty International rejected the proposals as showing an 'appalling and offensive disregard for victims'. Its Northern Ireland campaign manager, Grainne Teggart, said: 'Many victims are having their worst fears realised in these proposals, the government is closing down paths to justice.'[12]

The move was driven by the government's 2019 election pledge to end the historical prosecution of soldiers who served in Northern Ireland, but many victims said they could not believe veterans would want an amnesty that also applies to the very terrorists who murdered their comrades. And the debate raged on amongst veterans, their former commanders, and those who had held both military and judicial levers.

Ian Simpson, of the Northern Ireland Veterans' Association, said 'today is a shameful day', adding: 'Today, the veterans and innocent victims have been betrayed to the uttermost by Boris Johnson and the British government. People who held the line in Northern Ireland, who gave us peace in Northern Ireland, have been put on a pedestal with terrorists, people who went out on a daily basis to murder and to maim.' Veterans' Commissioner for Northern Ireland Danny Kinahan said that 'veterans on the whole want to ensure that the rule of law is followed and they don't want an amnesty either – they don't want equivalence. However, if we all look at this from a society point of view we are not getting anywhere through the courts cases, people aren't getting justice.' Kinahan said there are 'many forms of justice and some people won't even accept what would happen in the court if they don't get the justice that they actually want'. He added: 'What we have got to do is find a way forward and we know from comments from senior legal people in the past that we are not going to get it through the court system.'[13]

Lord Dannatt, a former Army chief who served in Northern Ireland during the Troubles, said the proposals represented the 'least worst option' and offered families a way to get answers about what happened. 'There is now a mechanism where questions can be asked, facts can be ascertained and they will be able to get some degree of closure in knowing what happened because the people answering those questions, whether they're paramilitaries or retired soldiers, will be able to answer those questions truthfully and honestly without the fear of being prosecuted and dragged through the courts.'[14] He and others also pointed out that army veterans had had more to fear from historic prosecutions because the British Army kept scrupulous records, while paramilitaries operated in the shadows with no paper trails leading to their crimes.

Jon Boutcher, a former chief constable of Bedfordshire Police and the current head of Operation Kenova, a team of officers which has been independently investigating a number of Troubles cases, said the government's plans were a 'miscalculation'. He went on: 'To take away the prospect, the potential, of justice for these families, and these are some of the most heinous crimes committed in the United Kingdom in modern history, certainly doesn't sit with me comfortably.' He said his operation's relationship with former soldiers has been 'a good one' and as a former police officer he believes 'it is the rule of law which sets us apart. It is, I think, a miscalculation to apply a statute of limitations in the name of the veterans,' he said.

Former director of public prosecutions in Northern Ireland, Barra McGrory, questioned the legality of the proposals in relation to inquests. 'This is a shocking proposal issued by a government which claims to adhere to the rule of law in that it seeks to abolish completely all meaningful and judicial accountable processes,' he said. 'We've heard many arguments recently in the courts about the sovereignty of parliament and that parliament can undo anything it has previously done, but to take a step that would abolish a historical and ancient judicial process by which controversial deaths can be examined, the legality of that is very questionable.'[15] Baroness O'Loan, who was Northern Ireland's first police ombudsman, said the proposals disregarded the rule of law and were simply designed to protect former soldiers from prosecution. 'I think there are very serious questions to ask,' she said. 'I think what has happened here is such a terrible, terrible betrayal of the victims. To deprive them of all their legal remedies simultaneously is a total abdication by government of their responsibilities for the operation of the rule of law,' she said.[16]

And the most senior Church leaders questioned the amnesty. Archbishop Eamon Martin, leader of the Catholic Church in Ireland, said the government's proposals would be 'seen by many victims as a betrayal of trust which denies justice to them and to their loved ones'. He added: 'I was particularly disappointed by Prime Minister Boris Johnson's naive comments in the House of Commons suggesting that his legacy proposals would allow Northern Ireland to draw a line under the Troubles. At this painful time I ask for prayers of comfort for victims suffering on all sides in the conflict, and for truth and justice to prevail in the interest of the common good.' The Reverend David Bruce, moderator of the Presbyterian Church in Ireland, had 'a genuine concern' about the proposals which he believed was shared among members of the Presbyterian Church. 'This is one more example of a government demonstrating its arrogance and its unwillingness to genuinely consult and to engage with people on the ground,' he added. 'It looks rather like a solution which has been arrived at on one of the other islands and imposed upon this part of the United Kingdom.' (BBC, 15 July 2021)

In Belfast, anger made strange cross-party bedfellows in subsequent days and weeks. First Minister Paul Givan urged Stormont parties to engage collectively and put their 'best foot forward' to oppose the government plans which he described as a 'further insult to victims'. The DUP assembly member (MLA) said he believed the government wanted to 'wipe the slate clean' on the past and that the next steps needed to be 'carefully thought through' as 'clearly this is going to be a battle that has to be fought at Westminster'. He urged Sinn Féin to end its policy of not taking its seats at Westminster, to help 'make the case' in London. Sinn Féin president Mary Lou McDonald said of the Johnson administration: 'They have clearly shredded the Stormont House Agreement and delivered an incredibly cruel and shameless body blow to victims and survivors across this island and beyond.' SDLP deputy leader Nichola Mallon called for the other parties to back a recall of the assembly from its summer recess to discuss the issue. She said: 'We want to demonstrate and say very loudly and clearly to the British government that as an assembly all of the parties are united on this, that we stand with the victims and survivors and we will not allow the British government to do this.'

Alliance Party leader Naomi Long said if the new law was passed her party would have to think about whether or not it could take on the role of justice minister again. 'We would have to reflect very carefully, if the system is to become so corrupted that people are to be denied justice, as to whether that's a system over which any member of our party would wish to preside in future,' she explained. 'There are many on Conservative backbenches who may feel less comfortable with the idea that those involved in terrorist organisations during the Troubles may be free not to face court charges,' she added. Mrs Long said she expected challenges to the proposals 'would be numerous and last for quite some time' in the courts.

There remained eight live court cases related to the Troubles being dealt with by the Public Prosecution Service (PPS) which at the time of writing said its work continues as normal in the absence of the new legislation.[17]

***

Like much of the tragic history of Northern Ireland, the moral justification for an amnesty is fraught with ambiguities and is an argument which cannot be conclusively won by either side. Can one equate a soldier shooting a paralysed civilian on the ground with a terrorist planting a bomb in a shopping centre? Are there any circumstances in which someone pledged to uphold the law can break the law with impunity? When does the chain of command justify the 'just obeying orders' defence and is giving such orders by gesture or implicit collusion amount to criminality – arguments deployed at Nuremburg and other war crimes trials ever since. Does political expedience carry with it an inherent statute of limitations? At what point does a terrorist turn into a statesman? And when does the fluid concept of the greater public interest overshadow the concerns of those still grieving their lost ones?

Often such questions – moral, pragmatic or political – can only be answered from a deeply personal perspective, as shown by the father of a twelve-year-old boy killed in an IRA bomb explosion who said while he did not support or approve the amnesty proposals, he did accept them. Colin Parry, whose son Tim died in the 1993 Warrington bombing, said it was important to focus on the future rather than the past. He said: 'I accept them because I think peace-building is a pragmatic business. We can't bring Tim back, and even if the bombers were disclosed or revealed, it certainly wouldn't make me any happier. In fact in many ways it might unsettle me far more.'[18]

During the Troubles, around 3,650 Britons lost their lives, more than the UK death tolls in the conflicts in the former Yugoslavia, Iraq and Afghanistan combined and more than the US suffered on 9/11. Unlike the American atrocity, in which almost all the casualties were fatalities, in the Troubles the price went far beyond the morgue. For every death, there were at least ten who lost limbs and genitals, sight and hearing, who were knee-capped in punishment beatings or who suffered severe mental trauma. Plus more who had their homes burned out or who were exiled by hate-filled neighbours. The Good Friday Agreement put an imperfect end to that and dealing with terrorists and fanatics was a price worth paying. But it was an uneasy fragile peace and Brexit negotiations showed that the bomb and the bullet were not necessarily consigned to history.

Boris Johnson's amnesty has to be considered in that light. But what sticks in the craws of all those affected is that he was motivated purely by pollical expediency, fulfilling a promise he made in the 2019 election which confirmed his premiership, and in subsequent by-elections. Such cynicism is hardly unusual, but given the grief surrounding the issue, it leaves a bitter taste.

Conclusion

'It's all been said.'

Most of the soldiers implicated in the deaths and woundings on Bloody Sunday remain living, albeit in anonymous retirement. Most were in their late teens and early twenties on that dreadful day. Given their supposed level of training and discipline, that was no excuse but can explain at least some of their behaviour. Behaviour which remained an indelible stain on the reputation of the Army, resulted in a truly terrible upsurge in violence, and boosted paramilitary recruitment.

Most, but not all, lied through their teeth in subsequent testimony from initial form-filling for the Military Police, through the Widgery cover-up, to the Saville Inquiry. Saville cut them some slack, however, saying that 'the fact that a soldier afterwards lied about what had happened does not necessarily entail that he fired without believing that he had identified a person posing a threat of causing death or serious injury, since it is possible that he was at the time convinced that he was justified in firing, but later invented details in an attempt to bolster his account and make it more credible to others'. When they disembarked in the Bogside the soldiers were in an open area where they had never previously been and which was overlooked by the large and high blocks of the Rossville Flats, believed by them to be a hotbed of republican paramilitaries. It is no wonder that they were highly alert to the risk of coming under lethal attack. Saville said: 'If these soldiers were not frightened, they must at least have been highly apprehensive.'[1]

The first shots fired by Lieutenant N over the heads of the crowd led some soldiers to believe that they were under fire and reinforced what they had been told about the likely presence of republican paramilitaries in the area. That also made them even more ready to respond in a knee-jerk fashion. In an urban area, where sound bounces off buildings, it is hard to know who is firing and from where, while the expulsion of a rubber bullet can sound like an explosive device. On Bloody Sunday such factors were magnified by what was known as 'the Derry sound' – the echoing effect created by the City Walls and adjacent buildings including the high Rossville Flats which multiplied the sound of gunfire and detonations. The same applied to civilians who were wrongly convinced that non-para soldiers stationed on the city walls also opened fire. Believing themselves under attack, some soldiers clearly lost self-control, forgot or ignored their training and fired without being satisfied that they had identified a person posing a threat of causing death or serious injury.[2]

That is perhaps understandable, to a degree. But nothing can justify, on the streets of the United Kingdom or anywhere else for that matter, shooting unarmed, panicking civilians as they ran or crawled away from heavily armed soldiers caught up in bloodlust. There was no possible justification for shooting Jim Wray a second time as he lay on the ground, for example.[3] Or for those shot while going to the aid of the wounded and dying. Members of 1 Para clearly believed they had a licence to kill which went far beyond the restrictions of the Yellow Card. The gung-ho culture of their barracks and training grounds exacerbated that and highlighted the 'them and us' mindset which ruled that there was little or no difference between demonstrators and terrorists. They were generally working-class lads from deprived areas across Northern Britain which could have made them more sympathetic to similar young men with different accents. It did not. Their talk on and off duty was of the 'honeytrap' murders, roadside bombs and other atrocities. They all knew someone who had become a casualty or knew someone who knew someone who had become a casualty. They had faced months of stone-throwing, petrol-bombing and abuse with limited opportunities to hit back. Frustration must have built up over the months. In at least some cases those who fired did so because of a belief they could fire with impunity, secure in the knowledge that the arrangements then in force – later criticised by the Lord Chief Justice of Northern Ireland – meant that their actions would not be investigated by the RUC, but by the Royal Military Police, their own police force, who would be sympathetic and who would not conduct a proper investigation. All of which made cocking a high-velocity weapon against instructions an almost automatic response.

And what of the senior officers? Major General Robert Ford was exonerated by Saville with the caveat that his decision to use 1 Para, which had a reputation for excessive violence, ran the risk of exacerbating the tensions between the Army and nationalists.[4] He claimed that he could not remember his notorious 'shoot selected ringleaders' memo. Ford relinquished his command in April 1973 and became Commandant of the Royal Military Academy Sandhurst. He was Adjutant General from 1978 to 1981 when he retired from the British Army.[5] For a year he was ADC General to the Queen. In retirement he chaired the Army Benevolent Fund; was Governor of the Royal Hospital, Chelsea; and vice-chairman of the Commonwealth War Graves Commission until 1993. 1989 to 1993. He died in November 2015.[6]

Major Ted Loden, the leader of Support Company also exonerated by Saville, subsequently held a number of airborne posts, including brigade major to 44 Para Brigade and commanding officer of 4 Para. On a visit to see his son, head of security for Barclays Africa, Loden was shot and killed during a suspected robbery in Kenya. One report said that he was 'in the wrong place at the wrong time'. He was seventy-three.[7]

In November 1972, Lieutenant Colonel Derek Wilford captured Ulster Volunteer Force leader Gusty Spence, then on the run from prison and wanted for his involvement in a series of sectarian murders.[8] Wilford had been regarded as a high-flyer within the British Army, but the shadow of Bloody Sunday never left him. The officer most criticised by Saville and known in Derry as the 'Butcher of the Bogside' considered that he had been made a scapegoat and appears to have been consumed by bitterness. He persistently defended his own leadership and the actions of his men. He claimed to have been abandoned by the military hierarchy and British government. Despite this he did not retire from the Army until 1983, although he stated he felt constantly passed over for promotion, ending his career only one rank higher than his 1972 position. He always maintained his soldiers were fired upon first and in 1992 in a BBC documentary he reasoned: 'If you get into an enormous crowd which is out to make mischief you are in the first instance a party to it.'[9] He resented the decision to call a new inquiry, saying: 'I feel bitterly betrayed by the Government. It seems that it believes in peace at any price – and the price is going to be our heads.' In 1999, speaking on BBC radio he angered the relatives of those killed and injured during Bloody Sunday by suggesting that almost all Northern Ireland Catholics were closet republicans. Although he later apologised for his comments, the Army distanced itself from him even further.[10] The Bloody Sunday families have always regarded it as an insult that Colonel Wilford was decorated by the Queen shortly after the atrocity. Wilford became estranged from his wife and divorced her to pursue a relationship with another woman he had met while he was posted in Belgium. In 2010 it was reported that Wilford had been living in Belgium for a number of years with his new wife and daughter. Following the release of the Saville report, he said: 'I don't want to talk about it. It's all been said.'[11]

Bloody Sunday did not blight the career of Mike Jackson. In 1972 he was a captain and adjutant to 1 Para, and by the time he retired in 2006 he was a General, had been knighted by the Queen and was Chief of the General Staff – the most senior officer in the British Army. Jackson was the last Army officer who served on Bloody Sunday to retire. Later he said he had 'no doubt that innocent people were shot'.[12]

Widgery blamed the civil rights organisers, but Saville cleared them of all responsibility, even though they must have realised that there would be trouble from rioters, on the grounds that they could not have forecast unjustified firing by soldiers.[13] Despite Saville's reasoned qualifications, however, there were many who, tacitly or actively, condoned paramilitary operations and cannot escape all responsibility.

They do not include Ivan Cooper, who at the height of his political career commanded the largest support of any nationalist Stormont MP. Cooper, who was opposed to all violence, increasingly found himself on the street trying to ease tension and prevent demonstrators from coming into contact with the police and Unionist factions. His outdoor oratory could reach to even the largest crowds, but on more than one occasion he was knocked out cold by bricks and stones. The high-water mark of his political career came in 1973 when he was elected to the power-sharing executive at Stormont, where he was given ministerial responsibility for community relations. But the executive was jinxed, foundering after only five months in office when the United Ulster Unionist Coalition brought it down with a general strike.[14] After service in the Constitutional Convention the following year, Cooper fought Mid Ulster for the SDLP in both 1974 general elections, splitting the nationalist vote and ensuring the defeat of the Independent Bernadette McAliskey (née Devlin). After boundary changes, Cooper stood aside in the new Foyle constituency to let in his colleague and friend John Hume. Disillusioned by the unceasing sectarian violence, he gradually shed his political career and became an insolvency consultant.[15] Cooper, despite declining health, strongly supported families of the bereaved in their campaign for truth and justice and continued to give pin-sharp interviews on the subject. He was present with the relatives when the Saville report was published and called for the soldiers concerned to be prosecuted. 'In my church the commandment says "thou shalt do no murder", and I believe that commandment,' he said. After a stroke, his health progressively deteriorated and he became wheelchair-bound. Nonetheless, much of the work that Cooper had done helped ultimately to smooth the way for the Good Friday Agreement.[16] He died in June 2019.

Inquiry chief Lord Saville remained active in his seventies, flying his own aeroplane, hiking in the American Rockies, solo white-water canoeing, sailing and tackling the computer age. His inquiry Counsel Christopher Clarke was knighted and appointed a High Court judge.[17]

Father Daly left Derry the year after Bloody Sunday to work as a religious adviser to broadcasters RTE, but he returned to the city a year later when he was appointed Bishop of Derry. Aged forty, he was the youngest Bishop in Ireland. Prior to Bloody Sunday, Daly had been sympathetic to the 'old' IRA, of which his father was a member, but the events of that day led him to believe that 'violence is completely unacceptable as a means to a political end'.[18] The Catholic bishops of Ireland discussed the possibility of excommunicating IRA members several times during Daly's tenure, often in the aftermath of a particularly bloody attack, though no decision was ever reached. Daly was always reluctant to excommunicate and used the motto 'better to communicate than excommunicate'. However, he introduced a ban on paramilitary trappings at Catholic funerals and in 1976 organised an interdenominational protest march through Derry city centre – a response to an increase in sectarian murders – which was unprecedentedly joined by almost all the clergy in the city.[19] During the Maze hunger strikes he lobbied the European Commission on Human Rights to intervene. But tensions with the IRA grew and came to a head following the October 1990 proxy bombings in which IRA members forced civilians to drive car bombs to their targets, killing the driver and anyone else in close proximity. Daly described the bombings as having 'crossed a new threshold of evil', and believed that while republican paramilitaries may claim to be Catholics, 'works proclaim clearly that they follow Satan'.[20] He retired as Bishop in 1993 after suffering a stroke and served as chaplain to the Foyle Hospice.[21] He was awarded the Freedom of the City by the local council in 2015 in a joint ceremony with Protestant Bishop James Mehaffey, with whom he had worked closely while the two were in office. He died in August the following year, aged eighty-two, in Altnagelvin Hospital after a fall; he had also been diagnosed with cancer. He was surrounded by family and local priests.[22] The incumbent Bishop of Derry, Donal McKeown, said that Daly 'served, without any concern for himself, throughout the traumatic years of the Troubles, finding his ministry shaped by the experience of witnessing violence and its effects'.[23] A message from Pope Francis was read out at the beginning of the funeral service. Hundreds lined the route from the cathedral to the grave. Obituaries described him as a 'fearless peace-builder' who left an abiding memory of 'a terrified but calm priest waving a bloodied white handkerchief' which proved 'the iconic image of Bloody Sunday'.[24]

The Provisional IRA, despite only limited deployment on Bloody Sunday, cannot wholly avoid responsibility, of course. During the Troubles the organisation killed more than 1,700 people with perhaps ten times that number injured by shootings and bombings, knee-capping and punishment beatings, with many more driven or burnt out of their homes. Protestant and Catholic civilians alike died at PIRA's hands and in the republican plot at Milltown Cemetery in West Belfast lie scores of graves of its own members killed during the conflict. 'All sides inflicted pain and suffering,' said veteran republican and former PIRA prisoner Sean Murray. 'I never ever want to see that inflicted upon any other generation. There were situations which happened which were of a sectarian nature – as a republican I must acknowledge that. That wasn't republican policy, or republican philosophy, but there were actions which could be viewed as sectarian.' Laurence McKeown, a former PIRA member who served sixteen years in jail for attempting to murder police officers, said: 'Once Bloody Sunday happened you are into full-blown guerrilla warfare. Yes, there were things done which republicans couldn't stand over but that doesn't take away, for me anyway, the legitimacy of the armed struggle.'[25]

As the career of the late Martin McGuinness showed, acknowledged paramilitaries engaged in the peace process and held posts in subsequent Stormont administrations. The IRA's political wing, Sinn Féin or 'Ourselves Alone' in Gaelic, continues to sit in Belfast and Westminster. In July 2002, on the thirtieth anniversary of the 1972 Bloody Friday bombings, the IRA startled its sympathizers and enemies alike by offering 'sincere apologies and condolences' to the families of its civilian victims. It and Sinn Féin continue to favour a United Ireland, but by peaceful means. The Royal Ulster Constabulary has been disbanded, Loyalist groups have largely laid down their arms, and most British troops have left for other battle zones. Tensions may still simmer, exploited by criminal gangs, Loyalist extremists and IRA splinter groups, and sectarian and political murders still add to the grief. But as comparable prosperity has changed Northern Ireland, and as a new generation has grown up, such violence is anathema to the general population.

Nevertheless, it is clear that 1 Para were deployed to teach a lesson to a community who at the time, and to varying degrees, supported violent resistance to what they considered an oppressive regime. At the very least the top brass knew that punitive action would involve the deliberate use of unwarranted lethal force or which they sanctioned with reckless disregard as to whether such force was used.[26] Saville found no conclusive evidence of that, but the General Ford memo is a giveaway.

It has long been claimed, and not just by grieving families, that the massacre was a deliberate political act, anticipated and planned for, by the Conservative government of Edward Heath. That, like most conspiracy theories, does not stand up. In the months before Bloody Sunday, genuine and serious attempts were being made at the highest level to work towards a peaceful political settlement in Northern Ireland. Any action involving the use or likely use of unwarranted lethal force against nationalists would have been entirely counterproductive. The Northern Ireland government had been pressing Westminster to step up the use of military force as the RUC had neither the manpower nor the resources to deal effectively with all security issues, but what happened on Bloody Sunday was never envisaged.[27]

Veteran journalist David Healy, who covered the Troubles for the Press Association, when asked to sum up, said: 'Bloody Sunday marked the day the British government lost the Northern Ireland propaganda war, at home and abroad and crucially in the United States. That sudden change of mood was clear to anyone who walked the streets of Derry and Belfast before and after Bloody Sunday. Nothing could counteract the image which went round the world of the local priest, Father Edward Daly, appealing for a stop to the shooting by waving a bloodstained white handkerchief as he tended a dying seventeen-year-old boy on the street. And it caused an intensification of the killing by all sides – that year more than double the number of people died, nearly 500, than in the previous four years of the Troubles added together. As Gerry Adams said, before Bloody Sunday the IRA had only minority support in the Nationalist population of Northern Ireland, after it money, arms and recruits poured in.'

No one on the nationalist side believed the British government's claim that the Parachute Regiment soldiers had been fired on and were acting in self-defence. From then on government statements were universally disbelieved by nationalists, and by a good many others. From Bloody Sunday onwards, the British government were on the defensive, politically and militarily. The deaths inflicted by British soldiers on that sunny January day were held to justify all the bloodshed which followed and many accused those soldiers of being directly responsible for the more than 3,000 deaths in the years to come. It took nearly forty years, two full-scale inquiries, millions of pounds and a peace process before the British government, in the shape of the Conservative Prime Minister David Cameron, admitted what many had known all along: British soldiers committed murder on the streets of Londonderry on 30 January 1972.

But only one soldier was prosecuted – the still legally unidentifiable Soldier F who allegedly killed with impunity on three separate sites of the

Derry battlefield – and he never faced trial. At the time of writing, it is presumed he lives in peaceful, untroubled retirement – unlike the victims of that awful day, and their families.

Perhaps the last word should come again from Lord Saville: 'What happened on Bloody Sunday strengthened the Provisional IRA, increased nationalist resentment and hostility towards the Army and exacerbated the violent conflict of the years that followed. Bloody Sunday was a tragedy for the bereaved and the wounded, and a catastrophe for the people of Northern Ireland.'[28]

And a fifty-year fight for justice will go on.

Notes

1 Flashpoint Derry

1. Gallagher, 227, 223
2. Purdie, chapter one
3. English, 91
4. Wilson, 37
5. Ruane and Todd, 126, 127
6. Lord Cameron, *Disturbances in Northern Ireland, Report of the Commission, 1969*
7. Purdie, 244
8. Hanley and Millar (2009), 103, 104
9. *Ibid.*
10. Cain.ulst.ac.uk
11. O'Callaghan, 22
12. Bew and Gillespie, 10
13. Alpha History website, *Political Violence in Northern Ireland, 1969-1972*
14. *Derry Journal,* August 18 2019
15. *BBC News*, August 13 1969
16. Coogan, 90
17. *Irish Times*, August 30 2019
18. *Derry Journal*, August 18 2019
19. *Irish Times*, August 30 2019
20. *Ibid.*
21. Cain.ulst.ac.uk
22. Paramilitary source to author, 1972

23. Crossman, 636
24. Bew and Gillespie, 19, 20
25. Alpha History website, *Political Violence in Northern Ireland, 1969-1972*
26. MacStiofain, 146
27. O'Brien, 166
28. Alpha History website, *Political Violence in Northern Ireland, 1969-1972*
29. Coogan, 143
30. White, 166
31. Walker, 190
32. Alpha History website, *Political Violence in Northern Ireland, 1969-1972*
33. Coogan, 126
34. Geraghty, 45
35. Kennally and Preston, 1971 pamphlet
36. McGuffin, chapters four and six
37. *Irish Times*, April 9 2019
38. *Daily Telegraph*, December 22 2009
39. *BBC News*, August 6 2013
40. *BBC News*, June 5 2014
41. Hamil, Introduction
42. *Irish Times*, April 9 2019
43. Taylor, 82
44. Coogan, 152
45. *Belfast Telegraph*, March 1 2011
46. Alpha History website, *Political Violence in Northern Ireland, 1969-1972*
47. Widgery, part two 10
48. Widgery, part two, 12
49. Saville, Conclusions, 2.3
50. Saville, Conclusions, 2.6
51. Widgery, part two, 13
52. Saville, Conclusions, 2.14-15

2 Honeytrap Killings and the Ballymurphy Massacre

1. Taylor, 89-91
2. *Belfast Telegraph*, February 26 2020
3. Geraghty, 40
4. *Daily Mirror*, March 9 2007

5. *Hansard*, March 11 1971
6. *Ibid.*
7. *Belfast Telegraph*, February 26 2020
8. *Sunday Life*, August 1 2006
9. *BBC Northern Ireland*, February 25 2020
10. *Daily Record*, February 26 2020
11. *Mail on Sunday*, February 9 2020
12. *Mail on Sunday*, February 16 2020
13. *Mail on Sunday*, February 9 2020
14. *Belfast Telegraph*, February 26 2020
15. to author, East Sussex, September 1972
16. to author, Southampton, 1974
17. to author, Winchester, 1974
18. *BBC News*, February 18 2011
19. *Guardian*, June 26 2014
20. ballymurphymassacre.com
21. *Ibid.*
22. *The Sun*, September 18 2018
23. *BBC News*, November 22 2016
24. *Ibid.*
25. *Ibid.*
26. *BBC News*, February 10 2015
27. *BBC News*, February 12 2016
28. *BBC News*, May 3 2016
29. *BBC News*, March 3 2020
30. *Morning Star*, March 21 2019
31. *BBC News*, March 13 2019
32. *BBC News*, September 9 2019
33. *BBC News*, February 26 2019
34. *Irish Times*, May 31 2019
35. *Belfast Live*, May 30 2019
36. *BBC News*, November 15 2018
37. Saville Report, Conclusions, 3.67-69
38. Army contact to author, East Sussex September 1972
39. *Irish News*, January 28 1972
40. *Guardian*, July 1 2019
41. Bardon, 650
42. *BBC News*, January 30 2002
43. Bardon, 660
44. *Secret History – Bloody Sunday,* Channel 4, January 22 1999
45. *BBC News*, June 10 2010

46. Rollcall, Paradata.com
47. *Belfast Telegraph*, June 21 2010

3 The Day

1. Guardian, June 11 2010
2. Widgery, Narrative, 9
3. Saville, vol 8, 147.3
4. Saville, vol 8, 147.94
5. Saville, vol 8, 147.99
6. Saville, vol 8, 147.100
7. Saville, vol 8, 147.101
8. *Ibid.*
9. Saville, Conclusions, 2.17
10. Widgery, Narrative, 16
11. Widgery, Narrative, 19
12. Saville, Conclusions, 3.1
13. *Ibid.*
14. Widgery, Narrative, 24
15. *BBC News*, January 30 1972
16. Saville, vol 4, 18.3
17. Saville, vol 2, 18.41
18. Saville, vol 2, 18.13
19. Saville, vol 2, 18.6
20. Saville, vol 2, 18.67
21. Pringle and Jacobson, 116
22. *Guardian*, January 11 2010
23. *Daily Telegraph*, March 30 2000
24. Saville, Conclusions, 3.14
25. Widgery, Narrative, 27
26. Saville, Conclusions, 3.17-18
27. Saville, Conclusions, 3.19-20
28. Widgery, Narrative, 33, 34
29. Widgery, Narrative, 42
30. Saville, Conclusions, 3.21
31. Saville, Conclusions, 3.22
32. Alphahistory.com/alana-burke
33. Saville, vol 3, 24.21
34. Saville, vol 3, 24.31
35. Saville, vol 3, 24.70
36. Saville, vol 3, 3.26

37. Saville, vol 3, 26.1
38. Saville, vol 3, 26.14
39. Saville, vol 3, 26.34-35
40. Saville, vol 3, 28.16
41. Saville, vol 3, 28.22
42. Widgery, Narrative, 47
43. Saville, vol 4, 55.4-5
44. Saville, vol 4, 55.47
45. Saville, vol 4, 55.37
46. Saville, vol 4, 55.24
47. Saville, vol 4, 55.45-6
48. Saville, vol 4, 55.19
49. Saville, vol 4, 55.65
50. Saville, vol 4, 55.77
51. Saville, Conclusions, 3.48
52. Saville, vol 4, 55.10
53. Saville, vol 4, 55.30-31
54. Saville, vol 4, 55.81
55. Saville, vol 4, 55.89
56. Saville, vol 4, 55.102
57. Saville, Conclusions, 3.48
58. Saville, vol 4, 55.130
59. Saville, vol 4, 55.86
60. Saville, vol 4, 55.141
61. Saville, vol 4, 55.150
62. Saville, vol 4, 55.162
63. Saville, vol 4, 55.145
64. Saville, vol 4, 55.168
65. Saville, vol 4, 55.212
66. Saville, vol 4, 55.228
67. Derry Journal, January 30 1992
68. Saville, vol 4, 55.240
69. Saville, Conclusions, 3.49-51
70. Saville, vol 4, 55.264
71. Saville, vol 4, 55.282
72. Saville, vol 4, 55.346
73. Saville, vol 4, 55.349
74. *BBC News*, August 18 2018
75. Saville, Conclusions, 3.52
76. Saville, vol 4, 55.312
77. Saville, Conclusions, 3.54
78. Widgery, 50

79. Widgery, 51
80. Saville, vol 3, 51.45
81. Saville, vol 3, 52.4-5
82. Saville, vol 3, 52.6
83. Saville, vol 3, 52.8
84. Saville, vol 3, 52.9
85. Saville, vol 3, 52.72
86. Saville, vol 3, 49.72
87. Saville, vol 3, 52.12
88. Saville, vol 3, 54.3
89. Saville, vol 3, 53.6
90. Widgery, 44
91. Saville, vol 5, 86.346
92. Widgery, 57
93. Saville, vol 5, 86.3
94. Saville, vol 5, 86.7
95. Saville, vol 5, 86.49-51
96. Saville, vol 5, 86.47
97. *BBC News*, March 14 2019
98. Saville, vol 5, 86.60
99. Saville, vol 5, 86.70
100. *BBC News*, March 14 2019
101. Saville, vol 5, 86.94
102. Saville, vol 5, 86.130
103. Saville, vol 5, 86.169
104. Saville, vol 5, 86.290
105. BBC News, March 14 2019
106. Saville, vol 5, 86.201
107. Saville, vol 5, 86.244
108. BBC News, March 14 2019
109. Saville, vol 5, 86.295
110. Saville, vol 5, 86.470
111. Saville, vol 5, 86.485
112. Saville, vol 5, 86.339
113. Saville, vol 5, 86.365-367
114. Saville, vol 5, 86.381
115. *BBC News*, March 14 2019
116. Saville, Conclusions, 3.58
117. Saville, vol 5, 86.415
118. Saville, vol 5, 86.421
119. Saville, vol 5, 86.426
120. Saville, vol 5, 86.439

121. Saville, vol 5, 86.448
122. Saville, vol 5, 86.563
123. Saville, vol 5, 86.566
124. Saville, vol 5, 89.71
125. Guardian, May 16 2001
126. Widgery, 59
127. Saville, vol 6, 3.33
128. Saville, vol 6, 104.2
129. Saville, vol 6, 104.8
130. Saville, vol 6, 104.10
131. Saville, vol 6, 104.5
132. Saville, vol 6, 104.140
133. Saville, vol 6, 104.151
134. Saville, vol 6, 104.166-168
135. Saville, vol 6, 106.203
136. *BBC News*, March 14 2019
137. Saville, vol 6, 104.208
138. Saville, vol 6, 104.215
139. Saville, vol 6, 104.309
140. Saville, vol 6, 104.309
141. Saville, vol 6, 104.290
142. Saville, vol 6, 104.294
143. Saville, vol 6, 104.597
144. Saville, vol 6, 104.466
145. Saville, vol 6, 104.482
146. Saville, vol 6, 104.502
147. Saville, vol 6, 104.513
148. Saville, vol 6, 104.498
149. Saville, Conclusions, 3.62
150. Saville, vol 6, 104.522
151. Saville, vol 6, 3.36
152. Saville, vol 6, 107.10
153. *BBC News*, March 14 2019
154. Saville, vol 6, 107.75
155. *Ibid.*
156. Saville, vol 6, 107.13
157. Saville, vol 6, 107.29
158. *BBC News*, March 14 2019
159. Saville, vol 6, 107.33
160. Saville, vol 6, 107.488
161. Saville, vol 6, 107.71

162. Saville, vol 6, 107.100
163. Saville, vol 6, 107.4
164. Saville, vol 6, 107.138
165. Saville, vol 6, 107.139
166. Saville, vol 6. 107.115
167. Saville, vol 6, 107.78
168. Saville, vol 7, 118.3-4
169. Saville, vol 7, 118.12-13
170. Saville, vol 7, 118.28
171. Saville, vol 7, 118.36
172. Saville, vol 7, 118.29
173. Saville, vol 6, 3.38
174. Saville, vol 7, 118.117
175. Saville, vol 7, 118.120
176. Saville, vol 7, 118.125
177. Saville, vol 7, 118.147
178. Saville, vol 7, 118.150
179. Saville, vol 7, 118.152
180. Saville, vol 7, 118.154
181. Saville, vol 7, 118.163
182. Saville, vol 7, 118.164
183. *BBC News*, March 14 2019
184. Saville, vol 7, 118.206
185. Saville, vol 7, 118.208
186. Saville, vol 7, 118.210
187. *BBC News*, May 23 2002
188. *BBC News*, March 14 2019
189. Saville, vol 7, 118.217
190. Saville, vol 7, 118.237
191. Saville, vol 7, 118.244
192. Saville, vol 7, 118.247
193. Saville, vol 7, 118.252
194. Saville, vol 7, 118.256
195. Saville, vol 7, 118.291
196. Saville, Conclusions, 3.65
197. *Guardian,* January 31 1972
198. *Ibid*.
199. Widgery, 42
200. CAIN timeline, 1972
201. Saville, vol 6, 107.7
202. *Guardian*, July 1 2019

4 Interlude: Martin McGuinness

1. *Daily Telegraph*, March 30 2000
2. Saville, vol 8, 147.207
3. *Guardian*, obituary, March 17 2019
4. *Independent*, March 15 2010
5. Saville, vol 8, 147.209
6. Saville, vol 8, 147.208
7. Saville, vol 8, 147.213
8. Saville, vol 8, 147.217
9. Security source to author, 2009
10. Saville, vol 8, 147.228
11. *BBC News*, December 5 2000
12. Saville, vol 8, 147.229
13. Saville, vol 8, 147.233-234
14. Saville, vol 8, 147.237
15. Saville, vol 8, 147.231
16. *BBC News Online*, March 27 2007
17. Saville, vol 8, 147.280
18. Saville, vol 8, 147.292
19. Saville, vol 8, 147.312
20. Saville, vol 8, 147.321
21. Saville, vol 8, 147.333
22. Saville, vol 8, 147.359
23. *Daily Telegraph*, February 21 2005
24. *Age of Terror*, BBC, April 21 2008
25. *Guardian*, obituary, March 17 2019
26. *BBC News*, March 7 2019
27. *Guardian*, obituary, March 17 2019
28. *BBC News*, January 9 2017
29. *Raidio Teilifio Eirean*, March 21 2017

5 Aftermath

1. *Guardian*, February 1 1972
2. Public Records Office, released January 1 2003
3. *Hansard*, January 31 1972
4. *Press Association*, January 31 1972
5. *Connaught Tribune*, February 1 1972
6. HistoryIreland.com January/February 2012
7. *Guardian*, February 3 1972

8. *Ibid.*
9. *Ibid.*
10. *Irish News*, February 2 2019
11. Coogan, 107
12. Wharton, 46
13. HistoryIreland.com January/February 2012
14. *British Journalism Review*, Volume 32, March 2021
15. *Hansard*, January 31 1972
16. AlphaHistory.com, timeline 1972
17. *Hansard*, March 24 1972
18. *Daily Telegraph*, January 1 2003
19. Bew and Gillespie, 48
20. AlphaHistory.com, timeline 1972
21. AlphaHistory.com, timeline 1972
22. CAIN – Conflict Archive on the Internet – Bloody Sunday 1972
23. Wood, 104, 105
24. *London Gazette*, October 3 1972
25. *Independent*, January 17 2010
26. *Times*, March 15 2019

6 The Widgery Cover-up

1. *BBC News*, June 11 2010
2. *Guardian*, November 26 2015
3. *Times*, obituary, July 28 1981
4. *London Gazette*, April 22 1971
5. Widgery, Introduction, 5
6. Widgery, Introduction, 7
7. Widgery, part 2, 21,22
8. Widgery, part 3, 32-34
9. Widgery, part 3, 54
10. Widgery, part 3,59
11. *Ibid.*
12. *Times*, Obituary, July 18 2020)
13. Widgery, Summary of Conclusions, 1-15
14. Widgery, part 3, 49
15. *Independent*, January 30 1998
16. *Guardian*, April 20 1972
17. *Times*, April 20 1972
18. Conway, 34
19. *BBC News*, June 11 2010

20. *Independent*, June 10 2010
21. *University of Western Australia Law Review* 1972, 411
22. *Economist*, June 4 1994

7 The Long Road to Calvary

1. CAIN, chronology 1972
2. *Hansard*, August 1 1972
3. Campbell, museumoffreederry-bloodysunday-justicecampaign
4. *BBC News*, November 21 2013
5. *BBC Panorama – Britain's Secret Terror Force*, November 21 2013
6. *Daily Mail*, November 17 2013
7. *BBC News*, November 21 2013
8. CAIN, chronology 1972
9. *Ibid.*
10. Whitehall source to author, 1979
11. Westminster source to author, 1979
12. Taylor, 265
13. Speech to Conservative conference, Brighton, October 1984
14. CAIN, chronology 1985
15. Westminster sources to author, January 1988
16. Campbell, museumoffreederry-bloodysunday-justicecampaign
17. *Ibid.*
18. Military sources to author, August-September 2007
19. Campbell, museumoffreederry-bloodysunday-justicecampaign
20. *Ibid.*
21. To author, April 2020
22. Blair, 154, 155
23. Blair, 157
24. Blair, 165
25. *Hansard*, January 29 1998
26. *Independent*, January 30 1998
27. Hansard, January 29 1998
28. *BBC News*, June 11 2010
29. *BBC News*, April 10 1998
30. *Dail and Seanad Official Report*, November 26 1998
31. *BBC News*, August 15, 16 1998
32. Author's reportage, August 1998

8 The Saville Inquiry

1. *BBC News*, June 15 2010

2. *Times,* June 14 2010
3. *Who's Who,* December 2009
4. *Ulster TV* archives, Bloody Sunday, key players
5. Van der Bijl, 52, 53
6. *Ulster TV,* June 11 2010
7. *Ulster TV* archives, Bloody Sunday, key players
8. *Ibid.*
9. *Guardian,* May 16 2001
10. *Ulster TV* archives, Bloody Sunday, key players
11. *Ibid.*
12. *Guardian,* May 16 2001
13. *BBC News,* January 30 2007
14. *BBC News,* April 3 2002
15. *Sunday Times,* August 14 2005
16. *BBC News,* October 24 2002
17. *Spectator,* January 12 2007
18. *BBC News,* December 16 2004
19. *Ulster TV,* June 11 2010
20. *BBC News,* September 24 2009
21. *Daily Telegraph,* May 29 2010
22. *Guardian,* June 3 2010
23. *Daily Telegraph,* June 12 2010
24. *Independent,* March 15 2010
25. *CNN,* June 15 2010
26. *BBC News,* June 16 2010
27. *Guardian,* June 11 2010
28. *Daily Telegraph,* June 16 2010
29. *Guardian,* June 12 2010
30. Saville, vol 3, 3.82
31. Saville, vol 3, 3.19
32. Saville, Conclusions, 5.14
33. Saville, vol 3, 3.82
34. Saville, vol 3, 3.80-82
35. *Daily Telegraph,* June 15 2010
36. Saville, vol 3, 3.90-91
37. *Daily Telegraph,* June 15 2010
38. *Irish Times,* June 15 2010
39. *BBC News,* June 15 2010
40. *Ibid.*
41. Saville, vol 3, 3.94-95
42. Saville, vol 3, 3.97-99
43. Saville, vol 3, 3.101

44. Saville, vol 3, 3.113
45. Saville, vol 3, 102-106
46. Saville, vol 3, 3. 108-110
47. Saville, vol 3, 113-115
48. Saville, Conclusions, 5.4-5
49. *BBC News Online*, June 15 2010
50. *RTE*, June 15 2010
51. *Wall Street Journal*, June 15 2010
52. Angus Reid Public Opinion, June 2010
53. *New York Times*, June 15 2010
54. *Daily Mail*, June 17 2010
55. Daily Telegraph, June 16 2010
56. museumoffreederry.com justice campaign
57. *Daily Mail*, June 16 2010
58. *Belfast Telegraph*, June 16 2010
59. *BBC News*, June 15 2010
60. *Belfast Telegraph*, June 16 2010
61. *Daily Telegraph*, June 16 2010
62. *Belfast Telegraph* online archive
63. *Daily Telegraph*, June 16 2010
64. *Ibid*.
65. *BBC News*, March 13 2019

9 Bloody Culture

1. Doyle, 53, 54
2. Ingham, 127
3. Doyle, 62
4. *Melody Maker*, February 19 1972
5. Doyle, 55
6. Ingham, 128
7. Woffinden, 64
8. Du Noyer, 64
9. Blaney, 68
10. Blaney 65
11. Du Noyer, 64
12. Howe, 183
13. Guila, 138
14. Oddie, 144
15. *Hot Press*, February 18 1983
16. *Rolling Stone*, June 9 1983
17. Stokes, 37-39

18. Lucy White, April 1 1983
19. *Rolling Stone*, June 9 1983
20. McCormick, 179
21. *U2 – Rattle and Hum, Paramount* DVD, 1999
22. *Daily Telegraph*, June 15 2010
23. *Guardian*, March 27 2005
24. *Tricycle Theatre* reviews, April 5 2005
25. *BBC News*, June 14 2010
26. *BBC News Online*, October 6 2002
27. *Bloody Sunday, Flixster* website
28. RogertEgbert.com, October 25 2002
29. *Guardian*, June 10 2004
30. *Guardian*, April 18 2016
31. *Irish Times*, January 27 2018
32. *BBC News*, June 10 2004
33. *Ibid.*
34. *Sunday, Letterbxed* website
35. *Sunday, IMDb* website

10 The Decision to Prosecute

1. *BBC News*, March 13 2019
2. *Belfast Telegraph*, January 19 2017
3. *BBC News*, November 11 2015
4. *Irish News*, March 15 2019
5. *BBC News*, March 15 2019
6. *BBC News*, March 14 2019
7. *Guardian*, March 14 2019
8. *Belfast Telegraph*, March 14 2019
9. *Ibid.*
10. *Belfast Telegraph*, March 15 2019
11. *Ibid.*
12. *Guardian*, June 11 2010
13. To author, March 2020
14. *Spectator*, March 14 2019
15. *Belfast Telegraph*, March 25 2017
16. *Mail on Sunday*, March 17 2019
17. *Hansard*, May 20 2019
18. *Hansard*, May 16 2019
19. *Hansard*, May 20 2019
20. *BBC News*, December 5 2019
21. *BBC News*, December 7 2019

22. *BBC News*, September 18 2019
23. *Mail Online*, September 18 2019
24. *Daily Telegraph*, September 18 2019
25. *Press Association*, February 24 2020
26. *Irish Times*, March 2 2020
27. *Daily Telegraph*, February 25 2020
28. *BBC News*, September 26 2019
29. *BBC News*, November 11 2019
30. *BBC News*, January 13 2020
31. *BBC News*, March 18 2020
32. *Ibid.*
33. *Irish Times*, March 27 2020
34. *BBC News*, May 13 2010
35. *Belfast Telegraph*, June 20 2020
36. *Belfast Telegraph* March 11 2020
37. *BBC News*, September 30 2020
38. *Daily Mail*, December 21 2020)

11 The Trial That Never Was

1. BBC Northern Ireland, February 19 2021
2. Ulster TV, March 15 2021
3. BBC, April 6 2021
4. BBC, April 24 2021
5. BBC, April 22 2021
6. BBC, April 12 2021
7. UTV, April 23 2021
8. BBC, May 4 2021
9. *Times*, May 5 2021
10. BBC, May 6 2021
11. *Ibid.*
12. BBC, May 11 2021
13. *Ibid.*
14. UTV, May 19 2021
15. BBC, May 11 2021
16. BBC, June 23 2021
17. UTV, July 2 2021
18. BBC, July 2 2021
19. BBC, July 4 2021
20. ITN, July 17 2021
21. Sky TV, July 13 2021

12 Amnesty

1. Hansard, July 16 2021)
2. BBC, July 14 2021
3. ITN, July 14 2021
4. Sky News, July 14 2021
5. Hansard, July 16 2021
6. BBC, July 16 2021
7. Sky News, July 16 2021
8. ITN, July 14 2021)
9. Sky News, July 15 2021
10. BBC, July 14 2021
11. Sky News, July 15 2021
12. BBC, July 14 2021
13. BBC, July 14 2021
14. ITN, July 15 2021
15. Sky News, July 15 2021
16. BBC Radio Foyle, July 16 2021
17. BBC, July 16 2021
18. ITN, July 16 2021

Conclusion

1. Saville, Conclusions, 3.87-88
2. Saville, Conclusions, 3.89-91
3. Saville, Conclusions, 3.109
4. Saville, Conclusions, 4.8
5. *Debrett's*, 1994
6. *Daily Telegraph*, November 26 2015
7. *Belfast Telegraph*, September 19 2017
8. Taylor, 112
9. *Sunday Mirror*, January 25 1998
10. *BBC News*, March 24 2000
11. *Derry Journal*, June 23 2010
12. *Ulster TV* archives, Bloody Sunday, key players
13. Saville, Conclusions, 4.33
14. *Guardian*, July 1 2019
15. *BBC News*, January 30 2002
16. *Guardian*, July 1 2019
17. *Ulster TV* archives, Bloody Sunday, key players
18. *Daily Telegraph*, August 8 2016

19. *BBC News*, August 8 2016
20. *New York Times*, August 8 2016
21. *Ulster TV* archives, Bloody Sunday, key players
22. *Irish Times*, August 8 2016
23. *Guardian*, August 8 2016
24. *BBC News*, August 8 2016
25. *BBC News*, August 14 2019
26. Saville, Conclusions, 4.1
27. Saville, Conclusions, 4.4
28. Saville, Conclusions, 5.5

APPENDIX 1

Speech of the Taoiseach, Jack Lynch

On Monday night on television and again on Tuesday in the Dáil I expressed the nation's grief at the happenings in Derry last Sunday. I expressed sympathy with those who were bereaved, those who were injured and with the people of Derry generally. I think it is true to say that grief and sympathy were hardly ever more sincerely felt, nor more widespread in this country, certainly not in my lifetime. I also announced on Monday night that the Government had called for a special day of mourning and I appealed to everybody who could in any way contribute to, or facilitate, that mourning to do so. I should like to express my appreciation of the manner in which those in positions of authority facilitated the day of mourning.

I appeal to everybody to respond to these tragic events with dignity and with discipline. There were demonstrations of sympathy in every part of the country. People in their tens of thousands responded magnificently and they attended church services. Indeed, it is true to say that the entire nation mourned. What was important too, was that the vast majority marked yesterday in peaceful demonstration, a demonstration of their grief, of their sympathy and of [908] their solidarity with the people who were bereaved and with their friends and, in general, demonstrated their sympathy and solidarity with the deprived minority in the North of Ireland. In this way they showed that in these difficult days there is a degree of unanimity and solidarity that was an example to the entire world and which gave encouragement and strength to the people in the North. For all this I commend all our people and congratulate them on the magnificent way they responded. I thank them for their wonderful gesture of solidarity and unanimity.

Regrettably, the situation had its dark spots. In Dublin yesterday many thousands of our people representing the different organisations, the trade unions, State bodies, students and, indeed people from every walk of life showed their sorrow in a most disciplined way. However, a small minority—men who, under the cloak of patriotism, seek to overthrow the institutions of this State—infiltrated what was necessarily a peaceful demonstration, infiltrated essentially peaceful groups and fomented violence. As we know the British Embassy has been destroyed but I want to say that the nation gains no credit from such an action. It was the action of people who are dangerous, who, above all, are a danger to our freedom, our democracy and to our institutions of freedom and democracy.

Unfortunately that incident was not the end of the matter and since then other danger signals have manifested themselves. Groups proclaiming to be members of illegal organisations have gone around intimidating people and seeking to give the impression that these organisations are now to have a free hand here to do what they like by way of intimidation or destruction. At the outset of what I intend saying, I wish to reassure those of our people who, understandably, may be apprehensive or who may have become concerned at some of yesterday's events, that the institutions of this State will be upheld without fear or favour. The laws will continue to be enforced and those who seek to usurp the functions of the Government will meet with no [909] toleration. I reaffirm those fundamental principles here today and I ask every member of the community and every Member of the Dáil to support the Government stand on this. The Government stand is the stand of the elected representatives of our people regardless of on which side of the House they sit and regardless of whether they are in this House or the other. In the days immediately ahead there is no doubt that those to whom I have referred will seek to play on the sympathies and on the emotions of ordinary decent people so as to secure support for their own actions and objectives. Many people in other countries—indeed throughout the world—are watching our reaction to the recent tragic events. The present situation is a test of our maturity as a nation. We must show the world that, with dignity and restraint, we can express our grief and our support for the minority in the North without, at the same time, playing into the hands of those who would destroy our own fundamental institutions. Therefore, I ask all men and women of goodwill and of responsibility and especially those in positions of influence and, perhaps, those who are engaged in the communications media, to be on their guard against the kind of danger to which I have referred.

This debate, perhaps, has been precipitated by the tragic events of last Sunday. Before the Government took action on Monday, we had received reports from sources that we believe to be absolutely reliable and since then we have been able to check these reports against more reports and especially against reports made by people who were eye-witnesses of these events, people who were actually on the spot. In this respect I would like to refer to the claim by the commanding officer of the British Forces in Derry last Sunday that 200 rounds were fired at his troops as well as nail bombs and other missiles. So far as I know and so far has been stated publicly, not one of these troops was injured either by bullets or nail bombs. They may have sustained minor injuries in scuffles but there were no casualties as a result of these alleged shootings and the throwing of bombs. The same officer claimed [910] that shots had come from flats, that there were snipers on the roofs of these flats which, I understand, were high rise flats in the immediate vicinity, but the stark fact remains that all those who were killed or injured were people on the ground and people who were about to attend, and some of whom had already attended, a public meeting which had begun already. Therefore, to that extent, what these people were doing then was not illegal according to the decrees of the Stormont Government. The march was banned. Therefore, one presumes that under their laws it was illegal to take part in the march but it had concluded at the time the paratroopers fired on these people attending the meeting who, at that stage, were about their lawful business and demonstrating in a lawful way even by Stormont's standards.

As I have said, reports that we received were confirmed by other independent sources and I would direct the attention of Members to the statement of an Italian journalist who must be regarded as being completely impartial and who, so far as I know, said that no shot was fired from the crowds that were demonstrating before the British paratroopers opened fire. I would direct the attention of the House also to a statement made by a very prominent journalist of a very prominent British newspaper who said that he was there all the time, that he thought he heard one shot that might have come from the direction of where the meeting was being convened. He wrote in his notebook "sniper" after which he put a question mark. This gentleman has said that that was the only shot he heard before the paratroopers fired and, obviously, by his own admission and by the record in his notebook, he was not convinced that the shot had come from the direction of the demonstration. It was on these facts that the Government took their decision on Monday to withdraw the Ambassador from London, to instruct our diplomats abroad to inform the Governments to which they were accredited of the facts of the situation as we had got them.

I also put forward the three proposals with which the House is familiar. I should like to repeat them [911] because I believe they are essential if any move forward is to be made. First, the immediate withdrawal of British troops from Derry and other areas in the North of Ireland where there is a high concentration of Catholic homes and the cessation of the harassment of the minority population. I believe that it was because of raids and repressive measures by the British troops in these areas that much of the violence that since has come about in the North of Ireland was caused. In speaking about harassment, I intended to cover the cratering of Border roads, which, I am convinced now more than ever I was, have no military effect or benefit whatever. It was done, as a result of repeated statements by a junior Minister in Stormont, to appease him, in the first instance, and to embarrass us in the second. Not only has it done both—it obviously has appeased the one and embarrassed the other—but it has incensed decent people on both sides of the Border against this type of activity, and has not prevented one person who had evil intent from crossing the Border. Therefore, not only was that kind of action undertaken for the reasons I said but it is militarily futile. The other two proposals I made were the end of internment without trial and a declaration of Britain's intention to achieve the final settlement of the Irish question and the convocation of a conference for this purpose.

I recognise that some of these proposals may not be immediately possible. I am certain that the withdrawal of the troops from the areas I mentioned is immediately possible and would be a first step towards the restoration of peace and the elimination of violence in the North. The second, too, the end of internment without trial, obviously will take some time because if those who are interned are brought to trial a suitable tribunal will have to be established. When I mentioned, having spoken to Mr. Harold Wilson on last Monday week, that I thought it might be possible to find a formula to induce the Nationalists and the SDLP [912] Members of Stormont into talks, and that this might be one of the ways. I want to say clearly that I was in no way dictating to these minority leaders as to what their attitude should be.

However, since the events which gave rise to these proposals resulted from a demonstration to establish civil rights, I would add one other proposal which I think would also be very quickly implemented. As Deputies are aware, especially Deputies who are delegates to the Council of Europe, some time ago the Council of Europe Assembly made a recommendation to the Committee of Ministers:

(1) To instruct the Committee of Experts on Human Rights to draft an additional protocol to the European Convention on Human Rights which would secure the equal treatment of persons in the enforcement of the law and prohibit discrimination in the exercise of the following rights:

  (i) the right to participate with equal voting rights in national and local elections based on the fair delineation of electoral boundaries;

  (ii) the right of access to employment, particularly in central and local government services, in State and semi-State companies and public bodies financed wholly or partly out of central or local government funds and in private industries partly financed or subsidised by State or local bodies;

  (iii) the right to the equitable allocation of dwellings and of resources required to provide dwellings wholly or partly financed out of public funds;

  (iv) the right of access to the public service.

The Assembly in their wisdom thought it necessary to add these to the Convention on Human Rights. I would now suggest to the British Government that they could amend their Northern Ireland legislation, which they have authority and power to amend, that is, the Government of Ireland Act, 1920 or the 1949 Act, to include these [913] specific principles, so that, instead of depending on the goodwill, the declaration, or whims, as the case may be of an administration in which people have lost all confidence, these people would legally enjoy those rights, and enforce such rights if they were not accorded to them. This, I suggest, could be done by simple amendment and done very quickly.

May I say in reference to demonstrations that I hope it will be possible to hold next Sunday's demonstration in a way that will not provoke the kind of action that we saw last Sunday in Derry, that it will not provoke the deliberate shooting down of innocent people by paratroopers. It may be that such a demonstration could be held within the law and equally effectively. That is not a matter for me to decide, but it is a consideration I would urge on those who are responsible and who rightly want to demonstrate to achieve those rights. It is known by now that I had a visit from the British Ambassador and this is one of the questions we discussed. It is not for me to say what passed between us. We also discussed the burning of the Embassy and I reiterated the Government's regret and our intention, as is the practice, to provide full compensation.

He did not indicate to me whether there was any response so far to the proposals that I put to the British Government last Monday.

I want to refer to the suggestion that the Leaders of the three parties should go to London, which Deputy Cosgrave raised in the House here on Tuesday. I had intended to discuss this matter with Deputy Cosgrave and Deputy Corish, but unfortunately the changed Order of Business and the visit of the British Ambassador precluded me from doing so. However, I hope to discuss it with them later. We, as political parties representing the people here, have publicly stated our unanimity and our solidarity and I would say we have the support of the vast majority of the people in our approach to this question. It may be that such a visit would endorse this solidarity, that as Deputy Cosgrave said, the meeting may do good but not do harm. I should like to consider this very carefully [914] before I would make any comment on such a visit.

Mr. Corish: The Taoiseach will make a decision before the weekend?

The Taoiseach: Not before I discuss the matter with Deputy Corish and Deputy Cosgrave. There is more we can do in this present situation. As I said, we are all solid and united in our approach to this problem. We are committed to a peaceful solution of the Northern Ireland situation. In talking of the future of Ireland, it is impossible not to reflect also on present policies being pursued in the North. Those lie at the heart of any discussions that we may have here amongst ourselves or otherwise.

The attempt to reimpose traditional Unionism, whose vision is narrow and self-defeating, will certainly end in total failure. I have no doubt about this. The political leadership of the non-Unionist community in the North have no doubt about it. Indeed, no objective observer—even though he might be British—European, American, or otherwise, doubts that this cannot happen either. It would be fair to say, in fact, that the published comments of most journalists, and the private views expressed to me and to the Minister for Foreign Affairs by most political leaders in other countries, are insistent that the policy of return to monopoly Unionist Government is now impossible.

The State itself was founded for the purpose of ensuring the ascendancy of one community there at the expense of another. I do not know of any other State—until the Eastern European countries were established after the last war—which was deliberately founded on the basis of keeping in power permanently one section of the population. I do not know either of any State which is less representative of the true meaning of Protestantism than the Northern State. The right to freedom of conscience was a fundamental of the Reformation. The practices of Government in Northern Ireland are certainly not in accord with these principles of Protestantism.

I know from many contacts I have that a great many Protestants in Northern Ireland seek peace and justice as much as their Catholic neighbours do. I also know that many of them have come to the belief that, within the limits of the Northern State, it is not possible to find peace with justice and that their minds, therefore, are turning in the direction of Irish unity. I should like to assure these people publicly, as I have done privately, that the unity which we seek is one which will be determined to find room for their talents as well as their sensibilities.

They owe it to themselves as much as they owe it to their neighbours to state how they would wish the institutions of Ireland to be formed. They will be their institutions as much as anyone else's. It is right that they should have a say in how they should be formed. If we are expecting moves or sacrifices from the Unionist majority in the North we, too, will have to face up to some change from our present stance and policy. In turning away from a failed system of government which was unworthy of them, if they do so, they will free themselves to undertake a task which is worthy of them, that of discovering out of the chaos of the present time the way forward to an Ireland which has been theirs for centuries and will be theirs again, as well as ours.

In addressing them publicly in this manner I am asking them to share in and to play an essential part in determining what Ireland should be. I have said harsh things about Unionism in so far as it has manifested itself in misgovernment in the North. It has never been my purpose to show hostility to Unionists, nor have I ever had any such feelings. To me the distinction is a vital one. Unionists are Irishmen who, to my mind, took the wrong course when the Irish nation insisted that Ireland should take charge of her own affairs. A moment of choice has come around again and Unionists can recapture their place in Ireland or continue down a road which will leave them without identity, without influence, and without happiness.

There are movements in Unionist circles which encourage me to believe that the right choice is on the brink of actuality. Certainly many Unionists —perhaps most Unionists—are prepared to support a non-sectarian State in the North. Many have the courage to advocate this despite the pressures exercised on them within their own society. In doing this they represent and speak for people Ireland needs in order to set in train Ireland's fulfilment. I would put a question to them: If the North should become a State capable of embracing the two communities there, in what essential manner could this context not properly be applied to the whole of Ireland?

It may be said in reply that the whole country is incapable of the resolution of problems in a manner satisfactory to the Northern majority for economic, social and other reasons. Laying aside the selfishness involved in a decision to keep a country divided for economic reasons, I consider that it can be truly argued that a united Ireland would not adversely affect the economic well-being of the North. In recent decades our economic development has been substantial, so much so, that far from being afraid of entering into the European Community—which among other things is a vast free trade area—we look forward to it confident of the acceleration of our economic expansion.

So far as social reasons go, Irish unity implies and, indeed, insists on a state of affairs equally satisfactory to the basic beliefs of all sections of the whole community. The North has nothing to lose from that. Therefore I would urge those thinking in the terms I have outlined to take the further step towards agreeing that their intention should be enlarged from trying to find a solution within Northern Ireland to one in which they will acknowledge that the proper goal is to find a solution for Ireland as a whole, agreeable to the Irish people as a whole.

I realise that I am limited to half an hour so I will just conclude. I want to refer again to the march next Sunday in Newry. I said that I hoped it would not provoke the same kind of reaction [917] as the Derry march did. I also want to say that I hope it will not provide any cloak or alleged excuse for the British Army to behave again as they did in Derry last Sunday.

Finally, I want to say again to our own people: let not present emotion, absolutely justified and justifiable, turn them away from what the overwhelming majority of the people know to be the only way towards unity. Above all, let not people who wish to exploit that emotion turn them away from what the great majority of our people seek, that is, the peaceful reunification of our country, the maintenance of our institutions, and the maintenance of our democratic institutions above all, so that all Irishmen, North and South, can enjoy living in economic well-being and happiness in a united Ireland.

Widgery Report, Summary of Conclusions

Summary of conclusions:

1. There would have been no deaths in Londonderry on January 30th if those who organised the illegal march had not thereby created a highly dangerous situation in which a clash between demonstrators and the security forces was almost inevitable.

2. The decision to contain the march within the Bogside and Creggan had been opposed by the Chief Superintendent of Police in Londonderry but was fully justified by events and was successfully carried out.

3. If the Army had persisted in its 'low key' attitude and had not launched a large scale operation to arrest hooligans the day might have passed off without serious incident.

4. The intention of the senior Army officers to use [1st Parachute Regiment] as an arrest force and not for other offensive purposes was sincere.

5. An arrest operation carried out in Battalion strength in circumstances in which the troops were likely to come under fire involved hazard to civilians in the area which Commander 8 Brigade may have under-estimated.

7. When the vehicles and soldiers of Support Company appeared in Rossville Street they came under fire. Arrests were made; but in a very short time the arrest operation took second place and the soldiers turned to engage their assailants. There is no reason to suppose that the soldiers would have opened fire if they had not been fired upon first.

8. Soldiers who identified armed gunmen fired upon them in accordance with the standing orders in the Yellow Card. Each

soldier was his own judge of whether he had identified a gunman. Their training made them aggressive and quick in decision and some showed more restraint in opening fire than others. At one end of the scale some soldiers showed a high degree of responsibility; at the other, notably in Glenfada Park, firing bordered on the reckless. These distinctions reflect differences in the character and temperament of the soldiers concerned.

9. The standing orders contained in the Yellow Card are satisfactory. Any further restrictions on opening fire would inhibit the soldier from taking proper steps for his own safety and that of his comrades and unduly hamper the engagement of gunmen.

10. None of the deceased or wounded is proved to have been shot whilst handling a firearm or bomb. Some are wholly acquitted of complicity in such action; but there is a strong suspicion that some others had been firing weapons or handling bombs in the course of the afternoon and that yet others had been closely supporting them.

11. There was no general breakdown in discipline. For the most part the soldiers acted as they did because they thought their orders required it. No order and no training can ensure that a soldier will always act wisely, as well as bravely and with initiative. The individual soldier ought not to have to bear the burden of deciding whether to open fire in confusion such as prevailed on January 30th. In the conditions prevailing in Northern Ireland, however, this is often inescapable.

April 10th 1972

Saville Report, Overall Assessment

The early firing in William Street resulted in two wounded casualties, neither of whom was doing anything that justified either of them being shot. It is possible that the soldiers concerned mistakenly believed that they had identified someone posing a threat of causing death or serious injury. Equally, each of those soldiers may have fired, not believing that his target was posing a threat of causing death or serious injury, but only suspecting that this might have been the case.

The soldiers of Support Company who went into the Bogside did so as the result of an order by Colonel Wilford, which should not have been given and which was contrary to the orders that he had received from Brigadier MacLellan.

With the exception of Private T and with the probable exception of shots Sergeant O said that he fired at someone on a balcony of Block 3 of the Rossville Flats and which, (despite his assertion to the contrary) did not hit anyone, none of the firing by the soldiers of Support Company was aimed at people posing a threat of causing death or serious injury.

We have concluded that the explanation for such firing by Support Company soldiers after they had gone into the Bogside was in most cases probably the mistaken belief among them that republican paramilitaries were responding in force to their arrival in the Bogside. This belief was initiated by the first shots fired by Lieutenant N and reinforced by the further shots that followed soon after. In this belief soldiers reacted by losing their self-control and firing themselves, forgetting or ignoring their instructions and training and failing to satisfy themselves that they had identified targets posing a threat of causing death or serious injury. In the case of those soldiers who fired in either the knowledge or belief that no-one in the areas into which they fired was posing a threat of causing death or serious injury, or not caring whether or not anyone there was posing such a threat, it is at least possible that they did so in the indefensible belief that all the civilians they fired at were probably either members of the Provisional or Official IRA or were supporters of one or other of these paramilitary organisations; and so deserved to be shot notwithstanding that they were not armed or posing any threat of causing death or serious injury. Our overall conclusion is that there was a serious and widespread loss of fire discipline among the soldiers of Support Company.

The firing by soldiers of 1 PARA on Bloody Sunday caused the deaths of 13 people and injury to a similar number, none of whom was posing a threat of causing death or serious injury. What happened on Bloody Sunday strengthened the Provisional IRA, increased nationalist resentment and hostility towards the Army and exacerbated the violent conflict of the years that followed. Bloody Sunday was a tragedy for the bereaved and the wounded, and a catastrophe for the people of Northern Ireland.

June 15 2010

APPENDIX 4

Speech of The Prime Minister, David Cameron

With permission, Mr Speaker, I would like to make a statement.

Today, my Rt Hon Friend, the Secretary of State for Northern Ireland is publishing the report of the Saville Inquiry...the Tribunal set up by the previous Government to investigate the tragic events of 30th January 1972 – a day more commonly known as "Bloody Sunday".

We have acted in good faith by publishing the Tribunal's findings as quickly as possible after the General Election.

Mr Speaker, I am deeply patriotic.

I never want to believe anything bad about our country. I never want to call into question the behaviour of our soldiers and our Army who I believe to be the finest in the world.

And I have seen for myself the very difficult and dangerous circumstances in which we ask our soldiers to serve. But the conclusions of this report are absolutely clear. There is no doubt. There is nothing equivocal. There are no ambiguities.

What happened on Bloody Sunday was both unjustified and unjustifiable. It was wrong.

Lord Saville concludes that the soldiers of Support Company who went into the Bogside "did so as a result of an order...which should have not been given" by their Commander...

...on balance the first shot in the vicinity of the march was fired by the British Army...

...that "none of the casualties shot by soldiers of Support Company was armed with a firearm"...

...that "there was some firing by republican paramilitaries...but.... none of this firing provided any justification for the shooting of civilian casualties"...

...and that "in no case was any warning given before soldiers opened fire".

He also finds that Support Company "reacted by losing their self-control...forgetting or ignoring their instructions and training" with "a serious and widespread loss of fire discipline".

He finds that "despite the contrary evidence given by the soldiers... none of them fired in response to attacks or threatened attacks by nail or petrol bombers"... and that many of the soldiers "knowingly put forward false accounts in order to seek to justify their firing".

What's more – Lord Saville says that some of those killed or injured were clearly fleeing or going to the assistance of others who were dying.

The Report refers to one person who was shot while "crawling... away from the soldiers"...

...another was shot, in all probability, "when he was lying mortally wounded on the ground"...

...and a father was "hit and injured by Army gunfire after he had gone to...tend his son".

For those looking for statements of innocence, Saville says: "The immediate responsibility for the deaths and injuries on Bloody Sunday lies with those members of Support Company whose unjustifiable firing was the cause of the those deaths and injuries"...

...and – crucially – that "none of the casualties was posing a threat of causing death or serious injury, or indeed was doing anything else that could on any view justify their shooting".

For those people who were looking for the Report to use terms like murder and unlawful killing, I remind the House that these judgements are not matters for a Tribunal – or for us as politicians – to determine.

Mr Speaker, these are shocking conclusions to read and shocking words to have to say.

But Mr Speaker, you do not defend the British Army by defending the indefensible.

We do not honour all those who have served with distinction in keeping the peace and upholding the rule of law in Northern Ireland by hiding from the truth. So there is no point in trying to soften or equivocate what is in this Report.

It is clear from the Tribunal's authoritative conclusions that the events of Bloody Sunday were in no way justified. I know some people wonder whether nearly forty years on from an event, a Prime Minister needs to issue an apology.

For someone of my generation, this is a period we feel we have learned about rather than lived through.

But what happened should never, ever have happened.

The families of those who died should not have had to live with the pain and hurt of that day – and a lifetime of loss. Some members of our Armed Forces acted wrongly.

The Government is ultimately responsible for the conduct of the Armed Forces. And for that, on behalf of the Government – and indeed our country – I am deeply sorry.

Mr. Speaker, just as this Report is clear that the actions of that day were unjustifiable…so too is it clear in some of its other findings.

Those looking for premeditation, those looking for a plan, those looking for a conspiracy involving senior politicians or senior members of the Armed Forces – they will not find it in this Report.

Indeed, Lord Saville finds no evidence that the events of Bloody Sunday were premeditated…

…he concludes that the United Kingdom and Northern Ireland Governments, and the Army, neither tolerated nor encouraged "the use of unjustified lethal force".

He makes no suggestion of a Government cover-up. And Lord Saville credits the UK Government with working towards a peaceful political settlement in Northern Ireland.

Mr Speaker, the Report also specifically deals with the actions of key individuals in the army, in politics and beyond… including Major General Ford, Brigadier MacLellan and Lieutenant Colonel Wilford.

In each case, the Tribunal's findings are clear. It also does the same for Martin McGuinness.

It specifically finds he was present and probably armed with a "sub-machine gun" but concludes "we are sure that he did not engage in any activity that provided any of the soldiers with any justification for opening fire".

Mr. Speaker, while in no way justifying the events of January 30th 1972, we should acknowledge the background to the events of Bloody Sunday.

Since 1969 the security situation in Northern Ireland had been declining significantly.

Three days before 'Bloody Sunday', two RUC officers – one a Catholic – were shot by the IRA in Londonderry, the first police officers killed in the city during the Troubles.

A third of the city of Derry had become a no-go area for the RUC and the Army. And in the end 1972 was to prove Northern Ireland's bloodiest year by far with nearly 500 people killed.

And let us also remember, Bloody Sunday is not the defining story of the service the British Army gave in Northern Ireland from 1969-2007.

This was known as Operation Banner, the longest, continuous

operation in British military history, spanning thirty-eight years and in which over 250,000 people served.

Our Armed Forces displayed enormous courage and professionalism in upholding democracy and the rule of law in Northern Ireland.

Acting in support of the police, they played a major part in setting the conditions that have made peaceful politics possible... and over 1,000 members of the security forces lost their lives to that cause.

Without their work the peace process would not have happened. Of course some mistakes were undoubtedly made. But lessons were also learned.

Once again, I put on record the immense debt of gratitude we all owe those who served in Northern Ireland. Mr. Speaker, may I also thank the Tribunal for its work – and all those who displayed great courage in giving evidence.

I would also like to acknowledge the grief of the families of those killed. They have pursued their long campaign over thirty-eight years with great patience. Nothing can bring back those that were killed but I hope, as one relative has put it, the truth coming out can set people free.

John Major said he was open to a new inquiry. Tony Blair then set it up. This was accepted by the then Leader of the Opposition.

Of course, none of us anticipated that the Saville Inquiry would last 12 years or cost £200 million.

Our views on that are well documented. It is right to pursue the truth with vigour and thoroughness...

...but let me reassure the House that there will be no more open-ended and costly inquiries into the past.

But today is not about the controversies surrounding the process. It's about the substance, about what this report tells us. Everyone should have the chance to examine the complete findings – and that's why the report is being published in full.

Running to more than 5000 pages, it's being published in 10 volumes.

Naturally, it will take all of us some time to digest the report's full findings and understand all the implications. The House will have the opportunity for a full day's debate this autumn – and in the meantime I have asked my Rt Hon Friends the Secretaries of State for Northern Ireland and Defence to report back to me on all the issues that arise from it.

Mr Speaker, this report and the Inquiry itself demonstrate how a State should hold itself to account...

...and how we are determined at all times – no matter how difficult – to judge ourselves against the highest standards.

Openness and frankness about the past – however painful – do not make us weaker, they make us stronger. That's one of the things that differentiates us from terrorists.

We should never forget that over 3,500 people – people from every community – lost their lives in Northern Ireland, the overwhelming majority killed by terrorists. There were many terrible atrocities.

Politically-motivated violence was never justified, whichever side it came from.

And it can never be justified by those criminal gangs that today want to drag Northern Ireland back to its bitter and bloody past. No Government I lead will ever put those who fight to defend democracy on an equal footing with those who continue to seek to destroy it.

But neither will we hide from the truth that confronts us today. In the words of Lord Saville –

"What happened on Bloody Sunday strengthened the Provisional IRA, increased nationalist resentment and hostility towards the Army and exacerbated the violent conflict of the years that followed. Bloody Sunday was a tragedy for the bereaved and the wounded, and a catastrophe for the people of Northern Ireland."

These are words we cannot and must not ignore.

But what I hope this Report can also do is to mark the moment when we come together, in this House and in the communities we represent.

Come together to acknowledge our shared history, even where it divides us. And come together to close this painful chapter on Northern Ireland's troubled past. That is not to say that we must ever forget or dismiss that past.

But we must also move on.

Northern Ireland has been transformed over the past twenty years... and all of us in Westminster and Stormont must continue that work of change, coming together with all the people of Northern Ireland to build a stable, peaceful, prosperous and shared future.

It is with that determination that I commend this statement to the House.

Bibliography

Adamson, Ian, *The Identity of Ulster* (Pretani Press, Belfast, 1987)

Ardagh, John, *Ireland and the Irish* (Hamish Hamilton, London, 1994)

Arthur, Max, *Northern Ireland Soldiers Talking* (Sidgwick and Jackson, London, 1987)

Bardon, Jonathan, *A History of Ulster* (The Blackstaff Press, 1992)

Barzilay, David, *The British Army in Ulster* (Century Books, Belfast, 1973)

Beattie, Geoffrey, *We Are the People: Journeys Through the Heart of Protestant Ulster* (Mandarin, London, 1993)

Bell, J. Bowyer, *The Irish Troubles: A Generation of Violence, 1967-1992* (Gill & Macmillan, Dublin, 1992)

Bew, Paul, and Gillespie, Gordon, *1968 – Northern Ireland: A Chronology of the Troubles, 1968–1993* (Gill & MacMillan, Dublin, 1993)

Bishop, Patrick, and Mallie, Eamonn, *The Provisional IRA* (Corgi Books, London, 1988)

Blair, Tony, *A Journey* (Hutchinson, London 2010)

Blaney, Aileen, *Remembering Historical Trauma in Paul Greengrass's Bloody Sunday* (History & Memory, Indiana University Press, 2007)

Blaney, John, *Lennon and McCartney: Together Alone: A Critical Discography of Their Solo Work* (Jawbone Press, 2007)

Bowyer Bell, J., *IRA Tactics and Targets* (Poolbeg, Dublin, 1990)

Brown, Terence, *Ireland: A Social and Cultural History* (Fontana Press, London, 1985)

Cameron, Lord, *Disturbances in Northern Ireland: Report of the Commission Appointed by the Governor of Northern Ireland* (HMSO, Belfast, 1969)

Campbell, Julieann, *Setting the Truth Free: The Inside Story of the Bloody Sunday Justice Campaign'* (Liberties Press, 2012)

Clarke, Liam, and Johnston, Kathryn, *Martin McGuinness: From Guns to Government* (Mainstream Publishing, 2003)

Conway, B., *Commemoration and Bloody Sunday: Pathways of Memory* (Palgrave Macmillan, 2010)

Coogan, Tim Pat, *The Troubles: Ireland's Ordeal, 1966-1996, and the Search for Peace* (Palgrave, New York, 2002)

Crossman, Richard, *Dairies of a Cabinet Minister* (Penguin, 1979)

Daly, Edward, *A Troubled See: Memoirs of a Derry Bishop* (Four Courts Press, 2011)

Darby, John, *Conflict in Northern Ireland: The Development of a Polarised Community* (Gill & Macmillan, Dublin, 1976)

Devlin, Bernadette, *The Price of My Soul* (Andre Deutsch, London, 1969)

Devlin, Paddy, *Straight Life – An Autobiography* (Blackstaff Press, Belfast, 1993)

Dillon, Martin, *The Dirty War* (Random House, 1991)

Doyle, Tom, *Man on the Run: Paul McCartney in the 1970s* (Ballantine Books, New York 2013)

Du Noyer, Paul, *John Lennon: Whatever Gets You Through the Night* (Thunder's Mountain Press, 1999)

Elliott, S. and Flackes, W.D., *Northern Ireland: A Political Directory 1968-1999* (The Blackstaff Press, Belfast, 1999)

English, Richard, *Armed Struggle: The History of the IRA* (Pan Macmillan, London, 2004)

Farrell, Michael, *Northern Ireland: The Orange State* (Pluto, London, 1976)

Faus, Jennifer, *Before Sunday* (Nonsuch Publishing, 2007)

Fields, Rona M., *Northern Ireland: Society Under Siege* (Transaction Publishers, 1977)

Foot, M.L.R., Fighting for Ireland (Routledge, London, 1995)

Foster, Roy F., *Modern Ireland 1600-1972* (Allen Lane, London, 1988)

Geraghty, Tony, *The Irish War: The Hidden Conflict Between the IRA and British Intelligence* (Johns Hopkins University Press, Baltimore, 2000)

Guila, Bob, *Guitar Gods: The 25 Players Who Made Rock History* (Greenwood Press, Westport, Connecticut, 2009)

Hamill, D., *Pig in the Middle: The Army in Northern Ireland* (Methuen, London, 1985)

Hanley, Brian, and Millar, Scot, *The Lost Revolution: The Story of the Official IRA and the Workers' Party* (Penguin Ireland, Dublin, 2009)

Harkness, David, *Northern Ireland Since 1920* (Helicon Books, Dublin, 1993)

Hermon, Sir John, *Holding the Line* (Gill and Macmillan, Dublin, 1997)

Howe, Stephen, *Ireland and Empire: Colonial Legacies in Irish History and Culture* (Oxford University Press, 2002)

Hume, John, *Personal Views: Politics, Peace and Reconciliation in Ireland* (Town House, Dublin, 1996)

Ingham, Chris, *The Rough Guide to the Beatles* (Rough Guides, London, 2003)

Jackson, Mike, *Soldier: The Autobiography* (Bantam Press, 2007)

Kee, Robert, *The Green Flag: A History of Irish Nationalism* (Penguin, 1972, 2000)

Kennally, Danny, and Preston, Eric, *Belfast August 1971: A Case to be Answered* (Independent Labour Party, 1971)

MacStiofain, Sean, *Memoirs of a Revolutionary* (Free Ireland Book Club, Daly City, 1979)

McCann, Eamonn, *War and an Irish Town* (Haymarket Books, 2017); *Bloody Sunday in Derry* (Brandon: Printing Press, 1998)

McLean, Raymond, *The Road to Bloody Sunday* (Guildhall Printing Press, 1997)

McCluskey, Colin, *Up off their Knees: A Commentary on the Civil Rights Movement in Northern Ireland* (Conn McCluskey and associates, Irish Republic, 1989)

McGuffin, John, *The Guineapigs* (Penguin First Edition Specials, 1974)

McKittrick, David, *Endgame – The Search for Peace in Northern Ireland* (Blackstaff Press, Belfast, 1994)

Mitchell, George, *Making Peace* (Heinemann, London, 1999)

Moloney, Ed, *A Secret History of the IRA* (W. W. Norton & Company, 2003)

Mullan, Don, *Eyewitness Bloody Sunday – The Truth* (Wolfhound Press, Dublin, 1997)

Murphy, Dervla, *A Place Apart* (John Murray, London, 1978)

Murray, Raymond, *The SAS in Ireland* (Mercier Press, 1990)

Norton-Taylor, Richard, *Bloody Sunday: Scenes from the Saville Inquiry* (Oberon Books, London, 2005)

O'Brien, Brendan, *The Long War – The IRA and Sinn Féin* (O'Brien Press, Dublin, 1995)

O'Brien, Joanna, *A Matter of Minutes – The Enduring Legacy of Bloody Sunday* (Wolfhound Press, Dublin, 2002)

O'Callaghan, Sean, *The Informer – The Real Life Story of One Man's War Against Terrorism* (Bantam Press, London, 1998)

O'Connor, Fionnuala, *In Search of a State: Catholics in Northern Ireland* (Blackstaff Press, Belfast, 1993)

Oddie, David, *A Journey of Art and Conflict – Weaving Indra's Net* (Intellect publishers, 2015)

O'Doherty, Shane Paul, *The Volunteer* (HarperCollins, London, 1993)

Patterson, Henry, *Ireland Since 1939: The Persistence of Conflict* (Penguin, 2006)

Pringle, Peter, and Jacobson, Philip, *Those Are Real Bullets, Aren't They?*

(Fourth Estate, London 2000)

Purdie, Bob, *Politics in the Streets: The Origins of the Civil Rights Movement in Northern Ireland* (The Blackstaff Press, 1990)

Rees, Merlyn, *Northern Ireland: A Personal Perspective* (Methuen, London, 1985)

Routledge, Paul, *John Hume: A Biography* (Harper-Collins, London, 1997)

Ruane, Joseph, and Todd, Jennifer, *The Dynamics of Conflict in Northern Ireland: Power, Conflict and Emancipation* (Cambridge University Press, 1996)

Ryder, Chris, *The RUC – A Force Under Fire* (Methuen, London, 1989)

Saville, Lord; Hoyt, William; Toohey, John, *Report of the Bloody Sunday Inquiry* (The Stationery Office, 15 June 2010)

Shriver, Lionel, *Ordinary Decent Criminals* (HarperCollins, London, 1992)

Stevenson, Jonathan, *'We Wrecked the Place' – Contemplating an End to the Northern Ireland Troubles* (The Free Press, Simon & Schuster, New York 1996)

Stokes, Niall, *Into the Heart: The Story Behind Every U2 Song* (HarperCollins, Australia, 1996)

Taylor, Peter, *Provos: The IRA & Sinn Féin* (Bloomsbury Publishing, London, 1997); *Brits: The War Against the IRA* (Bloomsbury Publishing, 2001); Loyalists (Bloomsbury Publishing, 1999)

Toolis, Kevin, *Rebel Hearts: Journeys Within the IRA's Soul* (Picador, London, 1995)

Van der Bijl, Nick, *Operation Banner: The British Army in Northern Ireland 1969-2007)* (Pen & Sword Military, 2009)

Walker, Graham, *A History of the Ulster Unionist Party* (Manchester University Press, 2004)

Walsh, Dermot, *Bloody Sunday and the Rule of Law in Northern Ireland* (Macmillan, London 2000)

Wharton, Ken, *The Bloodiest Year 1972: British Soldiers in Northern Ireland in Their Own Words* (The History Press, Stroud, 2011)

White, Robert William, *Ruairí O' Bradaigh: The Life and Politics of an Irish Revolutionary* (Indiana University Press, Bloomington, 2006)

Whitelaw, William, *The Whitelaw Memoirs* (Arum Press, London, 1989)

Widgery, Lord, *Inquiry into the Events on 30 January 1972 Which Led to Loss of Life in Connection with the Procession in Londonderry That Day* (Home Office, 1972)

Wilson, Andrew J., *Irish America and the Ulster Conflict, 1968-1995* (Blackstaff Press, Belfast, 1995)

Woffinden, Bob, *The Beatles Apart* (Proteus, London, 1981)

Wood, Ian S., *Crimes of Loyalty: A History of the UDA* (Edinburgh University Press, 2006)

Index